THE

EVERYTHING

INVESTING
BOOK

How to pick, buy and sell
stocks, bonds and mutual funds

Rich Mintzer & Annette Racond

Adams Media Corporation
Holbrook, Massachusetts

An Everything Series Book.
The Everything Series is a trademark of Adams Media Corporation.

Published by
Adams Media Corporation
260 Center Street, Holbrook, MA 02343

ISBN: 1-58062-149-X

Printed in the United States of America.

J   I   H   G   F   E   D   C   B   A

Library of Congress Cataloging-in-Publication Data
Mintzer, Richard.
The everything investing book / by Rich Mintzer.
p.   cm.
ISBN 1-58062-149-X
1. Investments—United States. 2. Stocks—United States. 3. Mutual Funds—United States.
4. Bonds—United States. 5. Finance, Personal—United States. I. Title
HG4910.M543   1999
332.6—dc21   99-15775
CIP

This publication is designed to provide accurate and authoritative information with
regard to the subject matter covered. It is sold with the understanding that the publisher is not engaged in rendering legal, accounting, or other professional advice. If
legal advice or other expert assistance is required, the services of a competent professional person should be sought.
     — From a *Declaration of Principles* jointly adopted by a Committee of the American
Bar Association and a Committee of Publishers and Associations

Illustrations by Barry Littmann

This book is available at quantity discounts for bulk purchases.
For information, call 1-800-872-5627.

Visit our home page at http://www.adamsmedia.com

CONTENTS

ACKNOWLEDGMENTS

Well-informed investing takes time and time is money. Therefore, we'd like to acknowledge those well-informed individuals who so generously offered us their time to help us with this book.

A special thank you to: Brad Sugarman, who was eager to offer his wisdom and insight right from the start; Richard Valentin, who is *always* there in a crunch; Ellie Karr, who we only wish had forced us to buy Intel, Cisco, and Lucent when she did; Jon Meigs who was always ready to help a friend. Linda London, who makes her office available around-the-clock; Felix Aguero and Nayda Rondon, who are generous with their time even when they're rushing off to the maternity ward; Hugh Tracey, who has an anecdote for every occasion; Maria D'Errico, who is on her way to brilliant investing; Esmael and Cindy Tahil, who have words of wisdom on any subject; Peter H. Voelkner of New York City-based KCM, Inc., who is *always* right there with an answer to any investment question; Scott Glover of Charles Schwab and Company; Charles Cremen of Fidelity Investments; Jerry and Muriel Mintzer for great last-minute proofing, as always; Harry Domash of *Winning Investments Newsletter*; Karen Alfest of New York City-based L.J. Altfest and Company; Daniel Pederson of *The Bond Informer* for invaluable help with savings bond information; Stan Chadsey, a New York-based financial planner with Capital Planning Associates; Paul Young of the Securities Arbitration Group, Inc.; Henry Block, financial analyst and president of 5Star Management; Michael Groupie of NAREIT; Rowena Itchon of T. Rowe Price; and Carol, Eric, and Rebecca for their patience.

INTRODUCTION

We are constantly hearing about ways to make our money "grow" on the one hand and ways in which the dollar is "shrinking" on the other. What is all this talk about the size of money fluctuating?

Despite the lower inflation rate of recent years, money does not buy as much as it once did. Nonetheless, more and more families are finding that they are now able to put a little more money aside, and that has led to an investing frenzy of sorts in recent years. Stocks—and particularly mutual funds—once thought of as investment vehicles for the "elite," are now accessible to the masses thanks to the ease at which they can be purchased and the proliferation of home computers.

The 1990s saw a major turnaround in investing. Television commercials geared at the general public are from Fidelity, Prudential, Paine Webber, and other investment firms, many of whom were rarely seen or heard from outside of the pages of the *Wall Street Journal*. Roadside billboards sport advertisements for mutual funds . . . who would have thought it? No longer is putting money away in a savings account the way of the typical American family. Today, the average family, the hardworking young college graduate, the senior citizen, and both the white-collar and the blue-collar worker have the opportunity to make their money grow.

We are now a society featuring a growing number of investors, wisely trying to plan for their own future and that of their families. Investing need not be in the glamorous high-risk investments that are creating a stir in financial circles but may be a simple 401(k) plan at work, a money market mutual fund, or the old standard U.S. savings bonds. The bottom line is that more Americans are investing than ever before.

INVESTING VERSUS SPENDING

Along with an increase in investing in profitable companies we have the other side of the equation, and one of the reasons why so many companies are surging forward: rampant spending. Millions of Americans are now deep in debt, particularly in credit card debt, because just as easily as we can invest our money and plan for the future, we can also spend our money. Whether it's by purchasing items online, through a shopping club, from one of numerous catalogs, or by phone on a toll-free number, people are spending money that they don't have. The media makes everything look so good on television that we have become a society with a mindset of "gotta have it now." In fact, the mutual fund craze is working on the theory of no-load purchases, funds that you purchase directly, often through a toll-free number, in effect making them an impulse buy. Some fund families are tapping into the fast-food mindset, but at least on a more positive note, offering potential earnings rather than just spending. The concern is that on either side of the equation, be it spending or investing, people are reacting rather than using self-control and planning ahead.

The idea of putting off immediate gratification to receive something more at a later date is hard for some people to swallow. The individual who wants immediate results plays the lottery and regularly goes to Atlantic City and Las Vegas. And while this can be fun within reason, it is not investing, but gambling, trying to get quick results by way of "chance." Investing is looking ahead, trying to see where you want to be in the future and making a plan as to how you will get there. The ones who have done the shrewd planning and figured out their future profits are the ones *offering* the casino games, not the ones *playing* them.

If you are successfully managing your finances to provide for yourself and/or your family, investing represents a real opportunity to make your money grow. Through investing, you take the money left after your necessary living expenses and put it to work for you to earn even more money

To invest, you will need to look at where you want to be in one, three, five, ten, and twenty-five years. For more risky investors the future might be the next forty-eight hours, but for most investors the future lies in the coming years. Because of the wide range of individual goals and dreams, and because your needs and those of your neighbors differ, your investment strategy has to be right for no one else but you. Therefore, prepared strategies and formulas don't always work. One person's financial plan and long-range goals and needs may be far more complicated than those of another person, which is why boilerplate financial planning does not work. This is why your investment plan is a personal decision.

Prior to investing, it's important that you:

1. Are not in debt beyond fundamental things like a mortgage and perhaps a car loan
2. Have some money already safely tucked away in accessible cash vehicles
3. Have money that is available to you specifically in case of emergency (Never invest your last dollar.)
4. Have a basic understanding of the different kinds of investments and the risks associated with those investments

Be prepared to be invested for some time and not expect instant returns. Impulsiveness doesn't usually work when it comes to investing. If you're looking for instant returns, bet on a racehorse. If you're looking to invest, buy a racehorse.

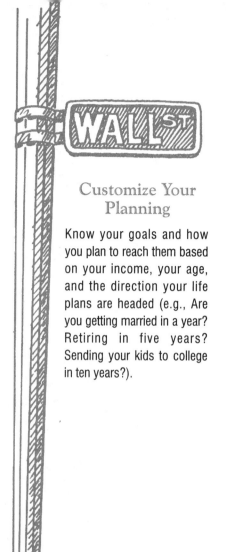

Customize Your Planning

Know your goals and how you plan to reach them based on your income, your age, and the direction your life plans are headed (e.g., Are you getting married in a year? Retiring in five years? Sending your kids to college in ten years?).

TWENTY-ONE QUESTIONS
(AND ANSWERS)

Here is a brief look at 21 of the most commonly asked investing questions with short answers. For more detail, look in the appropriate sections of the book.

Q: What is the first step in investing?

A: Determine your own financial situation, which includes evaluating your financial situation to determine how much money is available to invest. You then need to determine your financial goals and how long it will take to reach those goals.

Q: What is the fundamental differences between stocks and bonds?

A: Stocks mean you are buying shares of a company. Bonds essentially are loans by you to a company, municipality or to the United States Government. Stocks are more closely tied to the success of the company while bonds are tied to the issuer and to the interest rate. Bonds, as a general rule, are more conservative investments, but the rewards or income are usually lower.

Q: Are bond funds better than bonds?

A: You'll find plusses and minuses for each. Bond funds will allow you to diversify and have a piece of more bonds than you could buy individually, plus you'll have professional management. There is no assurance of a return of your principal investment in a bond fund. When buying an individual bond, you are paid a fixed rate of interest and there is a maturity date at which (usually) your principal will be returned. High grade or government issued bonds have greater guarantees, but bond funds can provide higher returns.

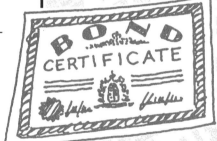

Q: Are municipal bonds good investments for retirement accounts?

A: Generally, no. One of the advantages of municipal bonds is that they are usually tax free. Once you are in a retirement account such as an IRA or 401(k), you are receiving tax deferred income. You should therefore go for higher yielding taxable bonds.

Q: What is the secondary bond market?

A: While many people buy bonds with the intent of earning income and cashing or redeeming the bond at face value (or for their initial principal) there are also numerous investors selling bonds on what is not actually a single market—like the stock market—but through brokers and dealers worldwide. That secondary market will tell you the value of your bond and allow you to sell it–or to buy a bond at the going rate. U.S. savings bonds are among the few bonds that do not have a secondary market.

Q: Is it true that the only time you pay taxes on a mutual fund is when you sell your shares?

A: No. This is a common misconception. You will pay taxes on money earned from capital gains by virtue of stocks sold within the fund. You will also pay on dividends you receive.

Q: What is asset allocation and how does it differ from diversification?

A: Asset allocation is the breakdown of where you are putting your assets. How much are you putting into long term bonds, short term bonds, intermediate bonds, stocks of large companies, stocks of newly emerging companies, aggressive domestic mutual funds, international mutual funds, bond funds, money market accounts, etc. It is important to allocate your funds in the most constructive manner for your own needs and goals. This means balancing risky and conservative investments in a way that suits you the best and is most profitable. Diversification is essentially how you spread out your investments among various stocks, various bonds or various mutual funds within a certain classification. By spreading your money into different asset classes, however, you are also (on a broad level) diversifying your investments.

Q: What are sector mutual funds?

A: These are mutual funds that invest in one industry such as medical, technical or automotive. If you think a particular industry is on the rise, you may want to invest in that industry. Naturally, this method means you are not diversifying greatly, but a "hot" sector, such as Internet stocks in recent years, can be profitable, whether it is through a fund or simply an area you are knowledgeable about and invest in through individual stocks.

Q: What are zero coupon bonds and why are they useful?

A: These are bonds that do not pay ongoing interest, but pay you interest upon maturity. The positive aspect is that you can buy them for a lot less money, or at "a discount." You might only pay $12,000 for a $20,000 Zero Coupon Bond. They are good for upcoming milestones such as saving for college and other such events.

Q: How do you invest in real estate if you can't afford to buy a property?

A: A REIT is the best choice. A REIT, short for Real Estate Investment Trust, is essentially a company that deals in the real estate business and offers the investor the opportunity to invest in real estate by investing in the company and not have to buy a property. REITs own office buildings or other commercial property, hotels and resorts, residential properties, etc. Investing in a REIT is like investing in a real estate stock company . . . in fact they are found on the stock exchange.

Q: What's the difference between a traditional IRA and a Roth IRA?

A: With a traditional IRA you can get deductions when you make your $2,000 annual contributions, but you will be taxed when withdrawing the money once you are over 59½. On a Roth IRA you cannot take deductions when you make your contributions. However, you are not taxed upon withdrawing the money.

Q: If you have a 401(k) plan at work and you leave your job or get downsized, what can you do with the plan?

A: You can roll it over within 60 days into an IRA or a new 401(k) plan if you've joined a new company and qualify to be in their plan. Make a trustee to trustee transfer or you could end up paying taxes on the money.

Q: What is the best way to play the stock market?

A: There is no sure fire answer. However, patience will usually present the best results. Over each decade since the 1930s the stock market has averaged an 11 percent gain. As for strategies, setting limits, buying low and selling high and dollar cost averaging—which means essentially putting in the same amount regularly regardless of the stock price—have worked well for many people, while trying to time the market has been ill advised for new (and even not so new) investors.

Q: What is the advantage to buying government bonds?

A: Government bonds are the safest of any bonds, being backed by the full faith of the United States Government.

Q: What does it mean to have "liquidity"?

A: Liquidity means how easily you can get your money out of an investment—technically, it means getting the total amount invested back. However, it is now commonly used to mean "getting some cash from an investment."

Q: What are the safest investments, in terms of not losing money?

A: Money market accounts, treasuries, treasury bills and savings bonds and CDs are among the safer accounts.

Q: What's the best way to save for college tuition?

A: Establish a plan as early as possible—giving yourself several years. You can establish a portfolio with an asset allocation of stocks, bonds and mutual funds that leans toward being aggressive at first and then progressively re-allocate and become more conservative as the college years approach.

Q: What's the difference between a load and a no-load mutual fund?

A: Loaded funds are purchased through a broker making a commission while no-loads are purchased on your own through a toll free number or online.

Q: If you want steady income-producing investments what should you look for?

A: Your best bets include either bonds that pay steady yields or stocks that pay dividends (which are usually large, well-established corporations).

Q: How many items should make up a portfolio?

A: There is no set limit or even suggested limit that makes up the blueprint for the ideal portfolio. One person might have two securities in their portfolio while another may have hundreds. The idea is to stay within your parameters regarding how much money you can have tied up in investments, and to allocate your assets, or investments, so that you are in different asset classes, that is, in stocks, bonds, mutual funds, money markets, real estate, etc. Within each group that you choose to allocate funds, you also want to diversify. As for how many stocks or mutual funds you own, it's important to have a level of comfort and to be able to follow closely all those that you own.

Q: Are some people simply not ready to invest?

A: The short answer is a fairly obvious yes, some people are not ready to invest. The two primary reasons are: (1) The person is in debt, working his or her way out of debt or does not have money at present beyond his or her living expenses or immediate needs, and (2) The person has not done some degree (even if minimal) of learning about investing, which includes organizing and evaluating his or her own financial needs and goals.

CHAPTER ONE

Welcome to the Wide World of Investing

Investment Smarts 1

Be leery of anything that looks "Too Good." Unfortunately, while this sounds like pessimism and paranoia, it's simply caution. There are numerous financial brokers and brokerage houses out there, and they want your business, as do real-estate brokers, art dealers, and other salespersons. The bottom line, however, is that no one is giving anything away. Low risk and high rewards do not usually go hand in hand. Offers that just don't sit in the same vicinity with other similar investments probably have a catch to them somewhere, like buying a home (as advertised on late night TV) or no money down. Be careful.

We invest to make life in the future, for ourselves, our children, our parents, and our significant others, easier. Investing wisely can also provide financial security—an important safety net in a rapidly changing world filled with uncertainty. Despite the lower unemployment rate of the past few years, people are still being downsized or let go from companies that are not faring well financially or have been bought by a larger company. There are other unforeseen emergencies. People whose homes are hit by hurricanes and other natural disasters will find themselves having to look beyond their insurance carriers and to their own savings.

On the other side of the coin, investing allows us to pursue our dreams, while allowing those we love to pursue their dreams as well. You may hope to someday open your own business, buy a home, or simply purchase a new car. You may wish to retire to a retirement community or travel around the world at some later time in life. Investing to send your son or daughter to college is investing in the future of your children. Investing takes us away from the everyday routine and allows us to look into our projected future. It is "projected" because neither life's best laid plans nor best intended investments are a sure thing.

Your reasons for investing reflect who you are as an individual. They are part of achieving your own personal goals and dreams.

Once you have set goals for yourself you should look at the time horizons for reaching each goal. The goal of sending your son to college essentially will be set for you by his age. A five-year-old will start college in twelve or thirteen years. Buying a home, however, is not time-defined. You could save up the money in one, five, ten, or twenty years. Determining both your goals and your time frame will allow you to look at the type of risk you can afford to take in your investments as well as the type of investment you want to make.

Investing is far from an exact science, which explains why the words "speculation" or the phrases "anticipated earnings" or "potential growth" are used. You, as an investor, have to take time for research and analysis, plus some intuitive thinking. You need to make informed decisions and have the tolerance and patience to find out if your choices were correct. There are a number of moves and strategies that you can make to safeguard your investments and to set the wheels in motion toward reaching your goals. However, there are also factors that remain out of your hands, such as sudden economic turns brought on by domestic news events, overseas events and other circumstances that are unforeseen. This explains why even the "forecasters" take a financial bath from time to time. The element of luck is part of investing no matter how you slice it. However, this doesn't mean that you are entering rocky waters and are in danger. It simply means that you should go into investing with your eyes open and with an understanding that you should not beat yourself up if all does not go as planned.

Anyone and everyone can invest. Newcomers are joining the investment world in great numbers thanks to online trading and other technology. And many are seeing marvelous returns. You, too, can be part of the successful investing world. It does not take an extensive knowledge of Wall Street or a large bankroll to watch your money grow. You can do it with a little effort, some patience, and an ounce of good fortune.

INVESTING IN STOCKS, BONDS, AND MUTUAL FUNDS

Stocks, bonds, and mutual funds are the three primary investment tools for the majority of investors looking to earn money outside of bank accounts. Even retirement accounts and college funds use these as the basis for much of their portfolios. At a basic level, stocks, bonds, and mutual funds are not particularly difficult to understand, nor do they require exorbitant sums of money. They are also easily accessible to purchase, to sell, and to follow thanks to computers, the financial media, and the Internet. There are numerous other investment options, such as real estate and commodities, but for the average investor, these are quite risky and far more complicated. Nonetheless, there are numerous investment options available—from rare coin or comic book collecting, to buying fine art, to backing a Broadway show, to owning a racehorse. We'll explore some of these in the book but in less detail, as proportionally there are far fewer "investors" in these areas and typically you need far more in-depth knowledge to invest wisely in a racehorse or the latest hot collectible.

Compared to bank accounts, stocks, bonds, and mutual funds tend to provide a far greater percentage of yield. This means, in short, that your money will grow much more quickly. Bank accounts may be earning at a rate of 3 percent, while common stocks over ten years (on the average) will earn more than twice that amount. Bond yields may see 5 percent, 7 percent, or even more, depending on the type and grade of the bond. Tech stocks such as Yahoo, Intel, and other Internet issues have seen unheard of gains, making people with modest investments wealthy in a matter of a couple of years.

INVESTMENT SMARTS

When it comes to investing, you might be on the naive side now, but it doesn't mean you can't learn some basic investing smarts. If you develop a solid understanding of your overall financial picture you will be off to a good start. As mentioned earlier, it's also important to double-check that you are in a secure financial position before investing. A little financial checkup may be in order. Do one final check to see that:

1. You are not behind in your payments on credit cards, or on outstanding loans or operating in the red.
2. You are not investing money that has already been earmarked to pay a line item on your budget.
3. You have some easily accessible cash in a bank account or money market for emergencies or unexpected cash flow problems.

Next, it's important that you understand some of the basics. A few key investment concepts for you to review are listed here.

1. ASSET ALLOCATION

According to a study in the *Financial Analysts Journal* in 1991, only 7 percent of successful investing depends upon the selection of specific stocks, bonds, or mutual funds. The other 93 percent of successful investing depends upon selecting the right asset classes in which to be invested, as well as when to be invested in them. The

Plan on Success

Investment success will depend on a number of factors, including: doing some investing homework; having the money to start with (without borrowing it); assessing your level of risk; and determining how much of your assets you wish to allocate in each type of investment.

question of whether you should be invested in CDs, the stock market, the bond market, real estate, money market funds, precious metals, global investments, and so on is, therefore, the tantamount question that precedes which mutual fund or stock to buy. Essentially, it's a matter of deciding which mode of transportation is best for you before deciding which airline to fly on or which car to rent. Henry Block, financial analyst and president of 5Star Management, a money management firm in Salt Lake City, Utah, notes that the wealth of advertising on television, radio, and in print is designed to promote specific investments, telling you how the investment has faired. "All of this is focusing on the 7 percent of the equation. Very little is done out there to help the average person on the street focus on the 93 percent of the equation, which is what I emphasize," explains Block, who adds that the 93 percent basically says that a rising tide raises all ships. "While an investor can run around deciding whether to invest in a tug boat, a sail boat, an ocean liner, or a cruise ship, he or she needs to appreciate the fact that all the ships will rise or fall with the tide, which holds true for investments in a particular asset class."

Within the broad grouping of asset classes (stocks, bonds, mutual funds, etc.) there are more specific asset classes. For example, equity mutual funds include large-cap stocks, medium or mid-cap stocks, and small-cap stocks ("caps" equate to the size of the company in regard to their assets), plus various sectors such as utilities, technologies, energy, and financial. There are cyclical stocks, and a host of industries such as the auto industry, airline industry, and so on. Each of these sectors and industries can be defined as a different asset class with very different behavioral characteristics. The stocks within that asset class will most often behave according to how that asset class is doing as a whole more than according to the fundamentals of a particular stock or bond. If, for example, IBM reports below-expectation earnings, then (in most cases) so will Apple, Intel, and the entire industry, unless there is a particular story centering around IBM, such as a merger or lawsuit, etc. The same holds true with funds. Asset classes perform in specific ways, the most notable being the tech stocks and tech stock funds of recent years. Surely, you can find an Internet stock that is the exception to the rule, but by and large, the sector has grown universally.

"Objective" Update

You should periodically review your portfolio in line with your goals, your financial plan and your overall "objective." Often investors will establish a financial plan and set certain goals only to find that after a couple years their investments do not match those goals. Just as your plans and goals will change in conjunction with your life situation, your investments may change as well. Small companies grow into larger ones, a less "risky" investment can become a greater risk or visa versa because of the direction in which the company is headed, competition can be outperforming the company you're invested in, or the interest rate can cause the value of your investments to change.

Conservative Approach

You've worked hard for years and now it's time to retire. A couple in your mid 60s, you want to enjoy your retirement years, play more golf, travel and do many things you always wanted to do.

You are looking for safe, low risk investments that produce income to dominate your portfolio.

The first place to turn is bonds, and to manage them effectively you should look to bond mutual funds for 60 percent of your portfolio. Income producing bond funds will be the mainstay of your portfolio. You may, if you are in a high tax bracket, look to put 20 percent in tax free municipal bond funds.

Once you are securely established in low risk bond funds, you want to have 25 percent of your money in the highest yielding money market fund you can find. Some are still over 5 percent.

Then comes the final 15 percent which goes into equity funds. Large cap blue-chip funds that handle the largest-tried and true, most prof-itable long standing companies in the world are a good place to start. You can also look at index funds or balanced funds which invest in both large company stocks (not necessarily blue chippers) and high-grade corporate bonds and/or U.S. Government Bonds. A couple of funds, 10 percent in the large cap fund and 5 percent in the balanced fund, will suffice.

The bottom line is that you first have determined your asset allocation, 60 percent bonds/bond mutual funds, 25 percent money market funds and 15 percent equity (stock) mutual funds. Then look at what the funds are made up of. Government bonds, high grade corporate or municipal funds, tax free municipals, blue-chip stocks, utility stocks or stock in necessities such as food products are your best bets. Aggressive growth funds, high yield bond funds, stocks of new emerging small companies, or anything in the global arena should not be your choices.

Asset allocation, therefore, means determining how much of your assets you are putting into each kind of asset class. You will ultimately allocate your assets into stocks and/or equity funds, bonds and/or bond funds, money market funds, real estate (including REITs (Real Estate Investment Trusts), or other types of investment vehicles based on the following factors:

1. Income level
2. Amount of money you have available to invest
3. Level of investing sophistication
4. Ultimate use for the investment, or goal (retirement, college, etc.)
5. Age
6. Time frame until reaching your goal
7. Level of risk/tolerance

But how do you distribute them?

Combining these factors, you'll determine what is the right breakdown across asset lines. For example, you might want an 80-20 split between equities and bonds or vice versa.

Generally, as investors get closer to their goals, they will become more conservative, particularly if money is earmarked for retirement. Approaching retirement, many investors will put a higher percentage of assets into safer investments with lower fundamental risk. The thinking is often that if you lower your amount of assets in equities and switch to bonds and cash instruments as you approach retirement, you will have a steady flow of income with less risk.

Another theory, however, would be that since on the long term the stock market has always done well (and the average life span may be twenty years beyond a retirement at age sixty-five), you might be just as well off keeping a reasonably high percentage in equities. The equities will grow, and if you should need income you can always sell a stock. Retirees need not invest so conservatively that the money is no longer growing over the next twenty or even thirty years. Karen Altfest of L.J. Altfest and Company, New York–based financial planners, notes that many people are also investing for two generations. "Many people want to invest for their children, and they don't want the money to stop growing or stop

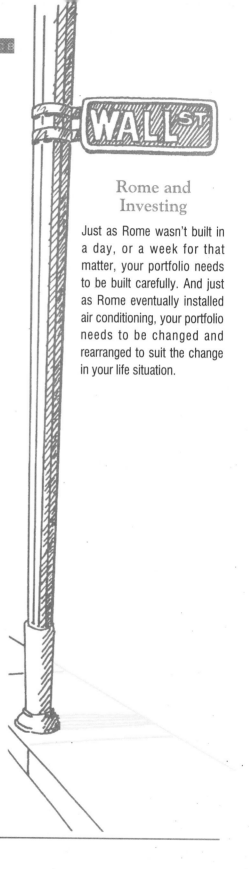

Rome and Investing

Just as Rome wasn't built in a day, or a week for that matter, your portfolio needs to be built carefully. And just as Rome eventually installed air conditioning, your portfolio needs to be changed and rearranged to suit the change in your life situation.

producing when they die." Retirees today need a certain amount for living expenses and various wants and needs, so that part is invested in a more conservative vehicle. Beyond that, the approach may be somewhat more aggressive to build up money for the next generation. Ms. Altfast adds, "It's not only a case of leaving money to family." She cites one client who does not have a family but wants to leave his money to an animal shelter that he cares very much about. "People have plans beyond their death," she notes.

The theories vary, but the main idea is to allocate your assets in line with the factors mentioned here and remember that everyone's situation is different. Do not let financial planners talk you into more-or-less conservative investments that are not right for your personal needs.

Some Suggestions

While I can't emphasize enough that your investment strategy must be based on your individual needs and goals, we still offer a few *broad* portfolio planning strategies for allocating your funds. These are merely a few allocation breakdowns to give you a ballpark look at what you could do in various situations, tailoring them to meet your needs, income, age, etc.

1. If you have a long-term plan, with a ten- to fifteen-year goal, you might start with a more aggressive approach to asset allocation, going with at least 85 to 90 percent in equities, including 25 percent in an international fund and 20 percent in emerging growth funds or small-cap companies.

2. If your goals are coming up in seven to ten years, such as having a child in grade school and saving for college, you can still be somewhat aggressive, with a small amount of international holdings as part of an 80-20 or 75-25 equity-bond split. You can balance your bond fund between conservative and aggressive bonds or bond funds and have some cash investments as well.

3. If you are looking at reaching your goals in four to seven years, such as having a high-school-aged child heading for college, you may want to lean toward an even split between safer bond investments and equities. In this case, however,

you should be opting to invest in more established companies (even some that pay dividends) than going for the higher-risk stocks.

4. If you are reaching retirement, it's usually, though not always, the time to go in the low-risk safe direction. A 75-25 split with bonds leading the way may be the right approach. Once you've established a safe, income-producing portfolio, however, unless you are adverse to risk, you can use the last 5 to 10 percent to play with a riskier equity fund.

These are just some very basic allocation ideas. There are a variety of ways to split up or allocate your assets within the stock or bond market, and real estate, cash instruments, and other investments will also come into play. The overall asset allocation that is right for you will depend on your specific goals, needs, and time frame to reaching your goals. Investment experts agree that allocating your assets properly will provide piece of mind as well as a good game plan toward reaching your overall goals.

2. RISK/TOLERANCE

Some people keep their money in a vault and visit it so infrequently that they barely remember the combination. Others make frequent deposits into the slot machines in Las Vegas and Atlantic City. How risky you choose to be with your money is part and parcel to your personality. Risk means taking a chance, with the outcome not guaranteed to be in your favor. In life, most things require some degree of risk, no matter how minimal . . . you can slip and get injured taking a shower. Financially, you can lose money. Your tolerance is how comfortable you will feel with an unfavorable outcome. When we take greater risks we need to know from the onset that the chance of losing money is greater. However, the rewards are usually greater too.

Risk versus tolerance is one of the first determinants in how you should invest your money. It is a way to assess which investment route you wish to take: conservative or aggressive. Some investors will take much bigger risks looking for large gains, while others are content just having their money earn them a steady income. There are levels in between.

Not for Everyone

Investing, and particularly risk taking, is not for people in debt or for anyone who is living from paycheck to paycheck. To invest in the stock market or in mutual funds, you should first have some savings tucked away in cash instruments, preferably $10,000 or $20,000. If you have a 401(k) or similar retirement plan, you are already investing to some degree and your company is putting in money to build a retirement plan for you. Not unlike the sign at the racetrack that says "bet with your head, not over it," investing follows the same principle. You should not be taking any risk or playing the stock market with money you cannot afford to spend.

Investment Smarts 2

Don't be easily sidetracked. If you want to invest in a stock fund and someone is hell-bent on selling you on a balanced fund with stocks and bonds (although it may be a good fund), you are being diverted from what you have set out to do. This is not to say that if you sit down and research other options as they come up, you may not find alternatives to your initial choices. It is to say, however, that you need to take time to investigate (a) the alternative and (b) why are you being "sold" on the alternative. Often when a particular type of investment is not available, the broker will sell you lock, stock, and barrel on what is available and tell you why it is better.

Here are a few samples of risk-tolerance questions to help you begin to determine where you fall in regard to risk versus tolerance. Keep in mind there are no "right" answers, only "your" answers!

1. Your stock drops four points within the first few days after you buy it. What do you do?
   A. Sell it and take the loss.
   B. Sit tight and do nothing.
   C. Buy more shares at the lower price.
2. Which sounds better to you?
   A. A monthly 6 percent rate of interest and a principal that will be maintained.
   B. A monthly rate that could vary from 0 percent to 15 percent but maintains your principal.
   C. A rate of interest that after a month could be anywhere from 0 to 30 percent but does not ensure you will maintain your principal.
3. You have $1,000 to invest, and your choices are:
   A. An investment that after six months will pay you $200.
   B. An investment that after six months will pay you anywhere from 0 to $500.
   C. An investment that after six months could be completely lost or pay an unlimited amount.
4. Although gambling is not investing, there is a basic principle of risk inherent to both (obviously, it is greater with gambling). On the roulette table, would you prefer to put $20 on:
   A. Red or Black, a near 50-50 shot paying 2 to 1 or $40.
   B. One of three rows of numbers, a near 33.3 shot paying 3 to 1 or $60.
   C. One of thirty-six numbers or "0" or "00," a .3 shot paying 36 to 1 or $720 (it's actually 38 to 1 odds with "0" and "00" but the house keeps the remaining dollars).
5. Suppose you buy a mutual fund that boasts a 20 percent increase in return over six months, but you find out about another fund that gained 34 percent over that same time period. Do you:
   A. Stay put.
   B. Track the other fund but do nothing for a year.
   C. Switch to the other fund immediately.

6. You invest $5,000. In ten years you can accept that you will have:
   A. Between $5,000 and $9,000.
   B. Between $2,500 and $16,000.
   C. Between $500 and $30,000.

And on it goes. There are numerous questions to determine what your personality is when it comes to money. If you are answering "A" to most of these questions you are playing it "closer to the vest" and are looking to take less risk and seek out safer, more conservative investments such as bond funds, money market funds, balanced funds leaning toward bonds, and large-cap stocks. If you are answering "B" to most of them, you are being cautious but are willing to take some level of risk. You can play stock funds (primarily domestic); buy stocks leaning toward the larger, better-known companies, and even have some money in bonds to keep things feeling comfortable. If you are answering "C" to most questions, you are more comfortable taking a greater risk. You are willing to go with emerging companies in stocks or stock funds, have some money in international funds, and look at aggressive growth funds without trepidation.

But don't take our word for it. Here is a sample of a risk tolerance questionnaire courtesy of 5Star Management in Salt Lake City, Utah. The questions are once again designed to measure your tolerance for investment risk. These feature more extensive hypothetical situations.

SAMPLE PORTFOLIO RISK QUESTIONNAIRE

Used by permission of Henry Block of 5Star Management.
1. What is your age?
   • 35 years or under
   • 36–55
   • 55 or above
2. What do you expect to be your next major expenditure?
   • Buying a house
   • Paying for a college education
   • Capitalizing a new business
   • Providing for retirement

An Asset Allocation Tale

Although they can serve the purpose, financial advisors are not needed to remind you how important it is to spread your money around. One planner noted a gentleman who was investing for his daughter's college education. The planner suggested that the investor not only go with equities, as he was planning to do, but also have some bonds to round out the portfolio. As it happened, at the time his daughter was starting college, the market was dropping. Rather than having to sell one of the stocks, he was able to cash in a bond that reached maturity the August before the college term was about to begin. This is an example of asset allocation.

3. When do you expect to use *most* of the money you are accumulating in your investments?
   - At any time now. . . . So a high level of liquidity is important
   - Probably in the future . . . 2–5 years from now
   - In 6–10 years
   - Probably in 1–20 or more years from now

4. Over the next several years, you expect your annual income to:
   - Stay about the same
   - Grow moderately
   - Grow substantially
   - Decrease moderately
   - Decrease substantially

5. Due to a general market correction, one of your investments loses 14 percent of its value a short time after you buy it. What do you do?
   - Sell the investment so you will not have to worry if it continues to decline
   - Hold on to it and wait for it to climb back up
   - Buy more of the same investment . . . because at the new low price, it looks even better than when you bought it

6. Which of these plans would you choose for your investment dollars?
   - You would go for maximum diversity, dividing your portfolio among all available investments, including those ranging from highest return/greatest risk to lowest return/lowest risk
   - You are concerned about putting all of your eggs in one basket, so you would divide your portfolio among two investments with high rates of return and moderate risk
   - You would put your investment dollars into the investment with the highest rate of return and most risk

7. Assuming you are investing in a stock mutual fund, which one do you choose?

Some Investor Types

Investor A: Conservative Carl. Carl has 40 percent in a money market fund/cash instrument; 50 percent in bonds, mostly government issued; and 5 percent in stocks, primarily large-caps.

Investor B: Nearly Moderate Millie. Millie has 25 percent in cash instruments, including CDs, 25 percent in bonds; 15 percent in a bond fund; and 35 percent in two stock funds, one blue-chip fund, and one mid- and small-cap fund.

Investor C: Moderate Mac. Mac has 10 percent in a money market mutual fund; 30 percent in a bond fund; and 60 percent in three stock funds: an index fund, a large-cap fund, and a small-cap fund.

Investor D: Moderate to Aggressive Angie. Angie has 10 percent in a money market mutual fund; 25 percent in balanced bond funds; and 65 percent in equities: 50 percent in stock funds including 10 percent in international, and 15 percent in equities including several growth stocks.

Investor E: Aggressive Arnie. Arnie has 10 percent in a money market mutual fund; 5 percent in a bond fund; and 85 percent in equities, including small-cap, aggressive growth, and international equity funds.

Riskier and Sexier

As for risks versus payoffs, it's simple: The riskier, sexier investments (the ones that have people talking) are those with the highest payoffs. The less risky investments have less growth potential but provide greater assurance of maintaining your capital.

- A fund of companies that may make significant techno-logical advances that are still selling at their low initial offering price
- A fund that only invests in established, well-known companies that have a potential for continued growth
- A fund devoted to "blue chip," highly diversified stocks that pay stock dividends

8. Assuming you are investing in only one bond, which bond do you choose?
   - A "junk bond" that pays a higher interest rate than the other two bonds, but also gives you the least sense of security with regard to a possible default
   - A "treasury bond" which pays the lowest interest rate of the three bonds, but is backed by the United States Government
   - The bond of a well-established company that pays a rate of interest somewhere between the other two bonds
   - A "tax-free bond" since minimizing taxes is your primary investment objective

9. Your investment advisor expects inflation to return and suggests that you invest in "hard" assets such as real estate and cable TV, which have historically out paced inflation. Your only "financial" assets are long-term bonds. What do you do?
   - Ignore the advice and hold onto the bonds
   - Sell the bonds, putting half the proceeds in "hard" assets and the other half into money market funds
   - Sell the bonds and put all of the proceeds into "hard" assets
   - Sell the bonds, put the proceeds into "hard" assets and borrow additional money so you can buy even more "hard" assets

10. You have the opportunity to fund an underwater salvage operation to recover sunken treasure. The chance of finding the vessel and recovering the treasure is only 25 percent. But, if the operation is successful, you could earn 74 to 100 times your investment. How much do you invest?
    - Nothing at all

- One month's salary
- Three month's salary
- Six month's salary

11. You have just reached the $10,000 plateau on a TV game show. Now you must choose between quitting with the $10,000 in hand or betting the entire $10,000 in one of three alternative scenarios. Which do you choose?

- The $10,000 . . . You take the money and run
- A 50 percent chance of winning $50,000
- A 20 percent chance of winning $75,000
- A 5 percent chance of winning $100,000

Such a questionnaire can be graded by professionals and can help you determine the type of investments that best suit you.

When it comes to investing, many people will fall into each category. Some will move from one category to the other depending on their investment success and where they are in their life at the time they are looking to invest.

Your life situation will be a factor in what level of investment risk you choose to take. For example, you might seek out a higher-risk investment when putting money into a college fund when your child is three or four years of age. At this point you can build up funds more quickly since you have more time to adjust should the investments not be performing as you had hoped. However, once your son or daughter is four or five years from college, you may want to move your money into more sure-fire, lower-risk (lower reward) investments for safety. The level of risk you choose, therefore, depends on your financial goals and how much time you have to meet such goals.

An unmarried, 29-year-old corporate executive may have more money available to put into riskier investments than the married father or mother of three paying a mortgage and high living expenses. The executive is most likely at a point where his or her money can grow without drastically affecting long-term plans. When it comes to risk/tolerance, there is no real formula unless you factor in all the components: AGE, INCOME, SAVINGS, GOALS, and PERSONALITY.

3. LIQUIDITY

Liquidity is a way of asking, *How fast can I get out of my investment and have the cash should I need it?* When you have money in your bank account or in a money market account, it is accessible to you and therefore "liquid."

Stocks, mutual funds, and even most bonds are liquid in that you are not locked into them with a penalty of losing money as you would be with a CD or 401(k). When you sell a stock, fund, or bond (or redeem a bond), there is usually a short wait of a few days or perhaps a week until you see your check. If you plan accordingly, as advised here, and have some money set aside in cash instruments, you should not worry about the liquidity of this type of investing. The more worrisome investments, in terms of liquidity, would be areas such as owning real estate or dealing in fine art, where your only way of becoming liquid is to find a buyer. These are not savvy investments for the rookie investor.

If you are properly insured for your life situation (home owners' insurance if you own a home, and so on), you will be covered for major emergencies. In reality, you can still sell off a stock and probably see the money faster than you'll see the check from the insurance company. Having money available for emergencies is one aspect of liquidity. However, the other side is knowing when you are going to need the money. For example, if you know you are buying a house in the near future, you will want to have money liquid for the down payment. If you are approaching a down payment and are worried that a drop in the market will eat into the money you need for that down payment, then you should move your money into a money market fund. Returning to asset allocation, you want a portion of your allocated investments to be liquid. This is usually the case with most of the "traditional" investment options.

4. RETURNS

Closely tied with risk are returns. Traditionally, greater risk means greater potential returns. You can see a return on your investment in the form of a dividend, from interest, or from capital gains due to making a sale of shares of a fund, equity, bond, or other investment vehicle. Compare returns you can make from various investments based on the returns such investments have seen in the past, over several years. Short-term returns are hard to gage as they can be based on a sudden event or turn in the market.

Interest from bonds, as well as bank accounts or CDs, offer a steady (safe) way to see a return on your money. Your principal remains steady while your money grows. Preferred stocks and some common stocks will pay dividends whereby you will get a steady, although not glamorous, return on your investment. As long as the money is growing faster than the rate of inflation, this is a way of seeing a "comfortable" return.

Your level of risk/tolerance will enter the picture as you determine which investment is right for you. It's also worth noting that you do not have to fall into only one category. Many investors are receiving interest and/or dividends while holding stocks or mutual funds that pay neither but are growing steadily in value. They are bringing in high returns, or money back on your dollar, which can be turned into a profit when you sell.

It is worth noting that many investment planners and counselors will agree that chasing high returns is not generally considered a good investment strategy. Yesterday's high returns will not necessarily be the high returns of tomorrow. And, most often, significant returns take time to build, through compounding interest, or through being in the stock market for several years. Rather than chase returns, you will almost always be better off setting up your goals and following a set plan of action that has you allocating your money into different asset classes and diversifying within each asset class, which brings us to the next area, "diversification."

5. DIVERSIFICATION

To diversify means to "spread it around" or "not put all your eggs in one basket." When we vote, we look at several candidates and select one for better or worse . . . too often for worse. In the world of investing, there are several investment vehicles available, but unlike voting, you need not choose only one. Among the reasons why mutual funds are so popular these days is that they select several stocks, bonds, or other investment vehicles for you. Funds are managed by professional money managers who choose a variety of investment vehicles. In short, they diversify.

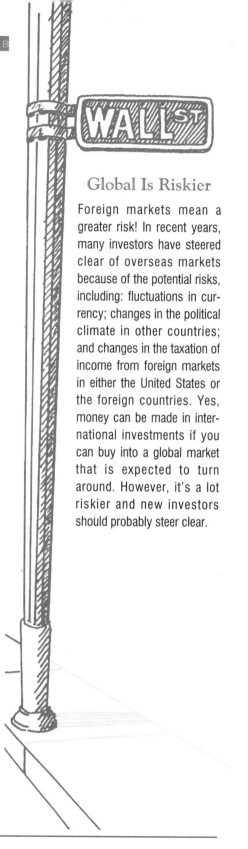

Global Is Riskier

Foreign markets mean a greater risk! In recent years, many investors have steered clear of overseas markets because of the potential risks, including: fluctuations in currency; changes in the political climate in other countries; and changes in the taxation of income from foreign markets in either the United States or the foreign countries. Yes, money can be made in international investments if you can buy into a global market that is expected to turn around. However, it's a lot riskier and new investors should probably steer clear.

Churning Is a No-No

The most important things to watch out for is a broker who is "churning" your account, which means that he or she is doing a lot of trading to run up the commission charges you will owe. This should not happen if you do not give the broker license to make transactions without your approval. Only in a case where you have established a comfortable rapport with a broker should you allow him or her to make transactions.

Owning a mutual fund does not mean you cannot also own stocks, bonds, or more than one fund. Tantamount to putting money on seven numbers on the roulette table instead of just one, you have better odds at winning. However, unlike the roulette wheel, which will have just one winning number per spin, you could win on several stocks.

The most prominent strategy is to mix high- and low-risk investment vehicles and to allocate the assets wisely, as cited in the examples in the previous risk/tolerance section. Once your funds are allocated into different asset groups, you diversify within that asset group. Buying stock means buying *stocks*, giving you a better chance at winners within that asset class. One investor who allocated a portion of his portfolio into mutual funds learned about diversifying just in time. Heavily into global funds in the early 1990s, the investor took the suggestion to branch out a little and try some new funds, including those in the areas of health and technology. Sure enough, his global funds took a downturn in the late 90s, his health fund brought him good returns, and his tech fund brought him excellent returns. Whereas this is also a story of allocating assets, it is a story of diversifying. Spread it around. That way, if one egg falls out of the basket, you still have enough left to make an award-winning omelet.

NOTE: One of the biggest mistakes an investor can make is putting everything in one pot.

6. COMMISSIONS AND COSTS

The primary cost associated with investing is that of paying commissions. Whether you are trading online or dealing with a real human being, commission fees will be attached to stock transactions. Mutual funds can be "no-loads," which means you do not pay a commission. However, there are operating costs associated with mutual funds. Many people don't bother to examine the operating costs associated with their mutual funds. Sometimes they can eat away at your profits, so they are worth checking out. Brokers dealing bonds will buy them at one price and sell them to you at another. The difference, or the spread, is in essence a commission of sorts for the broker. Buying government bonds on your own can eliminate this "spread."

DOING YOUR HOMEWORK

In school it meant a gold star or a good grade. In the investment arena, doing your homework can mean solid returns on your investment. There are countless Web sites and many important magazines, such as *Kiplingers*, *Money*, and *Smart Money*. There are also publications like the *Wall Street Journal* and *Morningstar*, which watch over the financial world and keep investors abreast of the latest news. The Financial Network, CNBC, and other networks also keep people up to date.

Doing investing homework, however, means more than just brushing up on the broad picture; it means looking more closely at the companies you wish to invest in. While you might not be doing too much of a background check before buying U.S. government bonds, you should look into the financial background of whatever company or municipality in which you are looking to invest. Surprisingly, many investors do not do much, if any, research. Even in the case of U.S. savings bonds there is a lot to learn about redeeming them, collecting the maximum interest, and so on.

Among the things you need to look at, besides the per-share stock quotes over weeks, months, and years, is the company's sales. Are they growing or are they flat? Look for a consistency or upswing in sales and earnings. A company can be making a profit but cutting costs. At some point, if they don't have a long trend of sales growth, they will eventually run out of places to cut costs. This can spell trouble. If sales growth is flattening out or if sales have been down, it will reflect in the company's stock.

It's important that, from the history of the company, you can make a fairly good prediction as to the company's future. Investments are based on the future. Newsletters, forecasters, and "experts" spend their days and nights forecasting—or trying to forecast—which company's stocks will perform well in the future. You will see when making your evaluations and studying the company's past history that companies react differently to changes in the economy. Some companies have experienced downswings but historically recovered quickly, while others have taken much longer. If you have patience, you can survive with stocks as most will recover over time. The market as a whole has always bounced back, whether it's

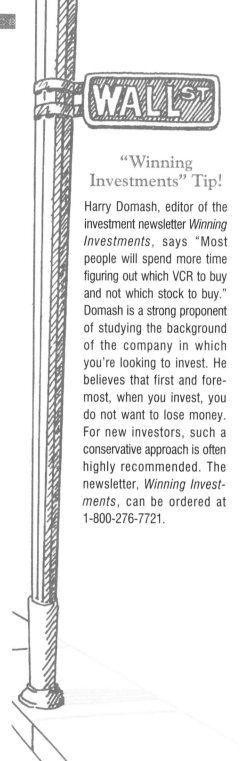

"Winning Investments" Tip!

Harry Domash, editor of the investment newsletter *Winning Investments*, says "Most people will spend more time figuring out which VCR to buy and not which stock to buy." Domash is a strong proponent of studying the background of the company in which you're looking to invest. He believes that first and foremost, when you invest, you do not want to lose money. For new investors, such a conservative approach is often highly recommended. The newsletter, *Winning Investments*, can be ordered at 1-800-276-7721.

in six months or two years. Sometimes companies are worth investing in during their down periods. Buying stock in a company that has done well but is struggling at present is called *value investing*. This too comes from research. Will the company grow again? Is the basic business sound? Can they correct their problems? Are they working on new technology or new products that will once again put them in the competitive market? Ahead of the market?

It is important that you look at the nature of the company and what it produces. Some of the brand new experimental (and "cutting edge") technology of this generation will be heavily marketed in the years to come, much the way VCRs and computers were on the rise some fifteen years ago. It's important that you judge which new industries are up-and-coming as well as which long-standing ones are still vital today. Common sense will tell you that a company making a faster Web server will be growing faster than one making type-writer ribbons. While most major corporations adjust and move along with the times, some lag behind. See what companies are up to. Sometimes an old company has new tricks up its sleeve in the way of new products that will bring it back to a previously enjoyed level of success.

You should also look at how a company holds up in its market. A company like Hewlett-Packard, for example, is part of the age of computers and electronic equipment. However, because of market saturation, it is not doing as well as one might have expected. Some industries grow at a rapid rate and not all the players (companies) can keep up. The golf industry has seen some mediocre results in the past couple of years. The game is more popular than ever. The technology has created first-rate new products. Numerous companies are manufacturing clubs, balls, and bags. The problem is that as fast as the game grows in popularity and people purchase new equipment, they cannot keep all of the companies blossoming at once. In the late 1990s more courses than ever were popping up, but some of the equipment manufacturers were having slow years. The problem was that there were too many manufacturers and, unlike a company making food products

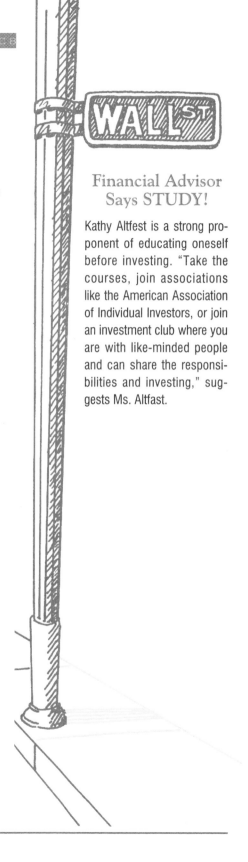

(an essential), new golf clubs are not essentials (but don't tell golf fanatics that).

One of the easiest ways to do financial homework is simply to open your eyes to what is new and being marketed widely around you. What are people talking about? What is generating the latest "buzz"? By learning about upcoming marketing and products, you are learning about a company and its future.

In early 1999, an investing magazine was hyping the company that owned the licensing of the children's toys associated with the television program called *Teletubbies*. Some of us with children saw the characters introduced over a year earlier as the most beloved characters in children's television in Great Britain.

When people thinking about "investing" see a new and innovative product that either is a time saver, fills a specific need, or has the potential to be well marketed and hyped to children, they ask themselves, "Who makes that?" Then they start thinking of investing in that company and look them up. The world around you can provide a lot of good investment tips that even the experts in their financial offices may miss out on.

CHECKING OUT BROKERS

While it's important to do your homework, one area is often overlooked. Having checked up on the company you are investing in, it is also worth your while to check up on the brokerage house and even on the broker who is doing your investing. Even when you are trading online, someone, or someone's computer system is at the other end of the transaction. Obviously, you should check out an unknown, smaller, or perhaps less-established brokerage house very carefully. You should also, however, ask questions and be well versed in what the investment process is within a large, established company. Many people make the mistake of assuming that because the company is a household name with numerous commercials featuring lions or bulls on your television set, they will automatically do well by you. These companies have massive lists of investors and you are, in effect, another number in their computer bank. This doesn't mean they won't make money for you. But, since your money is far more important to you than it is to them, it means that

Financial Advisor Says STUDY!

Kathy Altfest is a strong proponent of educating oneself before investing. "Take the courses, join associations like the American Association of Individual Investors, or join an investment club where you are with like-minded people and can share the responsibilities and investing," suggests Ms. Altfast.

you are entitled to ask questions and make sure you are comfortable with the responses. High-pressure sales pitches and an approach that makes you feel stupid for asking a question is not what you want from a firm in which you want to put your savings. A comfort level, therefore, is important to most investors, especially new ones.

Besides studying up on the companies you are investing in, you can research potential brokers. Large financial companies have been known to invest money in the wrong fund, neglect to start a direct deposit, or fail to send financial statements. Some have even completely lost an investor's entire account. Thank goodness this is not typical activity, but it happens. Humans make mistakes and so do computers, which are essentially at the hands of humans, no matter what others tell you when they quip, "Oh, the computer must have done that."

UNSCRUPULOUS BROKERS

Millions of investments are made every year without a hitch, and yours will very likely fall into that category. However, be aware that even if you've researched the firm and the broker to ensure that all is "legit" regarding licensing, there are still unscrupulous brokers. But there is something you can do about them. Therefore, we include this as an ounce of "prevention" before presenting several pounds of investments.

The area of securities arbitration and mediation is one in which you hope not to be involved. However, it does exist, and there are numerous cases that benefit from such types of intervention, and the needs are not always clear-cut. The issue is often not a matter of licensing or having proper papers filed.

Even the top Wall Street firm can have a broker or two that have a conflict between their desire for commission dollars and the goals and needs of the investor. According to Paul Young of the Securities Arbitration Group, Inc., who has been in the field of securities arbitration for twenty-one years, most cases are related to:

Suitability
Misrepresentation
Omissions of material facts about the recommendations
Commission grabs (also called churning)
Unauthorized transactions

Suitability is the most prominent issue in securities arbitration and mediation nationwide. It is the idea that the broker, in an effort to receive greater commissions, is selling an investor on an investment that is not suitable for that individual. Objective factors such as income, age, net worth, and health should be part of the equation. The always important subjective factor, risk/tolerance, should also be included. A dealer acting in the best interest of his or her client is supposed to be including these factors when selecting the appropriate, suitable investment.

An example of a classic "suitability" case stems from a major brokerage firm in the early 1990s. A sixty-seven-year-old man with a heart condition worked as a truck driver for more than thirty years. He and his wife purchased a home in the early 1950s, where they lived for some forty years until his retirement. They decided to sell their home and move into a condominium. The value of the home had grown over the years and was worth $100,000, which was far more money than the couple had ever seen before. Within two weeks a broker from a major firm sold him a thirty-year, long-term, non-liquid, high-commission, high-risk, limited real estate partnership (such partnerships were more popular in the early 1990s) that would not terminate until the man was more than one hundred years of age. Since partnerships paid much higher broker commissions than other investments, this was highly profitable for the broker, who sold the couple on this "fabulous investment opportunity" hook, line, and sinker. The couple, who had never invested before, trusted this broker, who, after all, was part of a major firm. Before they realized it, they found themselves out of all the money—all $100,000 that they had made from their home.

Fortunately, there was arbitration. The brokerage house fought hard, but the bottom line was that their broker had sold this couple, who knew nothing about investing, an investment that was com-

Knowledge Does Not Equal Positive Gains

For all it is worth and for all the benefits of being well informed, investors do, however, have to realize that they should not treat information as a supreme virtue. Information serves as a guide, but all the insights and past historical background you can possibly gather still does not take away the speculative aspect of investing—unless of course, you are getting your facts, figures, and numbers from a crystal ball!

Strategy for Starting Out

Once you've established that you indeed have at least the equivalent of six months expenses tucked away in a safe haven, being a bank account or money market account, you can start by setting up an investing plan.

Here are some basic steps.

1. Determine your financial goals and how long you have until you anticipate reaching them.

2. Plan to start with 10 percent of your annual income (assuming you are not in debt and can cover your living expenses). Take half of that amount or 5 percent (say $2,500, which is 5 percent of a $50,000 income) for your initial investment.

3. Take the other 5 percent, or $2,500, and invest it monthly over the course of one year which comes to (or round off to $225 or $230). You can have it invested by direct deposit from your bank account.

4. Select a balanced mutual fund, which will start you off with both bonds (safer investment) and stocks (more risky investment) OR select an Index fund, such as S&P, that covers a wide range of stocks and a bond mutual fund and split the amount between the two funds.

5. After six months, evaluate your situation. If you are seeing positive results you can increase the monthly amount being invested, particularly if you have had a pay increase. You can also take part of your profits and look into a stock, bond or mutual fund that meets your risk/tolerance level.

pletely unsuitable. In eight months they received their $100,000 back, plus interest, plus $50,000 in damages. This is the beauty of arbitration. There is no appeal in arbitration and cases like this can be won. As an investor, it's important that you know that you can fight back if you've been victimized.

"Misrepresentation" is where the broker is telling you something about a company or an investment to get you to purchase it, when in fact there is nothing to substantiate the (sales-related) statements. "But the broker told me" is the common phrase of investors who have purchased a stock or other security from brokers who misrepresented themselves. "The broker told me that small midwestern coffee franchise was going national like Starbucks," says the investor. The broker responds, "I never said that." To avoid such situations, you should ask for a written plan of action explaining where you are today and where you expect to be in X number of years to reach your goal. On the other hand, you must not take the broker's word at face value; investigate the source material from which the broker got that information. The broker should be able to tell you where you can look to find out that indeed this local coffee house is looking to go national. If the broker "can't tell you that," then there is something wrong with this scenario. Brokers are plugged into the market, but they do not have secret sources, unless they are doing insider trading—an entirely different matter to contend with. The bottom line is that a recommendation from a broker should be based on something that you can see in writing.

"Commission grabs," or "churning," is defined as making unnecessary transactions to grab more commissions. There is no set number at which churning begins. In one case it can be three transactions that need not have been made, and in another instance it could be forty. The bottom line is whether or not a broker is making transactions for the sake of running up commissions. This is not uncommon, so it's important to get valid reasons for transactions before approving them.

The easiest problem for investors to catch is the last one, "unauthorized transactions," which is simply where a broker has made a transaction without your authorization. You should always read your monthly statement carefully, even if they are difficult to read, or have someone look it over with you. If you see a stock or security appear

Investment Smarts 3

Don't chase yesterday's hottest news. We'll remind you of this periodically throughout the book. Yesterday's hottest mutual fund is not necessarily tomorrow's hottest mutual fund. Most investments, other than collectibles and art, operate solely in the future. You can use the past as a guidepost, but the recent past is not always a fair indicator. Look back a few years.

Be leery of cold calls. There are plenty of brokers relying on a percentage of their cold calls panning out. Don't be one of that percentage . . . or as Nancy Reagan used to say, "Just say No." At best, they should only get you to a point where if you hear something that sounds interesting you will request some written literature. Then study it, *but don't buy from cold callers.*

and no one ever discussed it with you, that is an unauthorized transaction. A broker cannot simply make moves, unless authorized to do so, without your permission. A statement such as "I couldn't reach you so I bought it in your best interest" is complete baloney. "Well, you hired me to take care of your finances" is equal baloney. A broker is hired to handle your account as advised specifically by you.

If a broker is going to work for you, you have the right to interview him or her. Don't be intimidated. You can ask for referrals, written research reports, and prospectus reports. Find out where the broker has worked previously and something about his or her background. You are entitled to know about the person who is handling your money. Just because the brokerage house hired the broker in good faith doesn't mean he or she is going to act in your best interest. Again, the majority of brokers do not fall into these categories, but as in any profession there are some rotten apples.

As the investor, you have a responsibility too: to tell the truth. If you have lied about your financial situation or in regard to other important factors, it can lose a case for you.

Mediation can also be used to settle a complaint. Unlike arbitration, where a panel of three arbitrators make a decision after a hearing (win, lose, or draw), in mediation both sides enter voluntarily and try to work out a settlement. The goal is to avoid arbitration by working out a solution that is satisfactory to both sides. It's more of a compromise than a situation with a winner and loser. If, however, one side does not feel he or she is getting a "fair settlement," that individual can always go on to arbitration. It's a growing area in the business that can, ultimately, save both sides time and money.

You can contact the Securities and Exchange Commission (SEC) at 1-202-942-7040. While the process is slow, they will listen to you and let you file your report. The government can terminate the license of a dealer, impose fines, or even send the broker to jail in extreme situations. The National Association of Securities Dealers (NASD) at 1-800-289-9999 is another place you can turn to get information about a particular securities dealer.

However, to get your money back if you feel you've been ripped off (and for faster service), you might call the Securities Arbitration

Group, Inc. Their hotline number is 1-800-222-4724. They are a non-governmental securities hotline designed to help the investor.

THE INTIMIDATION FACTOR

There are three common reasons why many people do not invest. First, they do not have the extra funds because they need every dollar to cover their living expenses—which is obviously a valid reason. Second, people do not know what to do when it comes to investing. For that there are this book and numerous resources available in the way of magazines and Web sites. And third, people are intimidated. This book will hopefully alleviate some of the intimidating aspects of investing. Often intimidation is linked to not knowing enough about investing. You do not need to know all the buzzwords, inside "lingo," investment strategies, and names of the major players or the names of the top mutual funds to be able to put your money into a stock, bond, or mutual fund and have it work for you. You need to know the basics:

> What investing is all about
> What to look for when selecting an investment
> How to follow your investment
> How to best position yourself for better results to meet your
> > goals
> How to get out when you choose to

It's amazing how many people hold onto an investment longer than they either want to or should because they are too afraid or intimidated to call a broker and say, "sell it." Any qualified financial planner, broker, or "analyst" (and we use the term loosely), should be working with you based on your needs and your level of "risk" when it comes to investing. In fact, you need not be intimidated because you need not work with anyone with whom you don't feel comfortable. AND in today's electronic world, you may not need to work with anyone at all. Web brokers, discussed later, allow you to make trades round the clock without ever having to deal with a broker. There are more than one hundred Web broker sites, and commissions generally run between $5 and $30 per transaction.

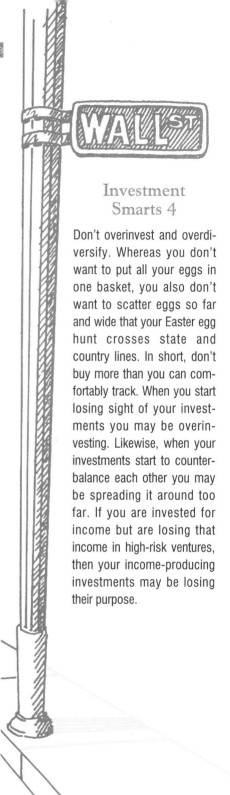

Investment Smarts 4

Don't overinvest and overdiversify. Whereas you don't want to put all your eggs in one basket, you also don't want to scatter eggs so far and wide that your Easter egg hunt crosses state and country lines. In short, don't buy more than you can comfortably track. When you start losing sight of your investments you may be overinvesting. Likewise, when your investments start to counterbalance each other you may be spreading it around too far. If you are invested for income but are losing that income in high-risk ventures, then your income-producing investments may be losing their purpose.

Hottest Mistake on the Rise

As they used to say on the music chart countdowns, "It's rising with a bullet on the charts." The hottest growing mistake made by investors, thanks to online trading, is over trading. It's moving up the list rapidly as new investors have fun wheeling and dealing at their home computers, often missing out on profits because they've traded too soon.

While electronic trading alleviates the "intimidation factor," it can cause other problems. Many online investors tend to get carried away and overdo it, simply because it's so easy. It's the same reason many television shopping club viewers have a garage full of junk—it was just too easy to buy it. In this day and age of computer games, playing the market can often feel like another version of poker or solitaire.

Some investors, therefore, appreciate the guidelines set by a broker's hours. Said one investor, "It makes me do my homework, knowing I've got to tell a broker what I plan to trade. He'll make the transition regardless, but I want to sound like I know something. In a way it serves as a speed bump to reckless investing." While some online traders are spending the bulk of their profits on commission costs, others use the Internet primarily for research and trade accordingly.

Keep in mind that your $1000 investment is just as significant to you as the $1,000,000 investment of a Wall Street tycoon. Plus, you might enjoy the notion that he or she has much more to lose. Also, remember that all the huge success stories you read about began with an initial investment, be it $100 or $1,000 or $10,000!

BE A GADFLY

A gadfly is a fly that doesn't leave you alone. When investing or transferring your investment from one account to another, it's important that you stay on top of the situation. DO NOT ASSUME EVERYTHING IS TAKEN CARE OF because a broker says "Don't worry, I'll make the transaction." The number of errors made by investing and financial companies is surprisingly higher than you would imagine. Almost every long-term investor can recount at least one tale of a transaction gone awry. Even the authors of this book can recount our own tales of ineptitude.

Yes, all the large firms use a wide range of technological wizardry. However, the old adage "Garbage in, garbage out" still applies. Take for example a major bullish investment company that accidentally deleted one woman's $50,000 account. Another investor talks about transferring $200,000 from one brokerage house to another.

The second house said, "We never received it," while the first house said, "We sent it." So where was his two hundred grand? On a smaller level, one couple invested $1,000 in a Merrill Lynch account in July with a certain amount to be transferred directly into the account on a monthly basis. By the following February the transfer had never been made, and while the $1,000 had earned interest, there should have been a lot more in that account. The representative, who phoned often to set up a meeting to get the couple to invest, apologized for not following through with this situation. However, he still didn't correct it for another three months. The point of these nightmares in investing is that if you do not call and make sure your transaction was made correctly, double-check, check once more, and check your statement quickly, errors can and will occur, and you will be at a loss.

When transferring an account from one brokerage house to another, you should not have to do a great deal of work; simply fill out an Automated Customer Account Transfer form in cooperation with your new broker. The new broker will ask you for a copy of your statements from your old brokerage house plus some additional proof of identity. Your transfer should be made in five to ten business days for regular accounts and ten to fifteen business days for IRA accounts and other types of retirement accounts. This is a process done electronically, but it starts with a human being. Since the new brokerage house wants your business they should be responsible. This doesn't always mean they are. It will take much longer if the paperwork sits on someone's desk for two weeks. Therefore you must check with the brokerage house and make sure they made the transfer and then look at your statement and make sure they transferred the account correctly. Some brokerage houses will charge you for closing an account. On the other hand, sometimes the new brokerage house, happy to get you on board, will pick up that fee—it can't hurt to ask. This is also the case with transactions. You can ask about waiving certain small fees if you are doing significant business with a firm. And if they've made an error, make sure you never pay for it. One investor told of the brokerage house transferring his money to the wrong account and then charging him a fee to move it into the proper place. He explained to the broker that he was going to write a letter to the president of the company, and the broker thought better of charging him to correct their own error.

Just so you know, the $50,000 and $200,000 examples listed here were both found—neither investor lost those large sums of money through brokerage house negligence. They did, as did the couple with the thousand dollars, lose interest income they could have been accruing.

The moral is to stay on top of your investments. Make sure they are where you want them to be. And remember that the SEC is a good place to turn to report companies that are not doing their job.

CHAPTER TWO

Investing: Getting In, Patience, and Getting Out

Financial Homework Is Introspective Too!

Doing financial homework means more than just deciding which stocks and mutual funds will bring you the best returns. Too many people forget that part of doing their financial homework is re-evaluating their own position. For example, a two income family that is now a one income family may have to stop contributing the same amount to their mutual fund every month for a period of time, or certainly stop buying the "new hot stock" for a few months. Someone who had been playing the market aggressively but now has additional financial responsibilities might need to look toward some more conservative options. Conversely, a family who has been paying for a full time baby sitter and investing minimally, may, now that their children are in school (and the sitter is no longer needed) have more money to put into investments.

Now that you have determined your financial goals, armed yourself with investment "smarts," determined how much risk you could tolerate, and accepted that your investment growth will not happen overnight, what do you do?

For your purposes, as the beginning investor, it's important to know three things: "*Getting In*," "*Patience*," and "*Getting Out*." BUT, before jumping into the water, it's a good idea to know how to swim. As an investor, it's important to lay the groundwork before diving into the investment pool. In the previous section we discussed areas such as asset allocation, diversification, liquidity, and risk/tolerance. As we approach the "ins and outs" of actually investing, it's important to see how these areas tie together and how "risk" (very often used as a broad term to explain a fundamental risk) can be broken down into various types of risks while building your portfolio. A good investment strategy begins with managing away, as best you can, six types of risk: four investment risks and two risks that will affect your investment strategies as well.

RISKS IN DETAIL

FUNDAMENTAL RISK

Fundamental risk, or business risk, is often (combined with technical risk) the primary risk referred to when risk is discussed. Fundamental risk applies to bonds, stocks, real estate, and all investments. It is the risk inherent within a particular business enterprise that relates to the company's financial strains, their position in the marketplace, their reputation, how they fare against their competition, and so on. It is more than the risk graded in the bond market, known as credit risk, which is more "black and white," determining the likelihood of the company defaulting or not. The fundamental risk is affected by how well-managed the company is and how they fare in their market.

The best way to manage your portfolio to minimize the effects of fundamental risk is to diversify. This is where you are investing in different companies in different industries within the same asset class.

On the More Conservative Side

Hugh
Healthcare Benefits Marketing Consultant
Age: 40

Hugh's investment philosophy melds with his overall philosophy about life. "I tend to be more conservative than most of my peers. This is true when it comes to investing, as well as the way I live my everyday life: Overall, I don't have a great tolerance for risk-taking." Hugh re-evaluates his tolerance for risk every few years and tends to grow even more conservative as time unfolds. "When I was in my thirties, I set aside a certain percentage of money for higher-risk investments, including aggressive mutual funds. I'm now moving away from even that level of risk," he explains. Hugh believes in the importance of taking your personality into account when devising an investment strategy. Some people, says Hugh, are better at dealing with

volatility than others. This needs to be part of the equation when developing an investment plan because you don't want to find yourself up all night worrying about whether you're going to lose a big percentage of your life savings. If one of his investments plummeted, this scenario would not sit too well with Hugh. Since he can't afford to lose his investments, he doesn't want to put himself in a position where this could actually happen. "I'd rather not look at my statement one day and find out that I've lost everything. To say the least, this would not be very comforting," he notes. If he had a lot of money to play with, he says that he might be a bit more willing to take investment risks. Let's hope that Hugh finds himself in this position in the near future.

Consistency and Discipline

If you've worked out a plan and have begun investing, it's important to stick with it for a fair amount of time— remember, smart investing means having some patience. Changing your investment strategy often can result in disaster. You need to give a plan time to work, and that means disciplining yourself to stay with it. If you've committed to investing $500 a month into a particular investment plan, by skipping months, or investing $100 one month and $900 another, you may be throwing off your initial strategy and find your plan is working against you. If you are in a bad investment, you need not stay there forever, but give your investments a chance.

TECHNICAL RISK

Technical risk involves measuring things such as unemployment, interest rates, the budget deficit, and various other economic and market indicators. All of these external factors play a part in the success or failure of your investment. Technical risk, also known as market risk, is how well the market of your investment fares in regard to these factors. The affects on the overall market will affect your investment—which brings us back to the all ships rise or sink with the tide analogy.

Managing technical risk means having a balanced portfolio. This is another way of diversifying across asset groups by having your dollars allocated into stocks, bonds, real estate, money market funds, CDs, and so on. Different asset classes also exist within the same market. Beyond that, there are numerous markets and they will react differently to the economic indicators listed here. Even in the bond market, there are different classes of fixed asset investments including long-term bonds, short-term bonds, high yield or junk bonds, municipal bonds, government bonds, global bonds, and so on.

Investors can work on the 93 percent of the investment puzzle by focusing on the area of asset allocation and then look at the "7 percent solution" by focusing on the specific investments. In other words, if you plan to spread your money across various markets and asset classes, you can lessen technical or market risk before focusing on the specific investments within each group.

INTEREST RATE RISK

Interest rate risk, which is also discussed in the section on bonds, is how your investment is responding to the direction in which the interest rate is heading and how fast the rate is going. Often people assume that this only affects the bond market. This is not true. There is strong correlation between interest rate risk and the stock market. While stocks have various other factors that directly affect them, they will frequently follow suit with bonds and react in the same inverse manner to the direction in which the interest rate moves.

You can manage away interest rate risk by having part of your portfolio in fixed principal investments with a guaranteed interest rate. Also, having a portion of your portfolio leaning toward short-term bonds (rather than long-term bonds, which will fluctuate more) will help you better avoid interest rate risk.

INFLATION RISK

Inflation risk is the risk that inflation will rise faster than your investment and that your dollars will be worth less in the future than they are today. In an effort to manage away inflation risk, or purchasing power risk, you need to look at stocks, real estate, and investments that will, over time, beat the inflation rate. During periods of moderate or low inflation the stock market performs well. During periods of high inflation the market can fall dramatically. It's hard to beat high inflation risk, but you can ride it out with investments that have a tendency to stay ahead of the projected inflation rate. An investment such as a CD that sits at a low rate would be your worst bet because often the CD is paying less than the inflation rate. For instance, if you put $10,000 into an investment vehicle yielding a 4 percent return and earned $400, after paying tax at 28 percent (or $112.00) you would be left with $288. Then factor in the inflation rate of 3 percent on the entire investment, or $300, and you are actually ending up with a total of $9988, or coming out at –$12.

For this reason, it's also important to gauge appropriately when looking ahead in retirement accounts. Many people do not factor in inflation. There's no way to know what the inflation rate will be in twenty years, but always remember to include it along with taxes (in investments that are taxed) to see if you are coming out ahead.

LIQUIDITY RISK

Liquidity risk is technically not considered an investment risk; it is not a risk based on the investment itself but on how much you need to be liquid. It is the risk that we will need our capital at a time other than we planned for. It deals with the risk of being able to rapidly convert our assets into cash. The full definition says that liquidity risk is how quickly your assets *are convertible into cash at full value. Getting back a few cents on the dollar does not make you rest assured that you are not at risk. Forced liquidations and auctions are the results of not taking liquidity risk into account.*

Do-It-Yourself Investing

Financial planners will tell you that you need professional help and guidance to invest. They get paid to do this, so why shouldn't they say it? You don't NEED help to invest. You may very well want someone to help you for lack of time or to be there as a guide. Most professional planners know their field very well and can be helpful if you choose to use one. BUT, you CAN do it yourself. All it takes is a commitment to investing. Just as you learn to cook, play tennis or golf, drive, or do any number of things that make up your daily routine, you can learn about investing and stay on top of it. If you have the desire to learn about investing, there is a ton of information available. All you need is time and a desire to be in control of your money.

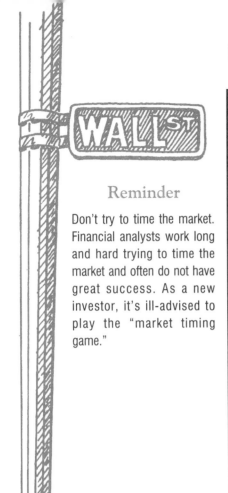

Reminder

Don't try to time the market. Financial analysts work long and hard trying to time the market and often do not have great success. As a new investor, it's ill-advised to play the "market timing game."

Liquidity risk is also based on, or balanced by, your need for the money in hand. You want to have a certain amount of your portfolio easily transferable to cash in the event that you need the money for an emergency. You also do not want to find yourself with no liquid assets for day-to-day needs. Beyond that, it is to some extent a state of mind or a level of comfort. Many people will prefer to have their money in stocks knowing that they can take out what they need for an emergency and not worrying about getting 79 cents or a full 100 cents back on the dollar if it's a matter of covering medical bills for a "real world" crisis. This takes us back to the various meanings of liquidity. Money back should I need it, versus full principal back, are two responses to different levels of risk and from different personality types.

Money market funds are the low end of liquidity risk, and actual real-estate investments along with locking money into retirement plans such as IRAs and 401(k)s are on the high end of liquidity risk. The best way to manage against the potential problem is simply to determine how much money you need in your budget for a certain time period, be it weekly or monthly, and make sure you always have that money available to you plus some reserve.

NOTE: People often comment that if their stock or bond falls they haven't lost the money unless they sell it. Actually, for the most part this is not true. If you've seen your stock drop from $90 to $72, when you do a new balance sheet those $18 per share will not show up on your list of assets. In this case, and with this type of investment, you are not liquid to the full value that you invested and there is no guarantee that you will be. This is a liquidity risk, in regard to full value—but by holding onto the stock you can get back to full liquid value.

TAX RISK

Tax risk is also not considered an investment risk; like liquidity risk, it isn't a risk to the actual investment, but more to the investor. You know ahead of time which investments are taxable and which are not. It is important to determine where you will land in the "tax bracket" game, and try to determine accordingly if some (and there aren't many) tax-free investment vehicles are a plus for your portfolio. As more singles and couples hit the higher tax brackets in a

time of higher wages and low inflation, municipal bonds and municipal bond funds have appeared more attractive to many baby boomers.

Most of the investment tax management, however, does not come from the investment itself, but rather from the vehicle in which the investments are made. IRAs, 401(k)s or 403(b)s, and variable life insurance are vehicles in which you make investments. The structure provides you tax-exemption or deferral to an extent dictated by the vehicle as well as by state tax laws. Often a tax-exempt or deferred vehicle directed at retirement also falls under the "not very liquid" heading. Nonetheless, from a portfolio-building standpoint, it is also important to address tax risk.

BY THE NUMBERS

All of the information just covered pertains to building a portfolio. This is important to consider even if "getting in" or starting out as an investor means buying a couple of stocks or bonds or perhaps a mutual fund. Understanding the importance of building a portfolio from the ground up will give you the investment edge you need to best position yourself to:

1. Manage away risk.
2. Seek returns.

In that order.

Interestingly enough, many investors look at #2 before #1. Brokers get commissions from selling you on #2, and although they will discuss #1, they are focused on seducing you with #2.

If you choose to build a portfolio, however, you will see the increasing value of #1. Often as we mature as investors, we begin to look at protecting ourselves. Safety becomes more significant than chasing the big reward. In a way we're like teenagers with new cars—first interested in looking sporty and going fast, and then, after maturing, beginning to focus more attention on safety features and comfort.

Okay, enough about the portfolio, or the "big picture." Let's talk about simply starting out, or "getting in."

All Planners Are Not Alike

If you should decide to hire a professional financial planner, keep in mind two things:

1. He or she is working for you, meaning you do not have to follow everything he or she says to the letter, or at all. You can even say, "We'll see," leave, and not return at all if you choose.
2. Financial planners are not all alike. Some may be too conservative in their nature for you or vice versa. Just as you ask for a medical second opinion, you can talk to a planner and decide to get a second opinion. Their word is not the gospel.

Strategy for Branching Out

If you receive a salary increase and wish to maintain a 10 percent level of your income invested, you might use that increase as an opportunity to invest in a stock or bond. If you are thinking more aggressively, look toward the stock market; if you are thinking more conservatively, think about a bond. Your age plus your life situation and risk tolerance level will determine which direction suits you the best.

GETTING IN

Now that you're ready to get into the pool are you going slowly, step by step; jumping into the shallow end; or diving in off the high board? New investors will commonly start off small and build as they feel more comfortable. There's nothing wrong with this approach. If your initial investment doesn't perform as you hoped, it may give you a "real" indication of your risk tolerance level. One investor will lose $1,000 in a good investment gone bad and shrug it off, saying, "I'd take the same chance again in a similar investment," while another might say, "I'll try something a little safer."

Dollar-cost averaging is popular with new investors, particularly in mutual funds. This has you investing consistently by putting in steady amounts. It allows you to maximize your number of shares when the price is low while also still investing when the price is high. By automatic withdrawal from a bank or money market account, the money is invested steadily for you, taking away the responsibility and decision of when to add more money into your investment. Here are some tips for GETTING IN:

1. *Set realistic expectations for your investments.* Unless you play the lottery or hit a "jackpot" you won't score big instantly. Investing is a way of watching your money grow, and growing takes time.

2. *Start sooner than later.* No, you can't turn time back and start young, but remember that money builds over time. If you are able to start investing regularly at age thirty-five, by the time you're sixty-five your money will have had thirty years of appreciation. This doesn't mean you can't do very well investing in your forties or even fifties, but it's always to your advantage to give your money time to grow.

3. *Prepare to be proactive.* The day you invest is not the day to stop doing your homework. Managing your assets is also not solely the job of a mutual fund manager, broker, financial consultant, or anyone else. Many people who are invested in 401(k) plans or other long-term retirement plans forget that they have the flexibility to move their investments around within the plan. Start off by being aware and ready to follow your investment.

The INVESTOR GAZETTE

Moderate – Middle of The Road Portfolio

You're in your mid-thirties, a couple with two young elementary school children. You want to invest for their future as well as your own. Several years away from college tuition payments, you have the luxury of having time on your side.

You're looking to allocate your assets so that you will be aggressively earning money toward goals like college for the kids, your own retirement and perhaps a new house, but you will also be keeping money in safe places for your own general family savings.

First, for the safe "cushion" you want and need with a family, you want to put 15 percent into CDs and money market accounts, which won't produce great earnings but will give you more money than a savings account and great piece of mind.

You can then put 20 percent in short term bonds and bond funds generating regular dividends.

Additionally, adding 15 percent in a balanced fund combining stocks and bonds will also be a way to generate income in a low risk area.

That covers the more conservative side of the portfolio. With years to go until college and higher future earnings potential for both halves of a working couple, the remaining 50 percent can go into long term growth funds, a major index fund and even some individual stocks, preferably large companies, blue chip or otherwise. Sector fund in the health sciences area and in technology could prove worthwhile, along with an emerging growth fund. Along with growth funds, you might seek out a value stock or two, since value investing is certainly a way to build. Look for a couple of stocks that are considered undervalued.

In the end, you want a portfolio that has 50 percent of your investments in the safer, less risky arenas ranging from CDs to money markets to high grade, low risk bonds and bond funds. The other 50 percent should be primarily in the more aggressive stock funds seeking rapid growth of capitalization. Then, as college, retirement and other milestones approach, you will readjust the more risky portion of the portfolio accordingly.

Reminder

Don't forget to follow your investment objectives. The best way to reach your goal is to keep it in sight and work towards it. One of the biggest mistakes investors make is deviating from their investment plan when building their portfolio.

4. *Just Do It!* This is not by any means saying that you should not do your homework, and is not contradictory to the previous advice. However, it means that there is a ton of information available and at some point you have to stop investigating and (once you feel you can make an informed decision) as Nike says, "Just Do It!" Too many people are at the starting line with a stock or mutual fund, only to wait just one more week . . . okay, just one more week . . . and so on and so forth. You need to reach a point where you are simply ready to get into the pool.

5. *Diversify.* The idea that diversification means you need to have large sums of money invested and/or be a more savvy investor is incorrect. Mutual funds can immediately, for even $500, have your money diversified. You too can take your initial investment and spread it around to some degree. You could, for example, take $2,500 and invest $1,000 in a bond, and $500 in a mutual fund, and $1000 in three different stocks. It's easy to diversify within an asset class and allocate your assets accordingly.

6. *Manage your risk.* Look at investments that best combat the risk you are concerned about, be it inflation, taxation, liquidity, or all of the above. Allocate your assets across different asset classes and try to cover the various types of risk associated with investing.

7. *Pay yourself first.* You've heard it said before, but it's true in investing as well. Once you've paid your monthly bills and made sure your expenses have been covered, you should then add to your investment. Having direct deposit from your paycheck makes this easier, but if it's up to you, make adding to your investment(s) a regular part of the process.

8. *Reinvest your earnings.* Many investments, including mutual funds, will do this for you, but it's to your advantage to keep your income working for you unless you need it for a specific purpose.

PATIENCE

Although you won't hear it mentioned in the same context as "risk" or "diversify," which are investment terms, good old "patience" is a major factor in investing—one that generally works in your favor.

A gentleman invested $1,000 in a stock on Monday. It dropped 5 points by Wednesday. He sold it and took a loss on Thursday. On Friday it went up 7 points. Suffice to say, a week isn't a great deal of time when it comes to investing.

It has been proven repeatedly that just as retail prices go up over time, so does the stock market. Patience is not easily found on Wall Street, but it is a valuable asset if you can find it. Being patient and letting time take its course is part of wise investment planning. Just as retirement funds succeed and grow over time, so will other investments. Playing the market on the short-term basis may work for shrewd investors who follow the details of the market and the financial updates very closely, but for others it's essentially gambling. World events over the course of a few days can send the market soaring or dropping and your investment along with it.

Time is one of the best allies of most investors. Bond holders, because there is a set maturity date, are more often aware of the idea of a "time frame." Unless a high-grade bond holder is looking to sell, he or she, because of the nature of a bond, should be comfortable with the element of time. The principal will be returned in time and that is comforting. There is no such comfort (no time table) when you own a stock or stock fund. Therefore, you need to make your own. Shrewd investors who work hard at following the market (stocks *or* bonds) and have a more calculated idea of when to buy and sell can play the investing game on a short-term basis. It is riskier, and one needs to stay very much on top of the business world to be successful. You need to look ahead at what is forthcoming in an industry, in a company, or in the market as a whole. Chasing after last year's hot stock or mutual fund generally does not work because the path of investing is to move forward and think ahead.

While looking toward the future, you need to understand that the road to your goal will not always be a smooth trip, just as you'll hit a bump or two while driving or some turbulence when flying. A

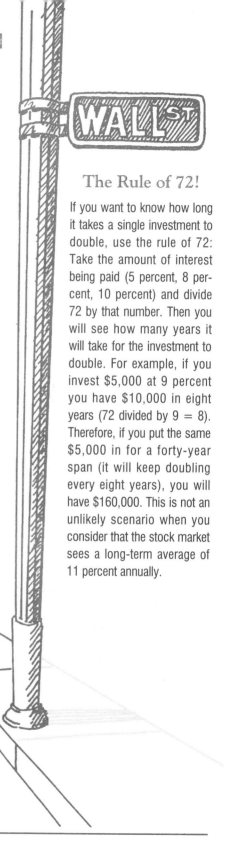

The Rule of 72!

If you want to know how long it takes a single investment to double, use the rule of 72: Take the amount of interest being paid (5 percent, 8 percent, 10 percent) and divide 72 by that number. Then you will see how many years it will take for the investment to double. For example, if you invest $5,000 at 9 percent you have $10,000 in eight years (72 divided by 9 = 8). Therefore, if you put the same $5,000 in for a forty-year span (it will keep doubling every eight years), you will have $160,000. This is not an unlikely scenario when you consider that the stock market sees a long-term average of 11 percent annually.

A Strategy for Jumping in

If you have just come into a lump sum of money, such as a $10,000 inheritance and want to invest, you might start with a three fold plan: mutual fund, stocks and bonds.

Once again it will depend on your age as well as your overall financial situation.

Putting $5,000 into a balanced mutual fund or index fund is a good starting point.

Then, look at two stocks, one blue-chip large company that you can hold onto and watch it grow and one newer company with good growth potential. Split $2,500 into the two stocks.

Finally, look at putting $2,500 into a high grade bond—perhaps a tax free municipal which will ease your tax burden a bit.

Evaluate your position in six months.

company, even a solid, long-standing blue-chip company, will have an occasional quarter where their earnings are off. Perhaps they issued a new product that didn't take off as they had hoped, such as "The New Coca-Cola." Some investors will jump ship; others will note the long history of success of a company and resolve that they will bounce right back with something else. Good investors will also see that many industries will have higher and lower periods. Beyond being patient, it's often to your advantage to pick up more shares of a solid company that you believe in when the stock price drops.

Tips for maintaining your PATIENCE include:

1. *Avoid impulsive reactions.* The opposite of being patient is being impulsive. You need to give yourself "stop orders" at times to ride out the volatility associated with most investments. Don't impulsively bail out. You also should stop yourself from buying impulsively without checking up on the stock first.
2. *Stick to your goals.* If you have set up goals for yourself, to have X amount of money in X number of years, remind yourself that these goals will not be reachable without patience.
3. *Smile at advice.* Everyone under the sun will always have a new and better way to spend or invest YOUR money. If you follow everyone's advice you'll be moving your money all over the place and never reach your goals. You can add new investments, but be patient with the ones you have (unless you know the company you're invested in is going out of business). Take advice with a grain of salt, smile, and listen to most well-intentioned friends, neighbors, relatives, and so on. Even the myriad of "experts" out there will have new-and-improved ways for you to invest. There's nothing wrong with investigating some advice that sounds feasible to your goals and needs, and even making some adjustments as you go along (in fact, managing your asset allocation can be important), but you should maintain and be patient with the core of investments in your portfolio. Don't be easily swayed.

GETTING OUT

There is a lot of talk and a lot written about investing your money—putting it *into* investments. However, there isn't a lot written about taking your money out. Sure, it's easy to put money into a 401(k) or a similar plan and know that at a certain age you will be required to take the money out, but what about selling off an investment? When do you sell your shares of a stock or mutual fund? For that matter, when do you sell off a piece of fine art? When you invest, you have three options: buy, sell, or hold. "Buying" occupies most of the magazine articles and is the basis for the advertisements for fund companies on television and in print. Buying into a fund family brings in business, and buying shares of a stock makes the stock more attractive. Selling, however, is what will transform the value of shares of stock or shares in a mutual fund into income. You can sell a bond at an attractive price, depending on the market. You can sell an investment for a profit or as a way of bailing out of a sinking ship.

Far too few investors are well-versed at selling. The two biggest mistakes, traditionally, are selling too soon and waiting too long with a losing proposition. Yes, holding onto stocks, overall, is usually to your benefit. However, that does not necessarily mean you hold onto them forever, nor does it mean that there are not exceptions to the rule. After all, if every stock went up and was a "winner," then there would be no level of risk involved, and that is not the case. Studies have shown that investors will far more quickly sell a wining stock and take the profits than accept they made a mistake and bail out of a loser. Everyone likes a good comeback story and there is always that ounce of hope that if you hang onto a sinking ship it might suddenly rise again.

Investing means knowing when to let go. One approach is sticking fast to your guns, as a person might do when they set a $500 limit before entering a casino, and simply decide that if the stock hits X amount you'll sell, or at least sell a certain number of shares and have a tidy profit, or if the stock goes the other way and hits X amount, you'll bail out and take the loss. "Stop market orders" are the term for setting up such limits. Some analysts say you should never hang onto a stock if it's lost 10 to 15 percent, while others will say 7 percent is time to get out. Naysayers will tell you to

Know Thy Planner

It's important that if you go to a planner you do some reading and be knowledgeable before your meeting. Too many people have walked away from planners with that unsettling feeling that they have just put themselves and their money in someone's hands and don't have a clue what this person is about to do with it.

ALSO, CHECK OUT THE PLANNER—GET REFERENCES!

Reminder

Don't buy last year's winners. Just as you can't predict next year's Super Bowl winner based on the previous year (few teams have repeated back to back), the hottest stock or mutual fund of the previous year is not necessarily the hottest for the coming year.

relax, that the market always rebounds. And while this is true, sometimes it can be a long wait.

On the other side of the coin is selling off winners. Of course, "greed" is the major nemesis when a stock goes up, leading to the overused phrase "If I'd only sold it when it was X." When the stock goes down, the problem is not wanting to admit defeat. Another significant way of knowing when to get out, or sell, is to have set goals predetermined. If and when you have achieved your goals, you can put your money into your new house, toward your retirement, toward paying off the tuition, and so on at the time you set up to do so. If, however, your plan is not working and you are not reaching your goal, you may need to get out of a particular investment and restructure your portfolio or asset allocation. Patience remains important, but not if mathematically you cannot reach your goal. Then it's a matter of getting out of certain investments and restructuring. Once you've done the long-term math to reaching your goal and straightened out your portfolio, you can return to being patient.

One of the biggest problems people face when they are in a losing investment, besides not knowing when to get out, is that they are losing time, as well as money, in their plan to reach their goal. If you've calculated a certain percentage of gain over X number of years, if you do not see any growth in the first two years of that investment you won't reach your anticipated goal. You will have then cut your ten-year plan down to eight. What's worse is that while your plan has not been working, your money could have been growing elsewhere. So not only are you not seeing gains with the bad investment, but you are losing the opportunity to be in a better investment.

The trick is to balance patience with the ability to admit making a mistake. Yes, often a blue-chip stock will rebound. On the other hand, a fledgling young company that is struggling may "fledgle" for another five years while your money could be growing elsewhere. Many investors simply do not want to say, "Okay I blew it," so they hold onto investments with the phrase "I just want to get my money back." Like a team that plays for a tie, you rarely come out even or ahead once that becomes your credo.

Knowing when to hold them, fold them, or buy more cards (which isn't a poker option) is also part and parcel of your level of risk and your investment personality. If the short-term player, buying

An Eye on the Future

Jane
Self-Employed Print Dealer
Age: 50

Jane inherited some money about six years ago, which she wanted to invest for her retirement years. After reviewing her options and interviewing various brokers, Jane decided to give her account to a broker who was new to the business, but who is the son of a very successful fund manager. "Although Richard was relatively new to investing," comments Jane, "I knew that his father, who has very extensive experience, would oversee his son's investment strategies. I also knew that I didn't have a big enough chunk of money to interest any of the major brokerage firms."

Jane worked with a full-service broker because she felt she needed help and support in devising her investment strategy. It was critical that Jane find someone who shared her investment philosophy. She wasn't interested in brokers who made a habit of churning accounts, which she had experienced several years back with an employee from a major brokerage firm. Determined to buy only good-quality companies, she felt comfortable working with Richard, who believed in a long-term approach to investment and was enthusiastic about investing in new technology.

After Richard suggested a stock to Jane, he gave her a background summary of the company and other relevant information. She reviewed this information, but she often did her own investigating, too.

Jane strongly urges investors to take an active role in the decision-making process by keeping up to date with both national and international events. "If you have an interest in the market," explains Jane, "you have a responsibility to read business publications and newspapers, along with watching financial news on cable television. It keeps you on top of trends. You become more conscious of how world events impact the financial markets."

Jane suggests that investors refrain from buying stocks based on a "hot tip" because this information rarely, if ever, pays off in the long run. Even with the best intentions, she says, you can't time the market and expect to circumvent every dip. Nor should you aim to buy at the bottom and sell at the top because this is an unrealistic goal. "Determine what you're willing to pay for a certain stock. If that stock reaches your desired price during a dip in the market and there's no serious underlying reason for the stock's price decline, you may want to view the situation as a buying opportunity," she says. Jane's investment instincts were right on target. In a little over six years, Jane has seen her money grow by more than 300 percent.

stocks for the short run, understands the nature of the investments correctly, he or she should be ready to wheel and deal, for better or for worse. Such investors come into investing looking to make moves and not to wait on their investments. The commodities market, which is far too rich and risky for beginning and even moderately skilled investors, means buying and selling fast, sometimes within hours as the prices rise and drop quickly —and you could lose a bundle in minutes.

The safer, less-risk-taking investor is looking to hold on and watch his or her earnings grow more steadily over time. This approach works fine as long as he or she can spot a fly in the ointment and get a potential loser out of the portfolio. Sometimes it's hard to spot a losing investment. An investment that is growing, but at less than the rising rate of inflation, is essentially losing money for you. If you invest in a fund that is growing at a rate of 2 percent over three years and the rate of inflation has climbed 4 percent, and a money market mutual fund could bring you a rate of 4.5 percent, you are sitting, for all intents and purposes, with a loser.

All in all, for many investors, it's much tougher to know when to get out than when to get in. One thing to consider when you are thinking about whether or not to hold onto a stock is the reason, or the reasons, you bought the stock in the first place. If you bought a tech stock based upon the news that the company was about to present a faster browser and the product has hit the market but was not at all what it was billed to be, then you may have overstayed your welcome, or investment, in this case. You might have bought a stock because it was outperforming others in its sector. But now you have found that the competition has caught up. Therefore, your motive for buying it, leading the competition, no longer holds true.

Fortunately, stocks and mutual funds are not an all-or-nothing proposition. You can sell off some of your shares while retaining others. In an area like collectibles, with a piece of art it *can* be all or nothing, but with a collection (unless the value is based on the entire set or printing) you can also sell some while retaining others. In areas such as collectibles and real estate, the market will dictate better and worse times for selling. A new shopping mall being built next to your commercial property might make it more attractive to someone looking to open up a restaurant. The market value of property can change based on numerous factors. If a person is buying real estate with the intention of reselling it for a profit, it's very important to know when to sell.

General tips on GETTING OUT include:

1. *Remember why you got in.* Evaluate why you got into the investment and see if the same reasons for being in it, or equivalent reasons, would have you buying it now.
2. *Be able to admit when you've made a mistake.* Forget bravado; even the biggest investors from Warren Buffet on down have blown a few.
3. *Remember moderation.* Sell some, keep some. You can always move from the deep end of the pool toward the shallower end without getting out.
4. *Set limits.* I sell at X and celebrate, or I sell at X and drown my sorrows.
5. *Remember your goals—stay focused.* If it's time to pay that college tuition, then use the money, or at least the portion necessary. If you can now afford the dream house, take the money and buy it. There's nothing wrong with continuing to invest, but the initial goals are why you are investing. As many a wise investor has said, "You can't take it with you," meaning it's not worth building the fortune if you can't enjoy it.
6. Try to gauge the future realistically. Look for a sound basis for holding onto an investment rather than sentimentality or a hunch.

DO ONGOING HOMEWORK

We've talked about it earlier, and we'll mention it again. When you are looking to invest, it's important that you do your homework— meaning research, analysis, and investigation. This does not mean that once you own a stock, fund, bond, or other investment you need not look beyond the day-to-day numbers. The numbers will keep you up to date, but they won't point to the future. Look up the stock you own on the Internet, find "company news," read their newsletter, read their annual or semi-annual reports, and ask your

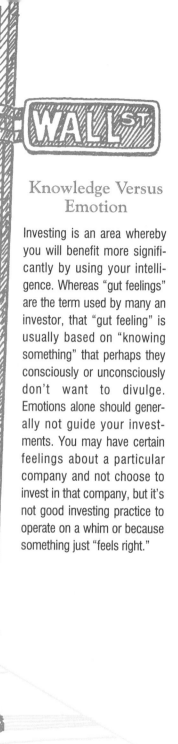

Knowledge Versus Emotion

Investing is an area whereby you will benefit more significantly by using your intelligence. Whereas "gut feelings" are the term used by many an investor, that "gut feeling" is usually based on "knowing something" that perhaps they consciously or unconsciously don't want to divulge. Emotions alone should generally not guide your investments. You may have certain feelings about a particular company and not choose to invest in that company, but it's not good investing practice to operate on a whim or because something just "feels right."

Speculating

When you invest, you need to be part sociologist and part philosopher as well as researcher. Therefore, you need to "speculate." Here is an example of questions you may ask yourself to get you thinking about the business behind the investments.

- In recent years technology has been the hottest sector in the market. But will this continue? Are there too many Internet providers to allow all of them to prosper?
- And what about the sheer number of software companies? Is the market oversaturated? Can a company prevail with too many competitors?
- The computer business has relied on the fact that models become obsolete dinosaurs within a year or two after purchase, causing a need for upgrades. What happens, however, when computers that last longer and are more easily adaptable to new software and upgrades become more popular? What happens when consumers with PCs decide they don't need

each and every new feature and simply hold onto their "dinosaurs" a little longer? This too could slow down the tech craze.

- On the other hand, just as notebook computers, laptops, PCs, and plenty of technology before them were the next great thing, a new emerging technology may be on the horizon—but from which company? Is live video-streaming for corporate use the wave of the future? Will the Internet move from consumer use to business-to-business usage?
- Perhaps the bio-tech and health and medical industry, with all the genetic testing and work being done with cells, will be the new direction. There are already promising entries in that area. However, in medical technology there is a fine line between what is being used for preventative health and what is thought of as experimental and even morally questionable. Cells from the umbilical cord of a newborn have been successfully stored and used later on to fight leukemia. This is essentially a major medical advance. On the

other hand, cloning a sheep makes the headlines, but for what purposes will such technology be practically used? Once again, it's worth checking out which companies are truly advancing science in a meaningful way. You can use this type of thinking to look into any industry. Will food manufacturers featuring foods lower in cholesterol but still maintaining a good taste be more profitable in upcoming years as sales of healthier foods increase?

This is just an example of how one can begin thinking about the future of investing. The next step is to do your research. Speculating, followed by well-researched, concrete proof (such as finding out that the XYZ Company is about to introduce some new technology that will make pigs fly in January of 2001) is what you look for. Then you need to determine if flying pigs is what the public, or the business community, needs. If so, then invest in it!

broker for any updated news he or she may have about the company. You need not do this daily or even weekly, but periodically checking up on what is going on with the company or municipality behind your investment is important. Too many people wait for some big news story such as a major lawsuit against the company before they bother to check out what is going on. At this point they find one distressing news item and panic—hence sell. If you're on top of what is going on, you may simply ride out the bad news. If you are an educated investor you can more likely be a patient investor—and one without high blood pressure.

Reminder

If you don't "get it," don't invest. Not understanding the ins and outs of a particular investment does not mean you are stupid. It simply means you do not yet have a grasp of all of the specific concepts involved. The problem arises when, instead of taking some time to learn about an investment vehicle, the anxious investor simply dives into it. This kind of "blind investing" is usually dangerous. It also explains why fraud in the penny stock industry has run rampant, thanks to shrewd "salespeople" preying on naive investors who don't understand what they are buying.

CHAPTER THREE

All About Stocks

Have you been indulging in Big Macs for as long as you can remember? When you're ready for a shopping spree, do you head to Wal-Mart? Is checking out one of AOL's chat rooms your idea of an exciting Saturday night?

We're all consumers, most of us with very distinct preferences when it comes to certain products and services. If you've found a consistently great product or service, odds are that you're not alone in your discovery. The stocks of superior companies that have stood the test of time are always in great demand. It's finding these companies that poses the real challenge to investors.

BUY WHAT YOU KNOW

The good news is that familiarity takes a lot of the anxiety out of picking stocks. It also gives you valuable insight about honing in on a specific company. In addition to your own experiences, observations are another way to gain valuable insight. During your recent trip to Japan, did you notice people consuming huge quantities of Coca-Cola? While waiting to pay for dinner at the local restaurant, did many of the patrons pull out American Express cards? Part of doing your homework, as mentioned earlier, is noticing the companies whose products and services are prominently displayed.

By being an informed consumer, you already have a better grasp of the market than you may realize. You probably have stock preferences and a better understanding of the business world than you would have guessed. However, knowledge of a given product or service is just the beginning of the process. Familiarity is a great entree to ensuring a bright investment future.

Putting serious thought into your investments early on will most likely pay off in the long run. Unfortunately, many people are introduced to the world of investing through a "hot" stock tip from their barber, buddy, or bellman. There's really no way to make an "easy buck," and by jumping into a stock because of a random tip, you'll probably end up shedding yourself of income in the process. Chasing that "easy buck" in the stock market is a mere fantasy.

Buying stock to purchase a house or to attend college within a year's time is also not advisable. Holding quality stocks for a minimum five-year period is recommended because you need enough of a time frame to ride out any bear markets (the term used to describe the market when it is down) or any other downturns that might come about. Often, a domino effect will have investors jumping ship and selling when the market is going down. Inversely, when there is a rising market, or a bull market, you'll see a trend towards stock buying. For those who understand the value of patience, staying in the market for the long term has been the most proven way to successfully invest.

No matter what type of stock fits your strategy, it's important that you have *"just in case"* emergency money set aside (preferably enough to cover expenses for six months) in a risk-free investment. Even the most prestigious blue-chip stocks come with inherent risks. After you've set aside an emergency fund and have reached the conclusion that you are not entirely adverse to risk taking, you can devise your own personal investment strategy.

Due to spectacular returns for most of the 1990s (with a few episodes of heavy "dips" mixed into an otherwise bright picture), the stock market has become the place where Americans turn when they want to boost their income. Many individuals in their mid-twenties are jumping on the stock market bandwagon. Although, for the most part, the market has been strong, it will inevitably take downturns and, in time, the odds are that it will rise back up again.

The earlier in life you start investing, the longer you can keep your money in the market. Although past performance is no guarantee of future performance, history has shown that time is probably going to work in your favor when it comes to investing.

If you had purchased two hundred shares of General Electric at the end of June 1995 for $5,640, by July of 1998 your investment would have been worth more than $18,000. General Electric is a fairly stable stock; other companies, especially smaller, less-established companies, can fluctuate significantly more in the short term.

Most analysts agree on this one universal truth: Market fluctuations, appearing in varying degrees, are inevitable, and it's merely part of the entire investing process. As with most things in life, no ride is completely smooth.

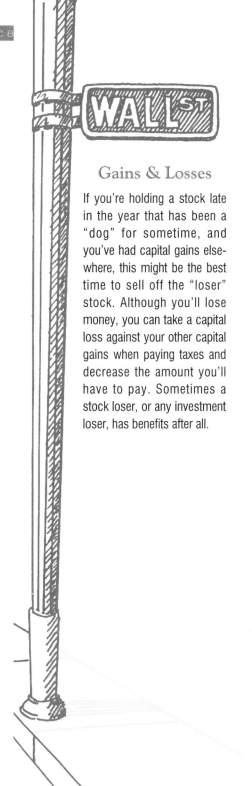

Gains & Losses

If you're holding a stock late in the year that has been a "dog" for sometime, and you've had capital gains elsewhere, this might be the best time to sell off the "loser" stock. Although you'll lose money, you can take a capital loss against your other capital gains when paying taxes and decrease the amount you'll have to pay. Sometimes a stock loser, or any investment loser, has benefits after all.

STOCK BASICS

Before you buy common stock, it's a good idea to understand exactly what that purchase represents. When you buy stock, you're actually buying a portion of a corporation.

Purchasing shares of stock is a lot like buying a business. That's the way Warren Buffet, one of the world's most successful investors, views it—and his philosophy is certainly worth noting! If you wouldn't want to own the entire company, then you should think twice before you consider buying even a piece of it. You are, indeed, buying a proportional share of the business when you purchase shares of stock. If you think of investing in these terms, you'll probably be a lot more cautious when singling out a specific company.

Most people wouldn't buy a business without conducting a thorough investigation of every aspect of the company. It's important to become acquainted with all of the details. What are all of the products and services the company offers? Which part of the business accounts for the greatest revenue? Which part of the business accounts for the least revenue? Is the company too diversified? Who are its competitors? Is there a demand for the company's offerings? Is the company an industry leader? Are any mergers and acquisitions in the works? Until you understand exactly what the company does and how well it does it, it would be wise to postpone your decision to rush into an investment.

Let's say you wanted to buy a convenience store in your hometown. You've reviewed such factors as inventory, the quality of the company's employees, and customer service programs. In addition to selling staple grocery items, the company also rents videos and operates a gas pump. The grocery side of the business may only account for a small percentage of the overall revenue. It would be in your best interest to value each part of the business separately in order to get a complete and accurate picture of the company's profit potential. Many companies may have traditionally been associated with a specific business, yet that same company may have expanded into totally new venues.

Disney, for example, has historically been associated with the Disneyland and Disney World theme parks. The reality is that Disney is also involved in a host of other ventures. Among other things, the multifaceted company also has interests in television and movie production, including Miramax Film Corp. and Buena Vista Television.

Behind the Scenes

Esmael
Lawyer
Age: 37

For Esmael, the most important factors to consider when reviewing a particular stock include the P/E ratio, dividends, and market share. "The bigger the player, the better position a company is in to make major moves," he says. He believes that new investors should become acquainted with fundamental analysis before they haphazardly buy and sell stocks. Becoming familiar with both fundamental analysis and technical analysis, according to Esmael, will give you the greatest profit potential.

Under certain circumstances, Esmael has found it advantageous to buy when the market dips. If a particular stock that you want to own has an excessive P/E ratio, you may want to figure out what you're willing to pay for it and see if it hits that price during an overall market dip. Many people panic and pull out during any and all market dips because they have no means of evaluating the situation. "It's the investors who have no knowledge about the mechanics of the market who start selling once the market dips. They're not really sure what's going on so they rush to sell. Sometimes," adds Esmael, "it's best to just hang in there."

Esmael says that many investors are completely naive when it comes to evaluating a company and, as a result, they rely upon someone else's research. Many investors, he explains, merely piggyback the current sentiment on Wall Street. He explains that if an individual sees big blocks of shares of a company being bought by an influential fund manager, he or she may jump on the bandwagon, "The problem," Esmael comments, "is that these investors are not doing their homework. It's important to find out about a company for yourself instead of just relying on someone else's legwork."

However, he does believe that it is extremely helpful to read what such master investors as Warren Buffett are doing. "A lot of people can't wait to get their hands on his annual report to find out what he's been up to in the way of investing," he notes. Esmael says that the market has undergone dramatic changes over the past three years. The prominence of day traders, according to Esmael, has had a major impact on the market. Such individuals buy and sell on momentum and account for a lot of the volume on the major exchanges. He explains that you can't always take what you hear as gospel. Esmael says that key financial figures may be touting a particular stock to better their own position. Says Esmael: "That individual may want to spark a buying spree on a certain stock because he or she may have just purchased a big block of that company." You're never too old to "do your homework."

Disney's ABC Inc. division includes the ABC TV network, as well as numerous television stations and shares in various cable channels like ESPN.

Philip Morris is commonly associated with tobacco products. The company also profits from food and beer subsidiaries, including Kraft (featuring popular brands like Jell-O, Oscar Mayer, and Post) and Miller Brewing.

Just like any other career, making money via investing requires work. The more research and thought you put into your strategy, the more likely you are to reap rewards. Although there are no guarantees in the world of investing, the odds will be more in your favor if you make educated and well-informed investment decisions.

When you make an investment, you will be putting your money into a "public" company, which allows you—as part of the public—to become an owner or to have equity in the company. That's why stocks are often referred to as equities.

TYPES OF STOCKS

Common stock are securities, sold to the public, that constitute ownership in a corporation. They come in all sizes—you can invest in a mega-company or a micro-cap company that has just begun to soar. While some individuals prefer to invest in well-established companies, other investors prefer investing in smaller, growth-oriented companies. No matter what type of company fits in with your overall strategy, it's important to research every potential stock you buy. Just because a company has been around for decades, it still might not be the best investment vehicle.

Companies are always changing, and it's important to make sure that the information you are reviewing is current. Mergers and acquisitions have practically become commonplace, and it's essential to know if a company you are considering buying is undergoing, or is planning to undergo, such a transaction.

It's also a good idea to research a company's market capitalization. The market value of all outstanding shares of a particular stock is synonymous with its market capitalization (or cap). Market capitalization is calculated by multiplying the market price by the number of outstanding shares. The number of outstanding shares refers to the number of shares that were sold and are, therefore, now shares outstanding. Larger companies will usually have a lot more outstanding shares than their smaller counterparts. Shares that are issued are outstanding until they are redeemed, reacquired, converted, or canceled.

A public company with 20 million shares outstanding that trade at $40 each would have a market capitalization of $800 million. Although there are no concrete rules to categorize stocks, they can be differentiated by the following:

Large-cap: $5 billion and over
Mid-cap: Between $1 billion and $5 billion
Small-cap: Between $300 million and $1 billion
Micro-cap: Below $300 million

There are also different categories of stock, which suit almost every personality. The variety includes blue-chip, growth, small-cap, cyclical, defensive, value, income, and speculative stocks, and socially responsible investments (SRI).

BLUE-CHIP STOCKS

These are considered to be the most prestigious, well-established companies that are publicly traded, many of which have practically become household names. Included in this mostly large-cap mix are IBM (NYSE: IBM), Disney (NYSE: DIS), and Coca-Cola (NYSE: KO). A good number of blue-chip companies have been in existence for more than twenty-five years and are still leading the pack in their respective industries. Since most of these organizations have a solid track record, they are good investment vehicles for individuals leaning to the conservative side when stock picking.

GROWTH STOCKS

As the name suggests, growth stocks comprise companies that have strong growth potential. Many companies in this category have sales, earnings, and market share that are growing faster than the overall economy. Such stocks, which currently include such companies as Lucent Technologies (NYSE: LU), Cisco (NASDAQ: CSCO), and Microsoft (NASDAQ: MSFT), usually represent companies that are

Warren Buffet

Warren Buffet is Chairman and CEO of Berkshire Hathaway Inc., a holding company owning subsidiaries engaged in a number of diverse business activities. One of the world's most successful investors, Buffet's investment philosophy is studied by investors of all levels. Warren Buffet is an advocate of buying good, quality companies and holding them for the long term. Buffet doesn't check stock prices on a daily basis because he believes that quality companies will prevail in all market conditions. He isn't concerned with minute-to-minute changes in the price of a stock, and he sticks to companies he thoroughly understands. If he isn't completely familiar with the mechanics of a company, he will pass on adding it to his portfolio. Although stock price isn't the primary factor in Buffet's investment strategy, he does look for quality companies at bargain prices. Buffet believes in purchasing a few good companies and sticking with them.

big on research and development. Earnings in these companies are usually put right back into the business. Growth stocks may be riskier than their blue-chip counterparts, but in many cases you can also reap greater rewards. Pioneers in new technology are often growth stock companies. In recent years, growth stocks have outperformed value stocks (defined later in this section). That has not been the case at times in the past, and the trend may well turn around in the future.

SMALL-CAP STOCKS

This category comprises many of the small, emerging companies that have survived their initial growing pains and are now witnessing strong earning gains with expanding sales and profits. A small-cap stock today may be tomorrow's leader—it can also be tomorrow's loser. Overall, such stocks can be very volatile and risky.

CYCLICAL STOCKS

Companies with earnings that are strongly tied to the business cycle are considered to be cyclical. When the economy picks up momentum, these stocks follow this positive trend. When the economy slows down, these stocks follow, too. Cyclical stocks would include companies like DaimlerChrysler (NYSE: DCX) and United Airlines (NYSE: UAL).

DEFENSIVE STOCKS

No matter how the market is faring, defensive stocks are relatively stable under most economic conditions. Stocks with this characteristic include food companies, drug manufacturers, and utility companies. For the most part, you can't live without these products no matter what the economic climate may be at any given time. The list of defensive stocks includes Merck and Co. (NYSE: MRK) and Johnson and Johnson (NYSE: JNJ).

VALUE STOCKS

Such stocks look inexpensive when compared to earnings, dividends, sales, or other fundamental factors. Included in the value stock mix are Diamond Offshore (NYSE: DO) and Alexander and Baldwin (NASDAQ: ALEX). When there is a big run on growth stocks, value stocks may be ignored. However, many investors

Warning–Pyramid Schemes

The simple message regarding pyramid schemes is this: They are illegal. They are not investments. These schemes are set up in a manner whereby more people put money into some non-existent "pot" and the ones who have been there longer get to take more money out as the pot grows based on someone's arbitrarily conceived "rules." Stay away, you can easily get burned.

believe that value stocks are a good deal given their reasonable price in relation to many growth stocks. Warren Buffet would probably vouch for that.

INCOME STOCKS

Income stocks, which include REITs (see Chapter Fifteen for more on REITs), may fit the bill if generating income is your primary goal. One example of an income stock is public utility companies because such stocks have traditionally paid higher dividends than other types of stock. As with any stock, it's wise to look for a solid company with a good track record.

SPECULATIVE STOCKS

Any company that's boasting about their brilliant ideas but doesn't have the earnings and revenue to back it up would be classified as a speculative stock. Since these companies have yet to prove their true worth, they are a risky investment. Speculative stocks include Yahoo (NASDAQ: YHOO), Amazon.com (NASDAQ: AMZN), and MindSpring Enterprises (NASDAQ: MSPG).

SOCIALLY RESPONSIBLE INVESTMENTS (SRI)

Another investment strategy that is growing in popularity is socially responsible investing (SRI). Here, investors put capital into companies that represent their personal values. Such individuals may avoid tobacco or liquor companies or any company with products or services that damage the environment. Socially responsible investors favor companies that have a positive influence on society.

PREFERRED STOCKS

Although it is a much less popular alternative to common stock, you can also purchase what is known as preferred stock. These stocks share more in common with bonds than they do with common stock. Essentially, this type of stock has a fixed dividend and a redemption date. Income received has nothing to do with the company's earnings. If the company goes under, holders of preferred stock have priority when it comes to dividend payments. You normally have no ownership as a preferred stock owner; however, it can be a viable option for income-oriented investors. This book will

Peter Lynch

From 1977 through 1990, Peter Lynch managed one of the all-time favorite funds— the Fidelity Magellan Fund. Under his direction, the fund grew from approximately $20 million to about $14 billion. He has since shared his wisdom with investors as an author, having written such books as *Beating the Street* and *One Up on Wall Street.* Essentially, Lynch believes in buying what you know. As consumers, Lynch believes that we are always conducting research and that this research could be put to good use. Among other necessary steps in the research process, Lynch believes in paying attention to company size and to the price of a stock relative to the company's value.

Standard Deviation!

Standard deviation is how far an investment's month-to-month total return will stray from its average total return at any given time. In other words, it will help you measure volatility and assist you in the area of risk management. If an investment has an average total monthly return of 10 percent, and the standard deviation is 3 percent, that means from month to month it should not go below 7 percent or above 13 percent. Of course, this is not an exact science. It's a way to compare apples and oranges, or different types of investments.

concentrate on common stock because, like its name, it's the far more common choice for stock investors.

PENNY STOCKS

Penny stocks are stocks that sell for five dollars or less and, in many cases, you're lucky if they're worth even that much. Most penny stocks usually have no substantial income or revenue. You have a high potential for loss with penny stocks. If you have a strong urge to invest in this type of company, take time out to follow the stock to see if it has made any headway. Learn all you can about the company and don't be tempted to act on a "hot" tip that may have been passed your way or one that you overheard in your travels.

PENNY STOCK WARNING

You've heard of the Six Million Dollar Man? Well how about the six billion dollar scam? That's the amount reportedly lost by investors every year in penny stocks and micro-cap stocks. Penny stock fraud, as of early 1999, had reached such a level that U.S. federal regulators found themselves adopting rule changes to head off the growing number of penny stock scams. The SEC vowed to make the fight against small stock fraud a top priority.

As we've just noted, the penny stocks, or micro-cap stocks, are small stocks generally trading for under $5.00 per share. They trade in either "pink sheets" operated by the National Quotations Bureau or on the NASDAQ small-cap market. Pink sheets, in brief, are listings and price information literally printed on pink sheets of paper that go to select brokers.

The companies behind these stocks are thinly capitalized and are often not required to file reports with the SEC. They trade over the counter and there is a limited amount of public information available. This in itself is reason for concern. How many astute investors want to put their money into an investment offering little to no information? Nonetheless, people do invest in these stocks.

One of the most interesting—and alarming—aspects of penny stock dealing is that brokers are not always acting as a third party but are setting prices and acting as the principals in the transaction. In other words, the broker selling the stock owns large chunks of it.

Aggressive Portfolio

You're young, single, and off and running in your new found career. Just shy of 30, you see this as the time to invest and build a portfolio before finding your "soul mate" and settling down . . . before added responsibilities.

First, you tuck away 10 percent in the money market fund, in case all else goes sour, or your new found corporate gig has you getting downsized unexpectedly.

Next, you spread out the other 90 percent of your investment among equity funds. For the steady growth you go with the old standards, putting 30 percent in large caps. Next you can put 30 percent in small cap funds, add 20 percent in mid caps and round it out with 10 percent in international funds.

Another approach is to put something into large caps (30 percent is good) and then just look for growth and aggressive growth funds, regardless of caps, and add in sector funds that you believe in,

focusing on tech funds and the emerging bio-tech market. You can also buy stocks in anything you have researched with a ".com" after the name. Internet stocks can be terrific if you hit the right ones. The field is wide open if you have the extra income to invest, so you can stock up on the investing magazines and surf the financial websites for the best value stocks and hottest growth options.

In essence you are putting 10 percent in a safe haven, 30 percent in the safer equity area and carefully picking your best bets for rapid growth for the remaining 60 percent. Be prepared to move some of this around since you are living more dangerously and may hit a dud on occasion. Youth and lack of numerous financial responsibilities allows you time to correct some mistakes. However, you should do your homework and not act impulsively when jumping into the arena of investing.

Patent Problems Can Affect Your Choices

One of the biggest drug companies in America, Merck is faced with a situation where some of the patents they hold on some of their top selling products will soon expire. What this means is that competitive companies can make less expensive versions of the same products. As a potential investor you need to determine—and this information is often hard to come by—just how long the company has the patent on a particular product. Similarly, if a retail company has made a licensing agreement to sell a particular item or line, how long will they have this exclusivity?

Penny stocks most often do not have a single price but a number of different prices at which you can purchase or sell them. Like bonds on the market, there are asking and bidding prices. Unlike bonds, you often cannot find the price listed that is being quoted to you by a penny stock dealer.

Okay, so there's little information about the company, the price, or anything else to investigate. But the guy on the phone—making a cold call—says it will be the next Starbucks! This is where they get you. Thanks to the Internet and the selling of phone lists, penny stocks dealers can reach out far and wide. They use high-pressure sales tactics and armies of callers to tell you anything to make you buy the stocks. (There's an episode of the old television series *Taxi*—now in syndication on Nickelodeon's *Nick at Nite*—where sleazy Louie DePalma, played by Danny DeVito, becomes a stock broker for a day. This show gets at the true gist of a penny stock dealer.)

Typically, unscrupulous brokers hype up and promote companies that have either no assets or minimal assets. The practice called "pump and dump" is where these hard-selling wheeler-dealers hype the stocks, making outrageous claims about the company that are substantiated by absolutely nothing. They bring the price up so that they can cash in on an artificial price that is high for a company that is worth nearly nothing, or not in business at all.

Fraudulent practices by brokers could also include unauthorized trading, churning, bait and switch, and other fun methods of pulling the wool over unsuspecting new investors. Their goal is to convince naive investors that these stocks are an incredible bargain. They are so cheap you can't pass them by. AND, when they become the next Lucent, you'll be rich!

All of this is not to say that there are no low-priced legitimate stocks on the market. They are usually small grassroots companies that, if you pick the right one and wait a while, can grow over time. You should invest cautiously and conservatively at first. Look for a new company with good leadership in an industry where you see growth potential. It's also advantageous to find a company that holds the patent on a new product. If the product may potentially take off, so could your stock. All of this is information you must seek out; it will not come to you via a cold caller.

All in all penny stocks are a *high-risk investment*, but in some instances it can payoff. Nonetheless, you should remember a few things about questionable investments in general:

1. Nothing that is a great deal needs to be hammered into you by a hard-line sales approach. No one called you on a cold call and told you to buy Intel or Yahoo. No one had to. Anything that good will sell without high-pressure tactics. In short, DO NOT BUY FROM COLD CALLS. The same holds true for the high-pressure online sales pitches of some penny stock brokers.

2. Anything worth investing money into should be easy to research and investigate. The SEC has updated information about companies registered with them. Call 1-800-SEC-0330 and ask for the form "10K," which is the annual financial statement for a public company. Moody's, along with Standard & Poor's, also have information on most investments (including penny stocks), so you can look at their financial history. Moody's and S&P are companies that provide financial information and ratings. They monitor the financial world.

3. Make sure you are dealing with a broker with a reputation you trust (get a referral)—*not another Louie DePalma*. And *not* someone who "specializes" in penny stocks.

The SEC offers a Web site at www.sec.gov to investigate any questionable activities. They also offer a host of free literature, complaint tracking, and a toll-free information line: 1-800-SEC-0330.

WHAT YOUR STOCK REPRESENTS AND STOCK SPLITS

Essentially, a share of stock represents the percentage of a company you own. If a company has 200,000 shares outstanding and you own 200 shares, then you own 1/2000 of the company. You become an official shareholder with your first stock purchase.

Small Beat Large Over Time

Despite the recent trend reversals, for some fifty years through 1997, the David's of the stock world (the small companies) have outpaced the Goliaths (the large companies) in annualized returns, with 12.5 over 11.0 percent.

If one share of a stock is selling for $50 and you buy 100 shares (known as a round lot), the price would be $500, plus any brokerage fees incurred. When a stock price reaches a certain level, the board of directors may vote for a 2-for-1 stock split. This means you now have double the amount of shares of that stock, with each share worth half the presplit amount. If you own 100 shares of Intel at $180 per share, you would own 200 shares of Intel at $90 a share after a 2-for-1 stock split. In some cases, there could be a 3-for-1 stock split, 3-for-2 stock split, or any other variation dictated by the board of directors. If you own 150 shares of Intel at $180 per share and the stock splits 3-for-1, you would own 450 shares of Intel at $60 per share after the 3-for-1 split. A company might do a reverse split if their stock is trading at an unusually low price. A reverse split can make the company appear to be more valuable to investors.

Corporations generally split their stock to make the price of a single share more appealing. The idea of buying 100 shares of a stock at $90 a share is a lot less intimidating than making the decision to buy 100 shares at $180 each. Many stocks will split and, subsequently, may split again in the not-so-distant future.

A stock can also undergo a reverse split, which *decreases* the number of shares. Therefore, each share of stock would have a greater value. If you have 100 shares of a stock worth $1 per share and there is a reverse split of 1-for-2 shares, you then have 50 shares of stock worth $2 per share.

Note: Stock splits do not result in a gain or loss of realization of taxable income to stockholders.

INVESTING IN AN UNPREDICTABLE WORLD

If a company's future looks promising and its products and/or services are in great demand, stock prices will normally rise. Conversely, the price may dip if the company isn't living up to its expectations. Keep in mind that even if a company's earnings rose during a given quarter, the stock price might not go up (or it could drop) if Wall Street analysts were anticipating even greater earnings. Buying and selling of shares will affect the stock price, and rumors—among other factors—can influence the direction of a stock price. If there are no major problems within the company, this is usually an example of a short-term decline. Due to market fluctuations, the value of your stocks will often change on a daily basis. In many cases, a stock's price may tumble or escalate for no significant reason.

If you find that one of your stocks has taken a turn for the worse, you need to examine the reasons behind this downward activity. Is there a significant reason for its drop in stock price or is it just down for the short-term? This is where turning lemons into lemonade could come into play. If it appears that the stock has been adversely affected for the short-term, a wise investor could take advantage of the situation by purchasing more stock rather than feeling like a victim. When a stock price drops for no substantial reason, you could consider the stock to be "on sale." If you've done your homework and understand the mechanics of the company, then you probably have nothing to worry about. Companies with great product introductions, attractive profit margins, and a phenomenal growth rate will, ultimately, prevail.

On the other side of the coin, if you did *not* do your homework and the company *does* have serious, long-term problems, it's often best to cut your losses and rid yourself of the stock. Think of it as a learning experience. Even if you did thoroughly study a company, there may be other factors leading to its lower stock price that could not have been foreseen. The company may have had a turnover in its key management team, new competition may have entered the arena, or demand for its product or service may have diminished. It's important to try to determine the specific reasons for a decline in a stock price.

Hopefully, your research will point you in the direction of stock that you want to keep for as long as you continue to invest. Tax considerations may be one of the best reasons to buy and hold quality companies. Although stocks can be held for the short-, mid-, or long-term, a capital gains tax may have to be paid when shares are sold if they were not held in a tax-deferred account, such as an IRA. You normally pay a capital gains tax on stock after it's sold (you may have to pay taxes on dividends on an annual basis).

The SEC in Action

Through 1998 and into 1999, the SEC had been using a multifaceted approach to combating the growing micro-cap fraud, including inspections, enforcement, regulation, and investor education/awareness.

The biggest focus of activity was in New York, Florida, and the Colorado/Utah areas. But with cold calling and Internet activity, the reach was far and wide for fraudulent brokers. In early 1999, new rules stipulated that small companies be required to disclose more information when they issue stock under special rules allowing them to do so without registering with the commission.

Ticker & Ticker

Every company is assigned a ticker symbol, which is the code used to identify a given stock. For example, Disney is identified as DIS and Compaq is identified as CPQ. When buying or selling stocks over the Internet, you may need to input this information. Since many of these symbols are similar, it's important that you jot down the symbol to avoid any confusion later on.

Capital gains refers to how much money you actually made from a given stock after it was sold. It usually does not include the initial price you paid for the stock or the broker's fee associated with its purchase.

SHAREHOLDERS

Once you become a common stock shareholder, you will receive quarterly and annual reports. Such reports feature a wealth of information, including new products and/or services, an earnings (gains or losses) report, and the names of key company executives. You also have voting rights with common stock ownership, usually one vote per share, and you're welcome to attend stockholders' meetings, where you can gain insight about a company's direction and about its recent performance.

Annual reports come in all shapes and sizes, from glossy, four-color magazines to publications resembling throwaway newspapers. Reports from young companies will probably not be as glitzy as publications coming from the more established blue-chip organizations. However, information contained in these reports is similar. Among other information, you'll normally find a letter from the chief executive officer; photos of company headquarters, the executive team, and beaming customers; and a listing of the company's complete line of products. Then, of course, you'll find pages of numbers revealing the company's activity over the past year. Included in the financial data you'll normally find the following:

Balance sheet. This reveals assets that a company owns or controls. Basically, the balance sheet gives shareholders a snapshot of a company's assets, liabilities, and capital during a specific period. It is a useful measure for value investors because it affords shareholders an opportunity to see the fundamental worth of the company.

Income statement. This states the dollar amount of goods and services sold. The income statement flows through from top to bottom, beginning with revenue/total sales and subtracting costs and expenses from this number. These expenses and

costs include everything from salaries to rental fees to cost of goods. Overall, shareholders can find out the economic results of the company for a designated period of time and can compare these figures to past years or quarters.

Cash flow. This shows how much actual cash a company has after expenses. The cash flow reveals what happened to the cash, such as whether it is in the bank, was paid out in dividends, or was used to buy back stock.

In addition to company reports, there is an immense amount of information available to individual investors. Whether you choose to go online, turn on your television, or pick up a newspaper, there is an abundance of information available to investors for little or no charge.

Shareholders and the Board of Directors

The shareholders of public companies elect a board of directors to manage the business as it grows. The board of directors represents all shareholders and, once elected, the board of directors elects its own chairman. In some instances, the chairman may also be the company's chief executive officer (CEO) or president. In addition to serving on the board, he or she may oversee the day-to-day operations of the company. In other cases, the board members may choose a chief executive officer or company president who is not on the board but who answers to it.

Annual meetings are conducted, and they are open to all shareholders. Such meetings give attendees an opportunity to, among other things, find out the direction of the company and how it fared during the course of the year. The meeting also includes the election of directors and a discussion of other considerations such as changes in the corporate charter. Even if they do not attend the annual meeting, shareholders can still voice their opinions. Such individuals can sign a paper that authorizes one or more of the officers or directors to act as their proxy, or representative, and vote on their behalf. Proxy statements, which explain the business to be con-

Electro Scam?

One example of a fraudulent scheme caught by the SEC was that of a company called Electro-Optical Systems Corporation. In the spring of 1997, the SEC obtained a TRO (Temporary Restraining Order), asset freeze, and preliminary injunction based on their findings of a market manipulation scheme. False and misleading information had been put on the Internet and had caused the stock to increase by a "mere" 1,000 percent in one day (hey, does that look suspicious?). They raised over $10,000 in three months, primarily from unsuspecting new investors who believed that the Internet was the place to do business. For some people it is, but as is always the case on the Internet, know with whom you are dealing. The Internet is large and invaluable for doing research and dealing with reputable companies. It is also, unfortunately, utilized by unscrupulous dealers. Be careful.

Buying on Margin: Tips

If you are buying on margin, which essentially means borrowing to buy, you need to use good judgement. Like options and futures, you are essentially buying more than you can afford and handling that larger sum of money in the stock market. Some "Margin Tips" include:

1. Set tighter stop limits and be stricter about them than you might be otherwise.

2. Do not use margin as a long term strategy.

3. Always have some cash reserve funds in case you need to pay off your debt.

4. Do not let margin call— or how much you are responsible for (your debt)—exceed 5 percent.

ducted and give shareholders a chance to vote, are sent out to shareholders prior to the meeting.

In some instances, the founder and/or owner of a publicly traded company can influence the outcome of elections if he or she owns a majority of shares. If such individuals own more than 50 percent of the total number of shares, they can control the company.

In a company that is not publicly traded, business is usually handled by the founder or owner, who normally hires a management team to run the day-to-day operations of the company. Once a company acquires some solid experience, the owners and/or founders may choose to go public at a later date.

CHAPTER FOUR

Inside the
Stock Market

Several markets make up what is known as "the stock market." Many stocks are traded on the New York Stock Exchange (NYSE), the National Association of Securities Dealers Automated Quotations (NASDAQ), and the American Stock Exchange (Amex). In addition, such cities as Boston, Chicago, Philadelphia, Denver, San Francisco, and Los Angeles have exchanges. You can also find exchanges in major international cities like London and Tokyo.

Also known as "The Big Board," the *New York Stock Exchange* is home to the most prominent players like IBM, AOL, and Disney. The Big Board is not for little league players. Among other requirements, a company must have at least 1.1 million public shares of stock outstanding, must show pretax income of at least $6.5 million over the three most recent fiscal years (each year has to be equal to or more than the previous year), and the company's market value of public shares must be at least $40 million to be on board. In addition, the company's most recent year's pretax income must be at least $2.5 million, and its net tangible assets must be a minimum of $40 million.

NASDAQ/Amex: The National Association of Security Dealers Automated Quotations (NASDAQ) and the American Stock Exchange (Amex) united in October 1998, creating the NASDAQ/Amex Market Group. The American Stock Exchange is now a subsidiary of the National Association of Securities Dealers, Inc. (NASD). By joining two of the world's top securities markets, there is now an alliance creating an even more globally competitive market. However, the NASDAQ and the Amex are still currently operating as separate entities.

NASDAQ is an over-the-counter (OTC) market, which is the term used to describe securities that are traded through telephone and computer networks as opposed to through an auction exchange (such as the American Stock Exchange).

THE INDEXES

The Dow Jones Industrial Average is the most prominent stock index in the world. The thirty stocks on the Dow, which are all part of the New York Stock Exchange, are established blue-chip companies like McDonald's, Coca-Cola, DuPont, and Eastman Kodak. Companies on the Dow Jones Industrial Average, which was created to mimic the United States stock market as a whole, represent a variety of market segments such as entertainment, automotive, health-care products, and financial services.

General Electric is the only company that was included in the original Dow Jones Industrial Average created in 1896 that is still part of its makeup today. However, General Electric was dropped in 1898, restored in 1899, taken out again in 1901, and then put back on the list in 1907.

The thirty stocks on the Dow Jones Industrial Average companies are all represented equally, each being added to reach a total number that is then divided by a "divisor." Due to stock splits and other market factors, this divisor will vary. The divisor was originally 30, but it has been reduced over the years to a value less than one. The important point to remember is that each company carries equal weight. The stocks currently in the Dow Jones Industrial Average are:

1. AlliedSignal Inc. (ALD)
2. Aluminum Co. of America (ALCOA) (AA)
3. American Express Co. (AXP)
4. AT&T Corp. (T)
5. Boeing Co. (BA)
6. Caterpillar Inc. (CAT)
7. Chevron Corp. (CHV)
8. Citigroup Inc. (C)
9. Coca-Cola Co. (KO)
10. DuPont Co. (DD)
11. Eastman Kodak Co. (EK)
12. Exxon Corp. (XON)
13. General Electric Co. (GE)
14. General Motors Corp. (GM)
15. Goodyear Tire and Rubber Co. (GT)
16. Hewlett-Packard Co. (HWP)
17. International Business Machines Corp. (IBM)
18. International Paper Co. (IP)
19. Johnson and Johnson (JNJ)

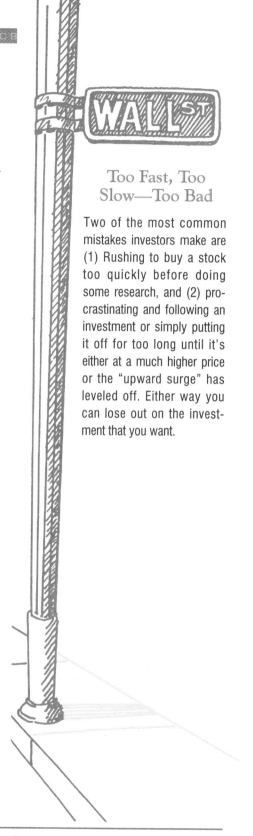

Too Fast, Too Slow—Too Bad

Two of the most common mistakes investors make are (1) Rushing to buy a stock too quickly before doing some research, and (2) procrastinating and following an investment or simply putting it off for too long until it's either at a much higher price or the "upward surge" has leveled off. Either way you can lose out on the investment that you want.

Take it Slow

You should never feel an urgency to jump into buying a particular stock even if you're feeling peer pressure to do so. There will always be investment opportunities, and it's usually counter-productive to behave impulsively because someone offers you a "hot" tip. It's vital that you research each and every "hot" tip before adding that stock to your portfolio. "Hot" tips often result in "cold" profits. When investing, there is no way to circumvent the research process.

20. J.P. Morgan and Co. (JPM)
21. McDonald's Corp. (MCD)
22. Merck and Co. (MRK)
23. Minnesota Mining and Manufacturing Co. (3M) (MMM)
24. Philip Morris Cos. (MO)
25. Procter and Gamble Co. (PG)
26. Sears, Roebuck and Co. (S)
27. Union Carbide Corp. (UK)
28. United Technologies (UTX)
29. Walt Disney Company (DIS)
30. Wal-Mart Stores Inc. (WMT)

The following section provides a brief description of ten of the thirty companies listed on the Dow Jones Industrial Average.

Johnson and Johnson (Symbol: JNJ)

Headquarters: New Brunswick, New Jersey
Telephone: 732-524-0400
Web Site Address: http://www.jnj.com

Johnson and Johnson founder Robert Wood Johnson teamed up with his two brothers, James Wood, and Edward Mead Johnson, who had formed a partnership in 1885. Two years later, the company was incorporated as Johnson and Johnson.

The company's first major introductions were ready-made, ready-to-use surgical dressings. This marked the beginnings of both Johnson and Johnson and the practical application of the theory of antiseptic wound treatment. To help fulfill a need for improved antiseptic procedures, Johnson and Johnson soon after developed a soft, absorbent cotton-and-gauze dressing that could be mass-produced and shipped in quantity to hospitals, physicians, and druggists.

One of the company's most widely recognized products was rolled out in 1921—BAND-AID Brand Adhesive Bandages. Around the same time, the company created JOHNSON'S Baby Cream. Another popular product, Pepcid AC, was introduced much later in 1995.

International growth was initiated in 1919 with the establishment of an affiliate in Canada. In 1924, Johnson and Johnson created its

first overseas affiliate, Johnson and Johnson Ltd., in Great Britain. On a more recent note, Johnson and Johnson is currently expanding into new markets such as the People's Republic of China and Eastern Europe.

Johnson and Johnson comprises more than 180 companies that market healthcare products in 175-plus countries. Its more than ninety thousand employees are engaged in producing products that serve medical needs ranging from baby care, first aid, and hospital products to prescription pharmaceuticals, diagnostics, and products relating to family planning, dermatology, and feminine hygiene.

Wal-Mart Stores, Inc. (Symbol: WMT)
Headquarters: Bentonville, Arkansas
Telephone: 501-273-4000
Web Site Address: http://www.wal-mart.com

Sam Walton's vision began in 1962 when he was convinced that consumers would support a discount store with a wide array of merchandise and friendly service. To this very day, the company retains its hometown spirit with a distribution system that allows many stores to customize merchandise to match the community's needs. In many locations, shoppers are personally welcomed by what has come to be known as "People Greeters."

The first Wal-Mart opened in Rogers, Arkansas, in 1962, with the first international store premiering in Mexico City in 1991. Sam's Club opened its doors in Midwest City, Oklahoma, in 1983, and the first Supercenter was built in Washington, Missouri, in 1988.

A small-town merchant who had operated variety stores in Arkansas and Missouri, Walton began what now is one of the world's leading retailers. Expanding into new arenas—grocery (Wal-Mart Superstores), international operations, membership warehouse clubs (Sam's Clubs), and deep-discount warehouse outlets (Bud's Discount City)—has opened various opportunities for growth.

Today, Wal-Mart caters to more than ninety million customers on a weekly basis in fifty states, Puerto Rico, Canada, China, Mexico, Brazil, Germany, Argentina, and South Korea. The company boasts more than 895,000 associates worldwide, with about 780,000 of these being United States employees.

Seeking Out Dividends in the Market

Yes, stocks still pay dividends. No, some of the hot Internet stocks are not about to lure you in with a dividend—they'll just get you the old-fashioned way: with big returns. But some of the big blue-chip stocks still do pay dividends, and if you are looking for the biggest, seek out the companies that need you as an investor the most. Industries such as oil, cars, and even banking are good places to look for dividends as these are not the "hottest" industries. Some REITs have been paying dividends as well. Look for stocks of major companies in industries that are slow at present but have potential to turn around. Until they do they may be paying out nice dividends. The tobacco industry stocks, if you're not of the social investing mode, are also paying out dividends to interest investors.

Rounding Off

Many investors like to buy stock in a round lot, which is 100 shares. This can make tracking the value of your portfolio simpler than if you were to buy shares in odd numbers.

Hewlett-Packard Company: (Symbol: HWP)
Headquarters: Palo Alto, California
Telephone: 650-857-1501
Web Site Address: http://www.hp.com

Founded in 1939 by Bill Hewlett and Dave Packard, Hewlett-Packard's first product was an audio oscillator—an electronic test instrument used by sound engineers. One of Hewlett-Packard's first customers was Walt Disney Studios, which purchased oscillators to develop and test an innovative sound system for the movie *Fantasia*.

The company's premiere computer was introduced in 1966 to gather and analyze data coming from HP electronic instruments. It branched into business computing in the 1970s with the HP 3000 midrange computer, launching a new era of distributed data processing, taking computers out of traditional "computer rooms" and making them accessible to employees in most departments.

Hewlett-Packard is a leader in computers and a producer of test and measurement instruments. Most of HP's revenue comes from computers—ranging in size from palmtops to supercomputers—plus peripherals and services. HP also manufactures and services networking products to help customers connect computers. The company's test and measurement instruments, as well as systems and related services, are used by engineers and scientists to design, manufacture, operate, and repair electronic equipment, including global telecommunications networks.

The company offers consumers more than twenty-nine thousand products. Hewlett-Packard also has networking products, medical electronic equipment, instruments and systems for chemical analysis, handheld calculators, and electronic components. The company employs more than 120,000 individuals, including about seventy thousand United States employees. Hewlett-Packard has major sites in twenty-eight U.S. cities, as well as in Europe, Asia Pacific, Latin America, and Canada.

Exxon Corporation (Symbol: XON)
Headquarters: Irving, Texas
Telephone: 972-444-1000
Web Site Address: http://www.exxon.com

One of the first multinational companies, Exxon was incorporated in 1882 as the Standard Oil Company of Jersey to succeed a business founded by John D. Rockefeller. In 1972, the company changed its name and principal trademark in the United States to Exxon.

The company has myriad divisions and affiliates, each with a specific operating responsibility. These include:

Exxon USA, an industry giant in oil and gas production

Exxon Chemical Company and its affiliates, one of the largest U.S.–based worldwide petrochemical companies

Imperial Oil Limited, Exxon's Canadian affiliate, a major force in the Canadian petroleum industry

Exxon Production Research Company, investigating new methods to find and recover energy supplies

Exxon is engaged in all aspects of the oil and gas businesses, from exploration and production to refining and marketing. The company is also a producer of petrochemicals and has interests in coal and minerals mining operations and electric power generation. Its affiliates operate or market products in more than one hundred countries on six continents.

Sears, Roebuck and Co. (Symbol: S)

Headquarters: Hoffman Estates, Illinois
Telephone: 847-286-2500
Web Site Address: http://www.sears.com

It all began in the mid-1800s when a Chicago jewelry company sent a shipment of gold-filled watches to a Minnesota jeweler, who ultimately did not want the watches. This turned into an optimal opportunity for Richard Sears. At the time, Sears worked at the Minneapolis and St. Louis railway station in North Redwood, Minnesota. When he purchased the unwanted watches from the jeweler and sold them on his own, history was made. In 1886, Richard Sears began the R.W. Sears Watch Company in Minneapolis.

De-fense! De-fense!

When the stock market is not faring well, or simply as a conservative measure, you may opt to invest in "defensive stocks" which are stocks of companies that provide necessities or necessary services such as electricity and gas. Food services or other such "staples" are examples of stocks that should hold their ground when the economy declines.

Buying on Margin Means Living Dangerously

Buying on margin means you are essentially borrowing money to make investments. It is something you need to do with the utmost of caution. You need to assess how much you can borrow against your total net equity based on your level of risk or tolerance. Never buy on margin unless you are prepared to follow your stocks on a daily basis. If you don't pay attention you can find yourself deep in debt. Also, do not use buying on margin as a long-term investment strategy.

Some important dates in Sears' long history include:

1888: The earliest catalog showcasing only watches and jewelry is rolled out.
1945: Sales exceed $1 billion.
1986: 100th anniversary is celebrated.
1993: "Come see the softer side of Sears" advertising campaign is introduced.

Sears operates about 833 department stores, many of which are situated in malls and regional shopping centers. More than 1,300 independently owned stores sell appliances, hardware, lawn and garden items, and automotive lines. The company also operates 1,325 furniture, hardware, and automotive parts stores. In addition, products are sold through Sears Shop at Home Service, including specialty catalogs through licenses with third-party distributors, and Sears HomeCentral, including repair services.

AlliedSignal (Symbol: ALD)
Headquarters: Morristown, New Jersey
Telephone: 973-455-2000
Web Site Address: http://www.alliedsignal.com

AlliedSignal was established in 1985 through the merger of Allied Corporation with the Signal Companies, Inc. In 1920, Allied Chemical and Dye Corporation was formed as an amalgamation of five American chemical companies that were established in the 1800s. In 1928, Signal was created as a regional gasoline company with oil-drilling activities.

Allied initiatives shifted the company out of its commodity business into more profitable, faster-growing businesses based on higher-value-added products and advanced technology. The year 1983 saw the acquisition of the Bendix Corporation. This acquisition augmented Allied's automotive products businesses and provided a significant entree into the aerospace industry.

The merger of Allied with Signal enhanced its aerospace, automotive, and engineered materials businesses. In addition, Allied sold a 50 percent interest in Union Texas Petroleum and began the divestiture of thirty-five nonstrategic businesses through the formation and spinoff completed in 1986 of the Henley Group, Inc.

AlliedSignal is an advanced technology and manufacturing company offering customers aerospace and automotive products, chemicals, fibers, plastics, and advanced materials. The following decades saw growth in both organizations. Allied had developments in the synthetic fibers business, entered into oil and gas exploration and production through the purchase of Union Texas Petroleum in 1962, and continued its chemical operations. Signal expanded through internal growth and numerous mergers and acquisitions.

McDonald's (Symbol: MCD)
Headquarters: Oak Brook, Illinois
Telephone: 630-623-3000
Web Site Address: http://www.mcdonalds.com

In 1955, Ray Kroc kicked off his first McDonald's location in Des Plaines, Illinois, which is now a museum boasting McDonald's memorabilia and artifacts. In 1963, Clown Ronald McDonald made his first television appearance. The Big Mac, created by one of Ray Kroc's earliest franchisees, was rolled out throughout McDonald's locations in 1968, and, about five years later, the Egg McMuffin was introduced. The Happy Meal made its debut in 1979, and today McDonald's Express locations can be found in more nontraditional locations like Amoco and Chevron stations.

Today, McDonald's is a leading global food-service retailer with more than 24,500 restaurants in approximately 115 countries. The company operates in a decentralized matter, with most stores owned and operated by franchises. The company continues to expand worldwide.

Eastman Kodak (Symbol: EK)
Headquarters: Rochester, New York
Telephone: 716-724-4000
Web Site Address: http://www.kodak.com

In 1881, George Eastman and businessman Henry A. Strong teamed up and formed the Eastman Dry Plate

Company. The company has been known as Eastman Kodak Company since 1892, when Eastman Kodak Company of New York was organized.

In 1883, the concept of film in rolls was brought before the public. The roll holder was adaptable to nearly every plate camera on the market, and the concept was well-received. In 1896, the 100,000th Kodak camera was manufactured. At the time, the pocket Kodak camera sold for about $5.

The foundation for the business was:

Mass production at the lowest possible price
International distribution
Intense advertising
Service to the consumer

Today, Eastman Kodak manufactures in Canada, Mexico, Brazil, the United Kingdom, France, Germany, Australia, and the United States. In addition, its products are marketed by subsidiary companies in more than 150 countries.

IBM (Symbol: IBM)
Headquarters: Armonk, New York
Telephone: 914-765-1900
Web Site Address: http://www.ibm.com

In 1911, IBM was incorporated as the Computer-Tabulating-Recording Company. Its roots can be traced back to 1890, during the height of the Industrial Revolution. It was in 1924 that the company became International Business Machines (IBM).

IBM initially focused on providing large-scale, custom-built tabulating solutions for businesses, leaving the market for small office products to other organizations. The year 1952 saw the IBM 701, the company's first large computer that was based on the vacuum tube. Transistors began replacing vacuum tubes in 1959, and the IBM 7090, one of the premier fully transistorized mainframes, could perform 229,000 calculations per second. At the time, this was a significant feat.

Data processing became a focal point in 1957 with the introduction of the IBM 305 Random Access Method of Accounting and Control (RAMAC), the first computer storage medium for transaction processing. IBM rolled out the System/360, the first large family of computers to use interchangeable software and peripheral equipment, which made upgrading possible.

Today, IBM remains a leader in computer hardware, and the company continues to enhance its offerings to keep up to date with the new technology.

General Electric (Symbol: GE)

Headquarters: Fairfield, Connecticut
Telephone: 203-373-2211
Web Site Address: http://www.ge.com

The beginnings of General Electric can be traced back to Thomas A. Edison, who established Edison Electric Light Company in 1878. In 1892, a merger of the Edison General Electric Company and the Thomson-Houston Electric Company created General Electric Company.

Foreseeing the advent of global competition, General Electric underwent a dramatic restructuring in the 1980s. The company proceeded to restructure, close, or sell businesses that weren't industry leaders. As a result, General Electric divested $10 million of marginal businesses and made $19 billion in acquisitions to provide its organization with the necessary tools to compete in the 1990s and beyond.

General Electric is a multifaceted technology, manufacturing, and services company, and is the only member of the Dow Jones Industrial Average that was part of the original index created in 1896.

Dating back more than 120 years ago, the company has grown to become a mega-organization operating in more than one hundred countries around the world, with approximately 250 manufacturing plants in about twenty-six different nations. The company employs 275,000-plus individuals worldwide, including more than 165,000 in the United States.

Full Service Brokers Have One Big Advantage!

In this day and age where Internet stocks come out of the gate at $12 per share and by the end of the trading day are at $57, one can only say "Damn, I wish I had gotten a piece of that!" That's where full service brokers can help in a big way... IPOs. If you trade regularly with a full service broker you may pay a little more in commissions, but when something like MiningCo.com suddenly issues their IPO which quadruples in one day, you'll forget all about those extra commissions.

As mentioned earlier, The Dow Jones Industrial Average made its debut in 1896 with only twelve stocks. General Electric was one of these twelve stocks, and it is the only original Dow stock that remains on the list to this day. The Dow Jones Industrial Average started out with:

1. American Cotton Oil
2. American Sugar
3. American Tobacco
4. Chicago Gas
5. Distilling and Cattle Feeding
6. General Electric
7. Laced Gas
8. National Lead
9. North American
10. Tennessee Coal and Iron
11. U.S. Leather preferred
12. U.S. Rubber

Later, in 1916, the number of stocks was increased to twenty, and it was increased to thirty stocks in 1928. Changes were made to the list, and in 1997 Hewlett-Packard, Johnson and Johnson, Travelers Group, and Wal-Mart replaced Bethlehem Steel, Texaco, Westinghouse Electric, and Woolworth. Over a year later, Travelers Group merged with CitiBank to form Citigroup, replacing Travelers Group.

The Dow Jones Industrial Average may be the index most quoted, but the Dow Jones Transportation Average was formed in 1884 before the Dow Jones Industrial Average. Union Pacific, one of the original nine stocks on this index, retains its place on the Dow Jones Transportation Average to this day.

Here are the twenty stocks currently in the Dow Jones Transportation Average:

1. Airborne Freight Corp. (ABF)
2. Alexander and Baldwin, Inc. (ALEX)
3. AMR Corp. (AMR)
4. Burlington Northern Santa Fe Corp. (BN)
5. CNF Transportation, Inc. (CNF)
6. CSX Corp. (CSX)

7. Delta Air Lines, Inc. (AL)
8. FDX Corp. (FDX)
9. GATX (GMT)
10. J.B. Hunt Transportation Services (JBHT)
11. Norfolk Southern Corp. (NSC)
12. Northwest Airlines (NWAC)
13. Roadway Express, Inc. (ROAD)
14. Ryder System, Inc. (R)
15. Southwest Airlines Co. (LUV)
16. United Airlines Corp. (UAL)
17. Union Pacific Corp. (UNP)
18. US Airways Group, Inc. (U)
19. US Freightways (USFC)
20. Yellow Corp. (YELL)

The baby of the three Dow Jones averages, the Utility Average entered the scene in 1929. Utility stock prices have proven to be greatly affected by interest rates. For many investors, a rise in utility stock prices signals a falling of interest rates. Since utility companies tend to take out significant loans, their profits are enhanced by lower interest rates.

Here are the fifteen stocks currently in the Dow Jones Utility Average:

1. American Electric Power Co. (AEP)
2. Columbia Energy Group (CG)
3. Consolidated Edison Inc. (ED)
4. Consolidated Natural Gas Co. (CNG)
5. Duke Energy Corp. (DUK)
6. Edison International (EIX)
7. Enron Corp. (ENE)
8. Houston Industries (HOU)
9. Peco Corp. (PE)
10. PG&E Corp. (PCG)
11. Public Service Enterprise Group (PEG)
12. Southern Co. (SO)
13. Texas Utilities Co. (TXU)
14. Unicom Corp. (UCM)
15. Williams Cos. (WMB)

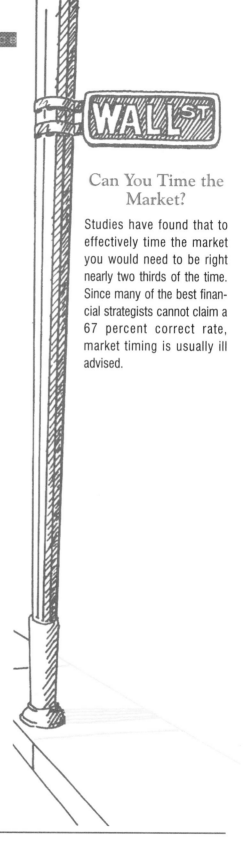

Can You Time the Market?

Studies have found that to effectively time the market you would need to be right nearly two thirds of the time. Since many of the best financial strategists cannot claim a 67 percent correct rate, market timing is usually ill advised.

A Bit of Trivia

The reason stock prices are quoted in sixteenths comes from the Spanish, who four centuries ago used gold doubloons as their money and they would cut them into halves, quarters, and sixteenths.

Some indexes are capitalization-weighted, giving greater weight to stocks with greater market value; others treat each stock equally. Other indexes include the following:

Standard & Poor's Composite Index of 500 Stocks. The Standard & Poor's 500 Index is a benchmark that is widely used by professional stock investors. The Index represents five hundred stocks—four hundred industrial stocks, twenty transportation stocks, forty utility stocks, and forty financial stocks. It consists primarily of stocks listed on the New York Stock Exchange, although it also features stocks that are a part of the American Stock Exchange (Amex) and over-the-counter (OTC) stocks.

Russell 2000. The Russell 2000 was created to be a comprehensive representation of the U.S. small-cap equities market. It measures the performance of the smallest 2,000 companies in the Russell 3000 Index.

MARKET IMPACT

The stock market comes with its surprises, many of which are difficult to predict. Since the auspicious start of the New York Stock Market, whereby twenty-four prominent brokers and merchants gathered on Wall Street to forge a securities trading agreement, the market has grown into the driving force behind the United States economy and has had a major impact on the world market. The world market has also had an effect on the New York and American exchanges.

Having set up shop at 40 Wall Street with their own constitution (in 1817), the stock market has been affected by major events and has subsequently left its mark in history. The market shut down for a week after the assassination of President Lincoln, closed early when President Kennedy was shot, and has seen significant fluctuations during times of major national or international crisis.

Worldwide financial news can have significant influence on the market because the world's economies intermingle with each other. Most financial news has an impact (or could potentially have an impact) on finance in some part of the world. Since we

reside in a global economy, international finance is affected via the "ripple effect."

A situation in one part of the world may very well have a major impact on another. For example, if a region in Japan is hit by a major earthquake and a company there is forced to shut down its computer parts manufacturing operations once its existing supply is depleted, this company will not be able to send parts to the United States. As a result, American companies will have to attempt to locate these parts elsewhere until the Japanese company can resume operations. American companies may be forced to slow down production due to a lack of computer parts, and this may cause a dip in the company's stock price, along with dips in the stock prices of retail stores carrying products using these computer parts.

Investors could either sell, stay put, or view this situation as a short-term problem and purchase more of the stock at the new lower price. Whichever approach investors take, trading can be significantly affected by Japan's earthquake.

Often the situation is not as clear-cut as the previous example. Political events abroad often lead to expectations of changes in laws and policies. They may also affect the stock market. Domestic lawsuits, such as an oil company being sued over a spill or simply needing to use massive amounts of funds on a cleanup effort, can affect the price of a stock and possibly the entire oil industry. New environmental laws may go into effect that force these companies to change their methods of transport. The ripple effect will impact this entire sector of stocks. Oil stock prices may go down and gas stock prices may go up; the transportation method that has been adversely impacted may go down while the new transportation method, as well as any related industries, may go up. If you had caught wind of the law a few months before its implementation, you could have bought the appropriate stocks at a low price as you sat back and waited for them to rise! New FCC regulations can affect the broadcast media. Businesses and the government are tied at many levels.

The market itself was the top news story in 1929 when the "crash" set off the Great Depression. In October 1987, a 508-point drop caused a second market crash, but the repercussions were not as severe. In the nineties the market made a major turnaround, but the decade was not without extreme periods of volatility.

S&P Success

Over the long haul, stocks are a reliable way of building your assets. The stocks in the Standard & Poor's 500 Index have averaged a return of about 9.8 percent annually since 1990.

Determining how much risk you can handle often dictates the types of investments that would be most appealing to you. In many instances, there is a direct correlation between risk and return. When you minimize your risk, you may also be minimizing your investment potential. The greater the risk, the more upside potential. Oftentimes, an established company won't witness the dramatic stock increases (or decreases) that a young burgeoning company might experience. However, you have to come to terms with how much risk you can tolerate.

THE SECURITIES AND EXCHANGE COMMISSION (SEC)

After the Great Depression, the Securities and Exchange Commission (SEC) was created to regulate the securities industry as a whole. It was during this time that Congress also passed the Securities Exchange Act of 1934. The SEC oversees the industry to ensure that no illegal activity is being conducted. In addition, the organization sets many standards for both brokers and investors. Companies trading on stock exchanges nationwide must be registered with the SEC.

Essentially, the SEC administers federal securities laws and issues rules and regulations. Its primary mission is to provide protection for investors and to see that the securities markets are fair and honest. The Commission makes sure that there is adequate and effective disclosure of information to the investing public. The Commission also regulates firms engaged in the purchase or sale of securities, people who provide investment advice, and investment companies.

Insider information is one of the issues reviewed by the SEC. Essentially, insider information (also known as insider trading) deals with the buying and selling of stock based on confidential information obtained from an "inside" source. Such information is not available to the rest of the public. The SEC also oversees trading activity to ensure that investors are getting the appropriate prices when both buying and selling securities.

The SEC requires that publicly traded companies publish regular financial reports. The reports provided to the SEC are called Form 10K or Form 10Q for annual or quarterly reports, respectively.

The Division of Enforcement, a division of the United States Securities and Exchange Commission, is charged with enforcing the federal securities laws. The Division's responsibilities include investigating possible violations of federal securities laws and recommending appropriate remedies for consideration by the Commission.

CHAPTER FIVE

More About Stocks

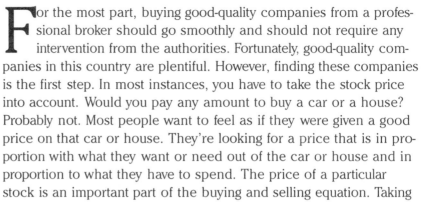

For the most part, buying good-quality companies from a professional broker should go smoothly and should not require any intervention from the authorities. Fortunately, good-quality companies in this country are plentiful. However, finding these companies is the first step. In most instances, you have to take the stock price into account. Would you pay any amount to buy a car or a house? Probably not. Most people want to feel as if they were given a good price on that car or house. They're looking for a price that is in proportion with what they want or need out of the car or house and in proportion to what they have to spend. The price of a particular stock is an important part of the buying and selling equation. Taking a business attitude toward investing is important—there has to be an emphasis on making wise investment decisions that incorporate a variety of factors. That's the only way to ensure profitability in the long run. You want high quality at a fair (or better) price.

While some investors are more inclined to be looking for "great deals," other investors prefer sticking with what's "hot." Hence, the terms *value investing* and *growth investing* were coined.

Essentially, *growth investors* want to own a piece of the fastest-growing companies around, even if it means paying a hefty price for this privilege. Buying on momentum is a common practice among this type of investor. Growth companies are organizations that have experienced rapid growth, such as Microsoft. They may have outstanding management teams, highly rated developments, or aggressive expansion plans into foreign markets. Such stocks rarely pay significant dividends, and growth investors do not frown upon this lack of dividends. Here, growth is the name of the game. Growth companies put a lot of their revenue right back into the business to accelerate even more growth. Among other things, those who follow this type of investing pay close attention to company earnings. If growth investing melds well with your overall investment strategy, look for companies that have had strong growth track records over the past several years.

Value investors are on the prowl for "bargains," and they're more inclined than growth investors to analyze companies using such vehicles as sales volume, earnings, and cash flow. The philosophy here is that such companies have already taken a beating, so the risk of them being hit again is unlikely. In other words, the value investor believes that such companies really have nowhere else to go but up. Dividends are more important to value investors. Such investors are often willing to ride out stock price fluctuations because of the extensive research they have done prior to committing to a particular stock.

Both styles of investing can be lucrative. The idea is to hone in on a style of investment that fits your personality and investment strategy. You need to make investments with which you can live—comfortably. In one instance, you may be leaning towards growth investing, while on another occasion you may feel that taking a value-investing approach is the way to go.

STOCK-PICKING TECHNIQUES

Investors generally follow one of two stock-picking techniques: *fundamental analysis* or *technical analysis.* Technical analysis relies on charts and graphs to determine stock movements. Fundamental analysis is the more commonly used method for beginning investors. It includes both growth and value investing.

Technical analysis involves charts and graphs containing information about past stock price patterns. Essentially, these are patterns that followers of technical analysis may use when investing. There are a number of patterns such analysts recognize to be historically recurring. The trick is to identify the pattern before it is completed. However, it's not as easy and clear-cut as one might be led to believe. Those who utilize this technique believe that you can forecast future stock prices by studying past price trends. Therefore, they buy and sell stock based on stock price movements. Such individuals tend to buy and sell stocks on a much more frequent basis than individuals who use fundamental analysis when making investment decisions. Technical analysts take into account things like moving averages, trend lines and even things like a "double top" or a "head and shoulders" pattern.

Fundamental analysis is a long-used, common way to review stocks. The technique involves an analysis of the company's ability to generate earnings and examines the value of the company's total assets. Value investing and growth investing are two subdivisions of

Stock Selection Tips, Part 1

Learn about all of the products and/or services offered by the company. A company may have one high-profile product and several other products and/or services that are not as visible. A high-profile product may be getting rave reviews and profits, but the company's lesser-known products may be taking a toll on the company's profits. Or it may very well be the other way around. A company's primary product may be suffering, but its other offerings may be reaping respectable profits. You need to closely examine all of a company's products and/or services to try to determine its future potential. Among other considerations, you want to invest in companies with high-quality products and/or services, a large market share, and good growth potential.

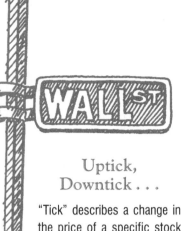

Uptick, Downtick . . .

"Tick" describes a change in the price of a specific stock from one trade to the next. If the last trade is higher than the previous trade, it is called an "uptick." Conversely, a "downtick" is used when the last trade is lower than the one that preceded it.

fundamental analysis. Proponents of fundamental analysis believe that stock prices will rise as a result of growth. Earnings, dividends, and book values are all examined, and a buy-and-hold approach is usually followed. Fundamental analysis advocates maintain the view that stocks of well-run, high-quality companies will become more valuable as time unfolds.

UNCOVERING GREAT COMPANIES

Once you've narrowed your focus to a handful of companies, you need to fine-tune your research even more. Simply put, one of the primary reasons to buy a particular stock is because of its fundamental outlook. As we explained earlier and want to continue to emphasize, it's wise to buy and hold onto a stock for the long term. That's why buying quality companies is so important. Among other factors, you want to purchase stock in a company that you believe has the following:

1. *A sound business model.* A solid foundation is at the core of the majority of most thriving businesses. You want to single out a company that has a solid business plan and a good grasp of where it wants to be in the years ahead—and exactly how it plans to get there. A company with a clear focus has a better chance of reaching its goals and, ultimately, succeeding than a company that just rolls along without a concrete plan.

2. *Superior management.* An experienced, innovative, and progressive management team has the best chance of leading a company into the future. Star managers have had a major impact on their prospective companies, and a company will often witness dramatic changes when a new management team comes on board. When key management leaves an organization, you will often see major changes in the way a company operates.

3. *A significant market share.* When a majority of individuals rely upon the products and/or services of a designated company, the odds are that the company has good insights about consumer preferences. If that company keeps doing what it's

Buy What You Know

Maria
Assistant Vice President at a New York–Based Bank
Age: 36

Maria's entree to investing was the result of a job she secured at a publicly traded company. As part of her employee benefits package, Maria is eligible to purchase stock in the bank as often as every pay period at a 5 percent discount. She notes, "You have a sense of ownership in more ways than one when you have stock in the company you work for. You also have confidence in your decision to purchase stock because you know firsthand how the company is run and how its business plan is being shaped and implemented. In addition, employees want to work that much harder because they have a vested interest in the company through their investment."

Maria didn't give much thought to investing prior to her position at the bank. The stock market, as Maria describes, essentially arrived at her office when she accepted the bank position. She now keeps up with financial news on a regular basis and is more comfortable with her ability to make sound investment decisions. When her bank stock drops, she often picks up more shares than she normally buys on a biweekly basis, when the money is automatically deducted from her paychecks. She is extremely confident of the bank's continued success and tries to buy additional shares at the best possible price. She's in it for the long-run and plans to keep her shares until retirement.

As far as new investments are concerned, Maria prefers established companies because she feels that such companies have the level of sophistication needed to serve consumers in the new millennium. However, she wants to buy good-quality companies at a reasonable price. "You want to buy a significant amount of shares without paying exorbitant prices," she says. Her prior employer, a health care benefits company where she worked for fourteen years was not a publicly traded company and Maria now feels that this was a disadvantage. "I wish I had been introduced to the world of investing at my last job," she says. "However, it's now a great time for investors—especially with the proliferation of the Internet. Today's investor has a lot of advantages that were not available just a few years ago. I'm ready to use all that technology has to offer to guide me in my future investment decisions. My investing career has only just begun."

In the News

been doing, then it will most likely continue to reap the rewards of maintaining a significant market share. Industry market leaders usually have a well-thought-out vision. Be careful and look more closely at markets with a glut of competitors. Also, determine where the company you are interested in sits among the competition.

4. *Competitive advantages.* A company that is ahead of the pack will often be on top of cutting-edge trends and industry changes in areas like marketing and technology. You want to single out those companies that are—and will continue to be—one step ahead of the competition.

5. *New developments.* If a company places a high priority on research and development, it's likely to roll out successful introductions. Those new introductions could be anything from a drug to treat arthritis to vegetarian chili to a quick-dry nail polish. If the product or service takes off, then the stock price may very well follow. Investors should always be on the lookout for new developments and introductions.

If the fundamental outlook for a particular company looks promising, then owning a portion of that company might very well make good business sense. As long as these catalysts are in place, and as long as those companies are able to execute on those catalysts, then holding onto that stock for the long haul may be your best bet.

Most individuals want to emulate the most successful investors. And why not? Warren Buffet has earned his claim to fame by investing in quality companies in lieu of relying on technical analysis strategies. Buffet is a firm believer that if you buy good-quality companies, you have no reason to sell your investments unless there is a serious underlying problem behind a price dip. Buffet believes that investors should understand the company and its industry before making any investment decisions. He says that this understanding is important in honing in on a specific company. Although Buffet wants to buy companies at prices below their potential, price is not the sole consideration in his stock selection process. Buying solid-quality companies for the long haul is key. If one of your star companies suffers a dip in its stock price, Buffet says, it might be a good chance to pick up some additional shares.

KNOW THYSELF

It may sound clichéd, but I'll say it anyway: Understanding yourself is an integral component in mapping out an investment plan. What's right for one person might be a disastrous strategy for another investor. If the market drops 20 percent right after you purchased stock, will you lose sleep? Will you be able to work the next day? Worse yet, will you "panic sell"? Determining how much risk you can tolerate is even more critical when dealing with stocks than it is with other types of investments such as bonds and mutual funds. Stocks have a tendency to be more volatile than the majority of mutual funds and a lot more volatile than bonds, where in most cases you're aware of how much profit you can expect right from the beginning.

However, buying high-quality stocks is a step in the right direction to a bright investment future. Knowing when to hold and when to sell a particular stock is an art in itself. You may have every intention of sticking with your investments for the long haul, but instead find yourself rushing to sell at the first sign of turbulence. History has revealed that holding onto solid stocks for a minimum of five to ten years has produced the best results. Therefore, buying good companies and holding them for the long term is a sound strategy for most investors.

The ability to stay the course is crucial, and it's a good idea to develop a strategy that you could implement if you feel like prematurely abandoning your plan. A good way to gradually enter the world of investing is through "paper trading." You can "paper trade" until you feel you have enough market exposure to make actual trades with your hard-earned money. Before you commit actual cash to an investment, test out your skills by buying and selling stocks on paper. By keeping a record of your trades on paper, you can get a feel for what it's actually like to invest. You can also get good practice in keeping your emotions in

Bull & Bear

The terms "Bull" and "Bear" are commonly used to describe the direction in which the stock market has headed. "Bull" means that the market is rising and doing well, while "Bear" is the term for the market dropping and not doing well.

The term "Bear" originated from bearskin sellers who would sell bearskins before having actually caught the bear. Eventually this term was used to describe speculators who would sell shares they did not own. They were speculating that the crops or commodities they were buying would drop in value. Subsequently they would buy after the price dropped and then deliver them to whomever they had promised to sell them to.

"Bull," thought to be the opposite of "Bear" in manner of aggression, was then considered to be the term used to describe the opposite, where people would speculate that the prices would go up.

check. If you purchased (on paper) 100 shares of stock on Monday that took a major dip on Thursday, you can find out how you react to volatility. This insight may very well help you in developing your long-term investment strategy with your hard-earned money.

If you find at any point, once you've invested, that you simply cannot handle the market's mood swings, you may want to re-evaluate your strategy. Your investment plan is not set in stone, but you should be fully aware of the reasons why you've chosen to stray from your original strategy. Maintaining realistic expectations will keep beginning investors from growing frustrated, disappointed, and disillusioned. It's unrealistic to want a 15 percent return on your investment if you aren't willing to take any risks. Understanding how the market works is a necessity that needs to be addressed early on in the learning process.

Once you have developed a strategy that you are comfortable with, don't analyze it on a daily basis and don't even try to predict stock prices for either the long or short term. Predicting actual stock prices for any period of time is impossible. No matter what the strategy, you have a good shot at success if you invest in high-quality companies that you believe will—among other things—continue a track record of good financial execution and financial management.

GETTING STARTED

Choosing the way you will conduct your investing is an important decision. Fortunately, you have several options, each equipped with both pros and cons. However, there is no universally "correct" way to invest. Whichever way you choose to conduct your investment affairs has a lot to do with level of investment interest and just how eager you are to partake in the entire research process.

If you are ready, willing, and able to investigate potential companies on your own, then a discount broker may fit the bill. Many individuals are finding that taking charge of their investments is an empowering experience. Once they become acquainted with all of the available information, many investors feel like they are in the best position to handle their investments and they are happy to be in the driver's seat.

Commissions charged by brokerage houses were deregulated in 1975, and this decision was truly the beginning of the ascent of the discount broker. Trades could be conducted for far less money than investors were used to paying at full-service brokerage firms like Merrill Lynch and Morgan Stanley Dean Witter. Discount brokers are now offering more services than ever before and, combined with all of the new and faster technology, investors have all of the investment information they need right at their disposal.

With the meteoric development and use of the Internet, the opportunity for self-education is virtually limitless. Beginning investors now have access to many of the same resources as full-service brokers. With this access to data, the demand for full-service brokers has been diminishing as the Internet continues to gain prominence. With a little enthusiasm and determination, you can find a wealth of information online that will keep you well-informed about everything from a company's new introductions to the ten most highly traded stocks on any given day.

Some of the best Web sites were created by financial institutions, and investors have access to everything with just the click of a mouse—from real-time quotes to analyst reports to stock market basics. You can even communicate with other investors, who may offer you some great investment ideas. The proliferation of online discount brokers has made trading possible around-the-clock for a nominal fee. In some cases, you can make trades for under $10. Trading online is ideal if you have done your homework and know exactly which stock you want to own.

If you want someone else to do most of the legwork, then you might opt for a full-service broker. Of course, full-service brokers charge a premium for their input. There is no guarantee that a full-service broker will steer you in the direction of massive capital gains; however, you can get his or her input. If you want to work with a full-service broker, it's advisable to get a reference from someone you know and trust. Be on the lookout for brokers that engage in "churning."

If a broker is overly eager to buy and sell your stocks on a continual basis for no apparent reason, you may be the victim of churning. Churning is especially beneficial to brokers who work on commission— the more trades they make, the more pay they take home.

Find a broker who shares your basic investment philosophy and one who gives you several investment options to choose from. Feel

Stock Selection Tips, Part 2

Investigate the company's competition. Find out which other industry players are offering similar products and/or services, and how the competition stacks up to the company you are reviewing. Investigate the quality of the competitions' products and/or services, along with how aggressive they are in areas like advertising and marketing. Determine whether the competition is in the process of any mergers and acquisitions or any new developments that may influence the industry as a whole.

Keep Tabs on Company News

Besides that daily "share price," you need to keep track of news and announcements regarding the company in which you are a share holder. You can read financial sections of major newspaper or specific financial newspapers or magazines. Company news can include new product information, merger or acquisition news, buyouts, a potential stock split, etc. Examine what effect such news can have on your holdings. If you don't understand the correlation or are not sure, consult a financial advisor or your broker.

free to request current company reports if you are unsure about which stocks would best suit your needs.

It's perfectly acceptable to ask your potential brokers questions pertaining to how long they have been in this business and about their formal education, their investment philosophy, and what sources they use to get the majority of their information. You may want to find out which investment publications they regularly read and which they find most helpful (and why). Find out if they rely only on their brokerage firm's reports when making stock recommendations. It may be in your best interest to work with a broker with a minimum of five years of investment experience because you want someone who has witnessed (and traded in) both bull and bear markets.

Becoming acquainted with the fee structure is crucial. In many cases, you may be charged for services that you didn't know you were getting—and wouldn't use even if you knew you could. You also want to inquire about the fees associated with ending, maintaining, and closing an account; getting checks; participating in investment profiles; buying and selling securities; and attending various seminars. To circumvent potential discrepancies, it's important that you obtain this information in writing and in advance—and not after the fact.

The National Association of Securities Dealers (NASD) can answer your questions about the practices of a particular broker by looking up his or her past record regarding any disciplinary actions taken or complaints registered against the broker. They can also confirm whether the broker is licensed to conduct business in your state of residence. You can reach them at 1-800-289-9999.

The NASD Regulation, Inc. is the independent subsidiary of the National Association of Securities Dealers charged with regulating the securities industry and the NASDAQ Stock Market. Through its many departments and offices, NASD Regulation's jurisdiction extends to more than 5,400 firms with more than 58,000 branch offices, and more than 505,000 securities industry professionals.

With ease of access to the Internet, full-service brokers have been losing market share because it's becoming increasingly more difficult for them to justify their high rates. Some experts believe that if you have investments totaling more than $100,000, you may want to explore the possibility of using a full-service broker. However, many investors now realize that they can obtain the information necessary to make prudent investment decisions and, at the same time, benefit from the significantly lower fees offered by both discount and deep-discount brokerage firms.

Another option is to utilize the services of financial planners. Such individuals go beyond handling just your investments—they can aid you in matters relating to insurance, taxes, trusts, and real estate. The cost of doing business with financial planners can range considerably. If you opt for a financial planner, it may be in your best interest to utilize the services of a fee-based planner in lieu of one that works solely on commission. If an individual works on commission alone, it may be in his or her best interest to encourage heavy trading in the investment options for which they get a commission. While some planners charge a flat hourly rate, other individuals may charge a fee that is based on your total assets and trading activity. In this type of arrangement, you are responsible to pay the financial planner even if you do not follow any of his or her suggestions. Other planners operate with a combination of fee-based charges and commission. Here, you may pay less per trade but you are also responsible for paying additional fees.

When it comes to trading, it's important to determine how you like to operate. There are three main personality types:

1. *Delegators.* These individuals prefer to have someone such as a full-service broker handle their investments. They may not have the time or the desire to research companies, and they are comfortable with delegating this task to a professional financial consultant.
2. *Validators.* Those in this category want to take part in their investment future but need assurance from a professional. Such individuals are willing to do their own research, but they want a vote of confidence before plunging into a stock purchase.
3. *Self-directed investors.* If you're in this category, you prefer to be on your own and don't want anyone interfering in your investment affairs. An increasing number of investors are exploring online trading, and the options available continue to flourish.

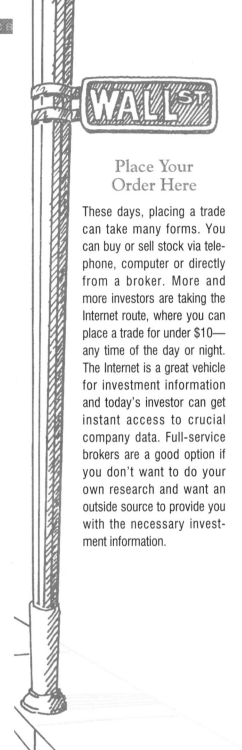

Place Your Order Here

These days, placing a trade can take many forms. You can buy or sell stock via telephone, computer or directly from a broker. More and more investors are taking the Internet route, where you can place a trade for under $10—any time of the day or night. The Internet is a great vehicle for investment information and today's investor can get instant access to crucial company data. Full-service brokers are a good option if you don't want to do your own research and want an outside source to provide you with the necessary investment information.

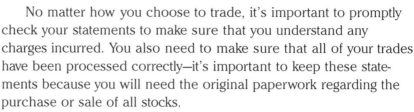

No matter how you choose to trade, it's important to promptly check your statements to make sure that you understand any charges incurred. You also need to make sure that all of your trades have been processed correctly—it's important to keep these statements because you will need the original paperwork regarding the purchase or sale of all stocks.

The Appendix at the end of the book contains a list of some of the many discount brokers.

KNOW THE BASICS

After you've narrowed down your focus to a handful of companies, it's a good idea to continue your research efforts by reviewing the following factors. This will give you greater insight into the stocks.

Earnings per share. Earnings per share is the company's net income divided by the number of common shares outstanding. It is the company's profit. Growth rate is often determined in terms of earnings per share. Finding a company with a strong earning growth is advisable. You also want to review the company's earnings per share over the past several years to see if the company is growing on a consistent basis.

Price/earnings ratio (P/E). Reviewing a company's price/earnings ratio is an integral part of the stock selection decision-making process. A P/E ratio is the stock price divided by the earnings per share. Essentially, it tells you how much investors are willing to pay for one dollar of the company's earnings. In most instances, you can find a company's P/E ratio in the newspaper. When investigating a particular stock, it's a good idea to compare its P/E with other companies in the same industry. Since every industry has its own unique qualities, you want to find out what the average P/E is for that sector. A P/E of 20 means that investors are paying 20 times earnings for the stock. If a company has an exceptionally low P/E (e.g., 4), you will want to find out why that is the case.

Book value. Shareholder's equity is another term for book value. Book value is defined as the company's assets minus its liabilities. The number you get from this equation is then divided by the number of shares outstanding. Hence, you have your book value per share. Many experts say you should look for a low stock price relative to the book value per share. This is how you find "value" stocks selling at less than book value.

Price volatility. Price volatility is often measured by beta. Beta shows you how a stock is moving in relation to changes in the Standard & Poor's 500 Stock Index. The index is fixed at 1.00. Therefore, a stock with a beta of 2 moves up and down two times as much as the Standard & Poor's Index. The stock with a 2 beta is expected to rise in price by 20 percent if the Standard & Poor's Index rises by 20 percent. Conversely, a stock with a 2 beta is expected to drop by 20 percent if the Standard & Poor's Index falls by 20 percent.

Dividends. Dividends are payments to shareholders that are not based on the stock price but are made simply because the company has reaped healthy profits and chooses to reward shareholders. Depending on the company's profits, the board of directors will decide whether or not to initiate a dividend to shareholders, as well as how often and when these dividends will be paid. Dividends are usually most important to investors looking for income (hence income stocks). Many companies pay dividends on a quarterly basis, and special one-time dividends may also be paid under certain circumstances.

    To be entitled to dividends, you must actually own the shares on the Record Date, which is when the board declares a dividend. Find out the current dividend and compare it with the dividend rate for the past five years. When a company's primary goal is growth, dividends may be small— or non-existent. Usually stock dividends are paid by large-scale companies.

Stock Selection Tips, Part 3

Review the company's growth pattern. This would include whether or not the company has met its own sales and revenue expectations. Determine what economic factors could potentially influence the success of this company. Such factors as international and national news, changes in legislation, and an increased or decreased level of product demand could have a great impact on a company's growth pattern.

Double the Fun

Stock splits do not increase the value of your investment. If you owned 50 shares of a stock that was worth $100 per share and it split two-for-one, you would now have 100 shares of stock worth $50 per share. Either way, your investment is worth $5,000. In many cases, however, a stock split is looked upon favorably by investors.

Number of shares outstanding. Shares outstanding refers to the number of shares issued to the general public, including company employees. It's a good idea to start your investing career by looking at companies with at least 5 million shares outstanding, because this indicates that the stock is heavily traded and, as a result, will not be difficult to sell if you should take that course of action.

Total return. Most investors in stocks tend to think about their gains and losses in terms of price changes, not dividends, whereas those who own bonds pay attention to interest yields and seldom focus on price changes. Both approaches are a mistake. Although dividend yields are obviously more important if you are seeking income, and changes in price play a greater role in growth stocks, the total return on a stock is extremely important. It makes it possible for you to compare your stock investments with similar types of investments, such as corporate or municipal bonds, treasuries, mutual funds, and unit investment trusts. To calculate the total returns, add (or subtract) the stock's price change and dividends for the past twelve months and then divide by the price at the beginning of the twelve-month period. For example, suppose you buy a stock at $42 per share and receive $2.50 in dividends for the next twelve-month period. At the end of the period, you sell the stock at $45. Your calculations would look like this:

Dividend: $2.50
Price appreciation: +$3.00 per share
$2.50 + $3.00 per share =$5.50
$5.50 divided by $42.00 = 13 percent
Your total return is a 13 percent increase.

BUYING AND SELLING STOCKS

When you're ready to place an order, either online or with a broker, you have several options: a market order, a limit order, a stop/limit order, or a stop/loss order. Any of these orders can be placed either for the day or GTC (good-till-canceled).

The INVESTOR GAZETTE

Here's to DRIPs

Felix
Financial Services Manager
Age: 30

"It all began in 1996 when I hooked up to the Internet. I had everything in the way of investment information at my fingertips, and I felt extremely empowered," says Felix. Prior to having access to the Internet, Felix was intimidated by just the thought of investing because he didn't know how to get the information he needed to make sound investment decisions. Now, he just logs on and his researching begins instantaneously. He does urge investors to make sure that the online information they are getting is timely and is coming from a reliable source.

Felix didn't have a large sum of money to invest all at once and was determined to find a way to circumvent broker fees. He was successful. "If you're not buying in round lots of 100, it isn't practical to buy from a broker. The fees cut into your capital gains," he explained.

Felix strongly advocates dividend reinvestment plans (DRIPs) because such plans enable you to invest minimal amounts of money on an ongoing basis for a nominal service fee. For example, Felix buys McDonald's direct from the company, and this strategy has been very practical. In some cases, however, you may have to already own at least one share in the company to use a particular DRIP. "Whenever I have extra money," says Felix, "I send in a check for additional shares of stock." He says that one downfall of relying on DRIPs is that you aren't buying stocks at up-to-the-minute prices. Most of these programs won't purchase shares until your check has arrived. This hasn't been too much of an inconvenience for Felix because he says that the difference in a stock's price between the time he sends in his check and the time the sale is made won't be a significant factor in the long run.

Depending on the specific DRIP program, Felix says, investors can often sell shares of stock on the spot by calling a toll free number. What he likes most about these programs is that it helps him stick to his investment strategy, which is to buy minimal amounts of shares on an ongoing basis. This keeps him active in the market. However, Felix is taking a short hiatus from the world of investing because he is expecting a new addition to his family—one of the most wonderful investments you can make!

Market Order:

When you want to buy or sell a stock at the current price, you can place a market order. This means that you want to buy or sell a certain stock at the price the stock is trading for when the order reaches the floor. In other words, you're buying or selling a given stock at the "going rate." Depending on whether you're buying or selling, the market price may differ. This is known as the bid or ask price, and the difference between these two prices is known as the spread. For example, Coca-Cola may have a bid price to sell at 65^1/_4$ per share and an asking price to buy at 65^1/_2$ per share, making the spread one-quarter. Unlike Coca-Cola, securities that are thinly traded often have bigger spreads. For playing the role of the middleman, dealers in a security generally keep a large part of the spread. Middlemen are in the business of selling goods at a higher price than what they initially paid. Stock prices, especially in heavily traded stock, can change in just seconds. By the time your order is filled with a market order, you might find a slight difference in the price you were quoted.

LIMIT ORDER

Limit orders are placed if you don't want to purchase stock for more or sell a stock for less than a predetermined price. A limit order, along with other types of orders, can be placed as a day order or as a good-till-canceled (GTC) order. A day order is only good until the end of the trading day; a GTC order is good until it is canceled. Your order may not fill with either one of these two options; however, you have a greater chance of your order being filled with a GTC order since it can remain open for a longer period of time.

Buy

If you want to buy a stock for a specified price, you can place a limit order. If Cisco is currently trading at $105 and you want to buy 100 shares of Cisco if it dips to $100, you can place a limit order for 100 shares of Cisco at $100 per share. The order may fill for $100 per share if the price dips to that level. If it does not, your order will remain

unfilled. Your order to buy stock may be filled for less than $100 per share if the stock hits $100 and trades at a lower price after it hits $100 per share. However, your order will not fill for more than $100.

Sell

If you own Cisco and want to sell the stock if it dips to $95 per share, you can place a limit order to sell. In this case, your order will fill for $95 per share. Your order to sell the stock may be filled for more than $95 per share if the stock hits $95 and trades at a higher price after it hits $95. However, your order will not fill for less than $95 per share.

Stop Order

Once your stock reaches a target figure in a stop order, it becomes a market order. Stop orders are a viable vehicle for investors who own a stock and are concerned about it falling too low.

Sell

If you purchase Disney at $40 per share, you could place a stop order for $30 to sell that stock if the price drops to $30. If the next trade after the stock reaches $30 is 29½ per share, you would sell your Disney stock for $29½ per share if your order is filled. The stop order turns into a market order as soon as the exchange price hits the predetermined figure. After the stock reaches $30 per share, it will be sold at the market price, which is the price of the next trade. This could be higher or lower than $30 per share.

Buy

You can also place a stop order to buy. If Disney is currently selling at $35 per share and you want to purchase the stock if it climbs to $40 because you think the price will continue to rise, it becomes a market order once it hits $40 per share. If the next trade after it reaches $40 per share is $40½, you would buy your Disney stock for $40½ per share if your order is filled. After the stock reaches $40 per share, it will be bought at the market price which is the price of the next trade. This could be higher or lower than $40½ per share.

Set Target Prices–But Not in Stone.

If you've studied the past history of the stocks you're looking to purchase, you should have a good idea of the 52 week highs and lows. This will help you set target prices for when to sell. As the stock approaches the target price you can start selling off shares, and then gage to what degree you believe it might pass the target. Don't use the target as an absolute figure but a barometer. If a stock is showing consistent gains, you may sell off some shares and then watch closely until that pattern of gains begins to diminish. ALSO: Before selling, note why the stock is rising, or falling and determine if that is going to be a pattern or if there is company news that made the stock price react in such a manner.

Stock Trivia A-Z

All but four letters in the alphabet represent stocks as one digit ticker symbols. BUT, whereas F is Ford Motor Company, G is Gillette or H is Harcourt General, others are not as obvious as they may seem. For example, O is the symbol for Realty Income Corp., T is AT&T, X is US Steel and Y is Allegheny Corp. Thus, when you're not sure of the symbol for a stock you want to look up on the Internet, it can be very hard to guess.

DIVIDEND REINVESTMENT PLANS (DRIPs)

Dividend reinvestment plans offer shareholders a simple and inexpensive way to purchase stock directly through a company. This type of investment plan does not require the services of a broker. Such plans enable investors to purchase small amounts of common stock (in many cases, as little as $25) directly through the company. Depending on the company, there may be a small fee for handling your account, and you often need to have already purchased at least one share of the stock from a broker. Close to nine hundred companies have dividend reinvestment plans, most of them being blue-chippers. If you are involved in ten different dividend reinvestment plans with ten different companies, you will get ten different statements. This may not be ideal for individuals who like one comprehensive investment statement. Dividend reinvestment plans, however, may be a good choice for long-term investors who want to buy more shares of a certain stock on an ongoing basis. You can probably find a listing of companies that offer dividend reinvestment plans at your local library, or you can call a company directly to find out if they offer this service. Examples are:

> AlliedSignal
> AT&T Corp.
> American Express
> Caterpillar Inc.
> Coca-Cola Co.
> McDonald's Corp.
> Eastman Kodak Co.
> Walt Disney Co.

INITIAL PUBLIC OFFERINGS (IPOs)

When a company chooses to "go public," that means they are issuing stocks to the public at large. Looking to grow, they sell shares of stock to raise capital without creating debt. Investors, in turn, expect to earn profits by purchasing stock in such a company. An initial public offering (IPO) is held when a company issues stock for the first time. If a company has previously issued stock, a primary offering is conducted when that company issues additional new stock.

The detailed process of issuing stock is usually done through an investment bank, with whom a company works to determine how much capital is needed, the price of the stock, how much it will cost to issue such equities, and so forth. A company must file a registration statement with the Securities and Exchange Commission (SEC), who carefully investigate the company to ensure that it has made full disclosure in compliance with the Securities Act of 1933. The SEC will then determine whether or not the company has met all the criteria to issue common stock, or "go public."

Prior to the stock going public, the SEC must make sure that everything is in order (this can take some time), and a red herring is usually issued, which is a prospectus informing the public about the company and the impending stock offering. When the stock is ready to "go public," a stock price is issued in accordance with the current market.

The best way to find out about an IPO is to have a broker who has a pulse on all breaking financial news. *Investment Dealer's Digest* lists all IPOs that are registered with the SEC. Once the stock is issued, the publication gives you an IPO update. Companies awaiting an IPO will often call the leading brokerage houses and/or brokers they are familiar with who will inform their clients about such an offering. They are looking for investors who will hold onto the stock for some time. As is the case with anything new, these stocks can be very risky due to their potentially volatile nature. It's a good idea to wait until the stock settles before you determine whether it would be a viable investment. The vast majority of stocks that you will be researching have probably already been actively trading.

Company size or market capitalization is an important consideration when making an investment. As explained earlier, to determine a company's market capitalization, multiply the number of outstanding shares of stock by the price per share. If a company has 2 million outstanding shares of stock trading at $10 per share, then the market capitalization for that company is $20 million. Many blue-chip companies have market capitalizations in the billions.

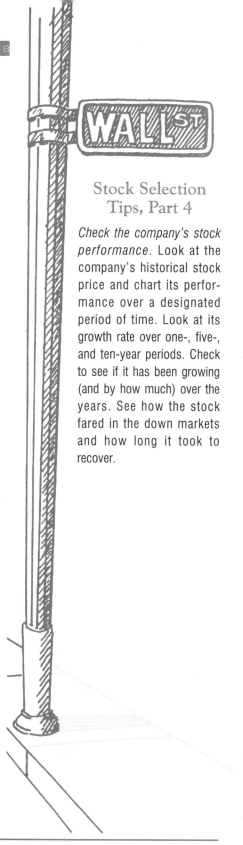

Stock Selection Tips, Part 4

Check the company's stock performance. Look at the company's historical stock price and chart its performance over a designated period of time. Look at its growth rate over one-, five-, and ten-year periods. Check to see if it has been growing (and by how much) over the years. See how the stock fared in the down markets and how long it took to recover.

REPURCHASING COMPANY STOCK

Companies may repurchase their own stock on the open market, usually common shares, for many reasons. In theory, the buyback should not be a short-term fix to the stock price but a rational use of cash, implying that a company's best investment alternative is to buy back its stock. Normally these purchases are done with free cash flow, but not always. If earnings stay constant, the reduced number of shares will result in higher earnings per share, which all else being equal will result, or should result, in a higher stock price.

INVESTMENT CLUBS

For close to 50 years, The National Association of Investors Corporation (NAIC) has been helping investment clubs get up and running—and their efforts have certainly paid off. Due to the growing popularity of investing over the past several years, the NAIC has witnessed a dramatic increase in its membership. As of December 1998, NAIC's membership boasted 730,000 individual and investment club members.

The Madison Heights, Michigan, not-for-profit organization provides members with an information-packed publication called *NAIC's Official Guide, Starting and Running a Profitable Investment Club.* The guide offers tips on starting and operating an investment club in the most optimal fashion. The organization's monthly magazine, *Better Investing*, covers a wide array of investment-related topics. In addition, members have access to sample agreements and brochures. There is a nominal annual fee per club to join the NAIC, plus a fee for each club member.

Overall, investment clubs can range in number from ten to twenty (or more) individuals of all ages and from all walks of life. With meetings normally held about once a month, members can include your neighbors, coworkers, friends, and relatives. Under optimal conditions, members should be able to work well together and should share similar investment philosophies. Recent NAIC statistics reveal that 67 percent of its members are female, with 33 percent being male. The median age of NAIC members is fifty years old,

Stock Portfolio Planning Tips

As an investor, you will need to develop a strategy that is optimal for your specific needs. Your investment time frame and your ability to handle volatility will play an integral role in this strategy. As noted earlier, there are a variety of different types of stocks that you can incorporate into your portfolio. The task is to identify quality companies that best fit into your overall strategy, whether that strategy is to save for your retirement or to finance your newborn's future education. Here are some tips:

1. *Design a personal plan*. Devote time to organizing a sound investment strategy based on your individual needs. Commit to whether you're looking for short-term, mid-term, or long-term investments and plan your strategy accordingly.
2. *Don't forget your goals*. Once you have designed a plan, you need to track your stocks on a regular basis to see if they are keeping you on track toward your stated goals. Re-evaluate your goals at least twice a year to make sure that your circumstances haven't changed since your original plan was implemented.
3. *Remember that research counts*. Study companies of interest, check indexes, and find out all you can about the industry and its competition. There is a vast array of valuable information that will help you in the decision-making process.
4. *Invest regularly*. Stay an active investor and incorporate it into your budget. It's also a good idea to reinvest your proceeds.
5. *Commit to diversification*. Diversification in the stock market is important, no matter what the economic climate may be at any given moment. Since different market segments tend to move at different times, one stock may be increasing in value while another may be slipping. The key is to make sure that your entire stock portfolio doesn't drop simultaneously.
6. *Stick with the winners*. Don't be tempted to invest in the cheapest stock around because it looks like a bargain. Go with stocks with a strong track record and a bright future. This is especially true for beginning investors. For growth, investing for the long term is a wise strategy for beginning investors. Once again, keeping good stocks for a minimum of five to ten years usually pays off. Ignore the urge to sell at the slightest setback if there isn't any major underlying reason for a stock's decline.
7. *Monitor your stocks periodically*. Check your stocks' returns against the appropriate benchmarks on an ongoing basis. Keep up with company news, including mergers and acquisitions, product rollouts, and new industry competitors.
8. *Stay in the driver's seat*. You should make the ultimate decision about when to buy or sell a given stock. Make sure that you give your broker prior approval before a trade is made on your behalf.

Wanna DRIP?

For those who would like to contact and buy stocks directly from the companies, which will set up a dividend reinvestment program, you can learn more from the magazine *DRIP Investor*. Call them at 1-800-233-5922 or go online to www.dripinvestor.com.

and the average investment club has been operating for four and a half years.

As in most organizations, investment clubs also elect various officers, and each member should take an active role in researching potential stock purchases and tracking existing investments. Individuals can be given specific assignments depending on their interests and preferences. Investment clubs tend to be most effective if members make a long-term commitment to the group.

Clubs of this type are a great way for both experienced and beginning investors to meet other individuals who all share a common goal—to reap the rewards of the stock market. The basic premise is to promote a spirit of partnership by ensuring that members work together to attain a common goal.

There is often a broad range of investment viewpoints expressed, which ends up a world of possibilities. You may be gung-ho about a particular stock until someone in the group talks about a news item that could potentially have a negative impact on the exact stock you were so excited about buying. If everyone makes a contribution, the overall researching process is a lot less labor-intensive for each member.

Some of the most successful clubs witness the best results when members have a cohesive investment strategy intact and stick with it. In most instances, a long-term strategy where stocks are bought and held has proven to be the most viable approach. Such an undertaking is a great way for new investors to get acquainted with basic investing techniques and for experienced investors to sharpen their skills. Members can share ideas, as well as learn (hopefully!) from others' mistakes.

The members agree on the actual investments that are to be featured in the portfolio. As a club member, a minimum monthly contribution of about $20 (this figures varies among clubs) is required. The value of each member's share of the portfolio is determined by the amount of capital contributions that were made. To get the most of the investment club experience, each member should partake in the decision-making process.

Investment clubs tend to invest in individual stocks. It is suggested that members invest a set amount on an ongoing basis, rein-

General Investing Tips

There is no easy way to become a successful investor. There isn't one single action you can take to "lock in" impressive profits. It takes a combination of actions, from keeping up with national and international news to reading up on specific companies and the competition to following the stock market on an ongoing basis.

Most important of all, you should stay within your budget and remember that there isn't one major opportunity. There are always opportunities to buy quality companies and, as we mentioned earlier, it's important to avoid impulsive behavior. The best time to invest is when you have a variety of information at your disposal and you feel confident that you've done your homework to the best of your ability. Here are some more tips:

- *Don't believe everything you read*. Many "hot" tips have gone askew over the years. Take every "you can't miss" candidate with a grain of salt and do your own research.

- *"Help, I need somebody"—or not*. If you are willing to do your own research, you can gain access to timely information from various sources. The Internet and many of the investment publications are a great starting point. Full-service brokers are a good option for individuals who do not choose to do research on their own.

- *Keep that business section*. From the *Wall Street Journal* to CNN to *USA Today*, there are myriad ways to follow the stock market. It's simple enough to do every day whether you prefer using traditional newspapers or online data.

- *Bargain hunt*. Keep an eye on stocks that have taken a dip in price for no significant reason. You may find yourself a good deal in the process. Investigate as to whether the company is planning to introduce some new technology, or a promising product or is in the process of a merger or acquisition.

- *Keep the word* risk *top-of-mind*. The greater the earnings potential, the greater the risk. If you want to be an aggressive investor, make sure that you understand the potential risks involved in committing to such an aggressive investment strategy.

- *Pay attention to company news*. Read the papers diligently to look for mergers, acquisitions, reorganizations, legal battles, management changes, and other factors that could impact your stock.

- *Insider trading does exist*. Be wary of any recommendations from an "inside source" regarding confidential information. Insider trading is illegal and punishable by fines and/or imprisonment.

- *Stay within your means*. If you have set aside $10,000 for investing and your stock has risen by 5 points, it's perfectly acceptable to invest the profits. On the other hand, if you lost money, don't beg or borrow to get hold of another $10,000 to reinvest.

Stock Selection Tips, Part 5

Explore other factors. Determine whether there are other factors that could potentially affect the company's progress. For example, find out if there has been any negative (or positive) press about the company or the industry as a whole. The media can have a great influence on public opinion regarding a company or an industry. Other factors to consider include lawsuits against the company, major changes in upper management, and potential mergers or acquisitions.

It's important to keep in mind that there is never an urgency to rush into the market. There is no "perfect" time to jump in. The best way to enter the market is when *you're* prepared. The time is right when you can honestly say that you understand how the market works and you've carefully studied any companies that you would like to include in your newly created portfolio.

vest dividends along with capital gains, and invest in a variety of different types of growth stocks. Such clubs make good use of dollar-cost averaging, investing a predetermined sum of money on an ongoing basis as opposed to making an investment in one lump sum. When a stock's price declines, the investor receives more shares for the fixed investment amount. Conversely, the investor receives fewer shares for the fixed investment amount when the stock's price rises.

CHAPTER SIX

Mutual Funds: The Basics

They are the hottest topic in investment circles and have even become a popular subject at cocktail and dinner parties. There are television commercials for them, between ads for Burger King and Mentos. Through the 1990s investing in mutual funds has been the "thing to do" with your money.

Despite their recent surge in popularity, they are not new. Mutual funds have been around for a while. In fact, they came into being more than seventy years ago. They were created to provide investors with a way to play the stock market without having to pick individual stocks. The first fund, consisting of forty-five stocks, was established in 1924. Within five years the market crash sent stocks and mutual funds reeling. As late as the early 1950s, less than 1 percent of Americans owned mutual funds. Nonetheless, the first international fund was introduced. Later, in the 1970s, although mutual funds were still far from "the rage," 401(k)s and tax-exempt municipal bond funds were introduced—with 401(k)s investing, in part, in mutual funds. By the start of the 1980s, however, money market mutual funds had become the rage. They offered decent returns, liquidity, and check-writing privileges. But would-be investors wanted more. Then, with computers and technology making information readily available at one's fingertips, the 1990s ushered in the age of "The Fund." The Internet allowed the financial institutions to provide a great deal more information than they could on television commercials or in print ads. They reached out to everyone, not simply those Wall Streeters who read the financial papers. People saw how easily they could play the market and have their money spread out in various stocks as well as bonds.

Diversification, the easy accessibility of funds, and the idea that a skilled professional money manager is working to make your investment grow are the three most prominent reasons why funds have become so popular.

WHAT IS A MUTUAL FUND?

A mutual fund is an investment vehicle that pools the money of many investors and buys stocks, bonds, or other securities, depending on the type of fund. It is a way to utilize the skills of a professional money manager, who manages the fund and selects the

specific investments that he or she feels will best lead the fund toward the goal the fund has set out to achieve. There are funds set up for a wide range of goals and financial plans. Funds can provide a steady flow of income or can be engineered for growth in the short or long term. The success of the fund depends on the sum of its parts, which are the individual stocks or bonds within the fund's portfolio.

Currently, the number of mutual funds is approaching eleven thousand. Consider that as recently as 1991 the number was just over three thousand and at the end of 1996 it was listed at around six thousand. As noted earlier, mutual funds have become extremely popular. Stock funds are growing as a way to play the market without having to make all the choices of when to buy and sell. However, bond funds are also growing, partly because of the complexities associated with understanding individual bonds, and as a way to hold more bonds than the average investor could afford if buying them on an individual basis. Money market funds offer a safe alternative to bank accounts, providing higher interest rates.

Every financial institution worth their weight in earnings has a wide variety of funds to choose from, and many business school graduates with MBA's from top universities are now finding jobs other than on Wall Street. Funds, as we enter the new millennium, see more than $4 trillion in investments, with nearly one quarter of American households owning at least one mutual fund. The number of accounts keeps growing, and there are now nearly 100 million individual accounts in mutual funds.

Here are a few more reasons why funds are so popular:

1. Tremendous overall rates of return in recent years
2. Ease of purchasing
3. Liquidity
4. Lower risk
5. Diversification

Some funds have seen returns of 30, 40, and 50 percent and higher in recent years. And while this trend may not last, over the three-year period of 1996 through 1998, the average domestic equity fund produced an annualized rate of return of 18.5 percent. Over the

Six Key Items to Look For in the Mutual Fund's Prospectus Before Buying

1. Check the date to make sure you have the most recent version of the prospectus.

2. Review the fund's investment objective: Be sure the fund's investment goals match yours.

3. Note the minimum investment.

4. Study the fund's past performance: You can request a copy of the Performance Section in the fund's Statement of Additional Information.

5. Consider the risks: Discuss the risks with your financial advisor.

6. Research the fees: The fee schedule will be detailed in the Summary of Fund Expenses.

Check It Out

Even if you work with a prominent full-service broker, you still
need to double-check all of
your transactions. When you
receive your statements, check
to make sure that your trades
were processed for the correct
amount of shares at the agreed
upon price. In addition, be
aware of all charges incurred
when placing trades.

five-year period of 1994 through 1998, the rate was 15.5 percent,
which—compared to other types of investments—is hard to beat. Even
domestic bond funds over the same period have averaged 5.5 to 6
percent.

Funds today are as easy to purchase as making a phone call or
a trip to your computer. Fund families (large investment firms or brokerage houses with many funds), seeing the serge in popularity and
wanting to make funds easily accessible to all investors, have toll-free
numbers and Web sites that make it easy for you to buy and sell
mutual funds. Transactions are also, occasionally, made by the old
fashioned method of "snail" mail.

Electronic trading has allowed investors to trade at all hours
from the comfort of their own homes. It's not hard to find the Top
10, Top 20, or Top 50 funds on your browser, as rated by some
leading financial source, and then buy them online. It is also not
hard to get "addicted to trading" and find yourself overdoing a good
thing. The accessibility and ease of trading online and through toll-
free numbers has led many overzealous investors into deep trouble.
Many new investors need to learn to be patient.

For those who need to put their hands on their money in a
hurry and convert mutual fund shares to cash, another benefit of
mutual funds is liquidity. A phone call allows you to sell your shares
in the fund at its current Net Asset Value (NAV, or posted rate per
share), and you should have your money in three or four business
days.

The risk of investing in a mutual fund is less than that of a
single stock because the fund is managed professionally and
because of diversification. Mutual funds offer you diversification
without making you do all of the work. Funds can hold anywhere
from a few select stocks to more than one hundred stocks, bonds,
and money market instruments. While some funds own as few as
twenty or twenty-five stocks, others like the Schwab1000 own one
thousand stocks.

The diversity minimizes much of your risk. If, for example, you
bought one stock on your own it could go either way. However, if
you bought six stocks, it would be less likely that all six would go
down. If three went down and three went up you would be even. If
you saw two dropping, you could sell them and buy something else,

For His Children

Selim
Architect
Age: 41

Selim started investing for the future college costs of his son. Starting early, he and his wife will have plenty of time; his son is just two years old. "I started with two investments, one being in an annuity, which is part of a life insurance policy and is long-term with penalties for early withdrawal. The other is a mutual fund," he explains. Like many people looking for their investments to grow over time, Selim set up a system of direct deposit with his bank to take the worry out of investing the money regularly.

"I chose a fund that was both growth and income," says Selim, adding that the fund included both domestic and international holdings and although it saw only a small gain in 1998, he was staying with it through 1999. "My advisor tells me to stay with it for some time. Over ten years you'll see positive results." Selim's advisor is a friend who is well-versed in the stock market and in mutual funds and suggested a good fund. "It was good to have someone to help me decide where to

invest since my time doesn't really allow me to study the market that carefully. It's very intricate, as it is in my own field, and it takes a lot of time to really learn it," he explains.

The annuity is helpful because the money it pays will help with his son's school costs until college. Then the mutual fund will go toward college tuition. Selim and his wife are also expecting their second child and may at some point, when his wife returns to work, start putting money into another plan. "We're also looking to buy a home in the next several years," adds Selim. "We're kind of gearing up to do that in the next five years. Right now the investing is based on my income, which is increasing over the years. Once she is also working, if we stay in good health we'll be able to build toward all our goals." With plenty of time until their young children reach college, and with plenty of income-producing years ahead for both Selim and his wife, they have very real and reachable goals.

The Fund Craze

The latest technological advances have gone hand in hand with the success of the mutual fund market as buyers have simply gone online to make their purchases. In short, convenience and a wealth of readily available information have also played a major role in the mutual fund phenomenon. Much of this ties into the information superhighway and those who use it. Many people are accessing more and more information from their PCs. Front and center on many Web servers is the latest in mutual fund news. Like most trends, information feeds on itself. More people are buying mutual funds and, therefore, more fund-related news is being posted online. The more news posted, the more new investors are attracted, and so on and so forth. There is also a tremendous amount of information available about mutual funds through magazines, newspapers, and in financial news reports.

while you were still earning money off the others. The mutual funds work on the same "safety in numbers" principle. Although there are funds with higher and lower risks, the comfort of many mutual funds is that they limit risk by balancing higher-risk investments with lower-risk/safer investments. Diversity acts to your advantage as it protects you against greater swings in the market, be it the stock or bond market.

One of the reasons mutual funds can diversify so successfully is that when you invest in a mutual fund you are pooling your money with other investors. Having a larger group of investors allows the fund much greater buying power. It also allows you as the investor to stretch your money much farther. Some funds allow you to invest as little as $500, which then gets divided up into the various ownings of the mutual fund. Your $500 is now investing in perhaps fifty stocks and ten bonds. You could not have done this by purchasing stocks and bonds individually—the individual commissions alone would have eaten up your money.

Further diversification can also come from buying more than one fund. You can also allocate your assets into different types of funds. If you buy into a few funds in different categories, you'll have that much more diversification and that much less technical risk. (It's usually not advisable to have more than six or seven mutual funds at a given time or you can start to counterbalance your efforts to construct a strong portfolio.) Your portfolio might include, for example:

> A more conservative bond fund
> A "tech" fund to cash in on a hot industry
> A more high-risk international fund
> A low-risk, blue-chip fund
> A growth fund

The idea is to balance your portfolio between more- and less-conservative—or higher- and lower-risk investments. Depending on your needs, you will diversify. One investor will have 10 percent in bond funds, 20 percent in growth, 30 percent in tech, and so on, while another will have 5 percent in tech and 40 percent in blue-chip. That's why there is no boilerplate investment strategy.

It seems odd to need to diversify your mutual funds since the job of the fund is to diversify the stocks, but it's all part of building a solid investment portfolio. Your mutual fund is the sum of many parts. Therefore, you may want another fund in your portfolio. Perhaps you won't want a sports car like your aggressive little small-cap fund, but an old station wagon that doesn't look sporty but gets you and your family where you want to go—a more conservative fund. The comparison ends there, because while cars depreciate in value, mutual funds—by and large—do not.

Another significant reason for diversifying your mutual fund investments is to spread your assets out across sectors, industries, and asset classes. A fund manager, no matter how skilled, is limited by the goals and the direction set forth by the fund.

FUND MANAGERS

Another reason for the popularity of mutual funds is that they are run by professional fund managers. During the last quarter of the twentieth century, Americans have heavily embraced the notion that if you want something done right, you should get a professional to do it for you. This is not a bad idea, particularly if you do not have the time to delve into the numerous financial papers to do the proper research necessary for finding individual stocks. Fund managers save you the trouble of sifting through thousands of potential stocks in an effort to build up your portfolio through one fund. Of course, as the number of funds grows, you will soon find yourself sifting through more funds than stocks. Nonetheless, it's the full-time job of the fund manager to select the right investments for the fund. These managers are well-versed in the intricacies of the national and international fund markets.

Following the success of a fund manager has become the financial world's equivalent to following the success of a top ballplayer. Managers of the hottest funds appear on financial talk shows, write books, and are the talk of the financial community—until, of course, their hot streak ends. Then they're yesterday's news.

To assess a good fund manager, you need to look at his or her background over several years. You want to look for consistency in management of the fund or previous funds. You also want to see that the fund manager is holding true to his or her fund's financial goals. If, for example, you are looking at a more conservative growth and income fund, you don't want to find out that the fund manager is making high-risk investments and taking the fund in a different direction (this is called "style drift"). It is more common than you might think to have fund managers with roving eyes—managers who look at and buy stocks that don't fit the fund's stated objective. On the other hand, if a fund is struggling, you may appreciate if the fund manager starts drifting for the sake of keeping your investment afloat.

You should also look closely at a mutual fund's portfolio. While you may not be familiar with each and every purchase, you can ascertain whether they are following the latest trends or bucking the system. If you have heard, for example, that a certain market, such as automobiles, is taking a downturn, and the fund manager is buying heavily in that area, it will mean one of two things: either he or she is buying now for an anticipated turnaround (value investing), or he or she is not keeping up with the market's news.

You should also look at how the fund manager fared during the down markets of 1990 and 1997. See how quickly their funds rebounded. Did he or she panic and make drastic moves or hold on tight and ride out the storm? Naturally it will depend on the type of fund and the particular holdings. The manager's response is worth taking note of, since the market does go through volatile periods.

You also need to check out a new fund manager if you own a fund and the manager changes. A new fund manager needs to show that he or she can work within the structure of the particular fund, holding true to the goal of that fund. Fund size and assets can matter as well. A manager who has handled a $2 billion fund successfully may not be as comfortable when handed a $20 billion figure in a larger fund. Some managers are only successful with a finite amount of funds. You might also want to know whether or not this fund manager is working closely with a team of analysts or doing it all on his or her own. If the latter is the case, you could be in trouble

when the manager moves to another fund and takes along his or her secrets.

Forbes, Kiplingers, Money, Morningstar, and other sources will rate the mutual funds and often give you the "lowdown" or profile on the fund manager. It's important to look for consistency. If the fund manager has bounced from one fund to another, it is not a good sign if you're looking to hold the fund for a long time period. It is also not to your advantage to have a fund with a different manager at the helm every year.

LOADS, NO LOADS AND OPERATING COSTS

Loads and no-loads is mutual fund lingo for "with a salesperson" or "without a salesperson." A loaded fund means you are paying a commission to someone who has helped you determine which fund to purchase. A no-load fund means you have bought the fund on your own, usually through a toll-free number. The choice is yours depending on how much help, guidance, or hand holding you are seeking when buying mutual funds. The investor who does his or her homework and knows which fund is designed to meet his or her goals and needs can simply dial the fund and buy it without paying an additional commission. There is certainly enough information available to support the choice of buying a no-load fund. However, if searching for the right fund is taking hours out of your potential income-earning time, or time spent on the pursuit of enjoying your life, you may be better paying a commission with a load fund and utilizing your time in other ways. As mentioned earlier, it's all up to you.

As is the case with everything these days, there are more than two choices. While no-loads have gained an edge on loaded funds, many companies have started offering loaded no-loads. Naturally these loaded no-loads have catches to them whereby you will be paying a fee somewhere down the line for the privilege of not paying a fee. Whether the costs are for some types of "special benefits," a personal finance report, or some other accompanying service, the bottom line is that these are not commission-free funds. There

Take Good Care of Yourself

Remember, your comfort level is important. If losing $5,000 is going to raise your blood pressure, then don't sink $5,000 into the high-risk fund; put $4,000 in the conservative fund, which will earn you enough in income to weather the storm if you lose the $1,000 you put into the high-risk fund.

"Oh Marge," said the woman to her friend, "I'm so happy. Now we can pay Fred's medical bills for his ulcer. The market soared this week."

"I didn't know he had an ulcer," responded the friend. "What caused it?"

"The market plunged last week."

Front- and Back-End Loads

Assessed when you initially invest, front-end loads will generally run you from 2 to 8.5 percent, while back-end loads (when you sell) can range from 1 to 6 percent.

are numerous ways that certain companies have found to slip fees and payments into their fund business. Read the prospectus carefully. If there are hidden costs that pop up, you might be best looking elsewhere. In short, "no-loads" by any other name are essentially loaded funds. Therefore, it's to your advantage as a new investor to buy either basic loads or no-loads. AND, when buying loaded funds, make sure you are told of each fee that can be charged; you deserve no surprises if the fund family wants your business.

Operating costs are also part of mutual funds. This is the money spent to keep the fund afloat. Along with administrative expenses, the analysts and fund manager also need to get paid advisory fees for their hard work investing your money. Expense ratios range from less than .25 percent to more than 2.5 percent. It is important to take note of the operating costs to determine how much of a bite they are taking out of your profits. This is an area that more savvy investors are taking note of as they compare mutual funds. In their favor, mutual funds buy in vast amounts and save you on broker fees, which would be accumulating if you were buying stocks individually.

UNDERSTANDING FEES AND EXPENSES

Generally listed as the "expense ratio" are several costs that shareholders will pay for services and management of the fund. While the Securities and Exchange Commission is closely monitoring funds to make sure that shareholders are aware of all the expenses related to their fund, it's important that you as an investor understand the basics behind these fees and have a sense of what to look for on your own. After all, there are thousands of funds, and some of them have devised new and inventive ways to "bill you," so to speak, while the vast majority are fairly straightforward about where the expenses are going. International funds often have higher expense ratios than domestic funds because they are dealing with companies overseas.

A mutual fund operates like a smaller business within the structure of the larger fund family. It is an entity unto itself in that the

Teamwork Versus the One-Person Show

Hillary Clinton said it takes a village to raise a child. It certainly does not take a village to run a mutual fund. However, the preference between one person guiding the fund on his or her own and a team of top-level analysts is a matter of comfort. One leader can make faster moves unilaterally. He or she can set a path and not be steered off the course. While all managers have people working around them, the individual go-getter can make the key choices and take the fund in the direction necessary for good results. Of course, the flip side to this is a fund manager overreacting or not having the data or second opinion to possibly secure a better deal or make a better move. The manager working more closely with a team can utilize the "ten heads are better than one" approach to finding the right option to guide the fund, especially when the going gets tough. It's important to ascertain, if possible, how much a fund manager is a soloist with backup support or the leader of a well-run team. How does he or she utilize the other expert analysts that make up the nucleus of the fund management team?

Index funds, essentially, go without a leader on board, on automatic pilot. Yet they are often successful. After all, if the fund managers are measuring their success by an index, then why not go with the benchmark by which they are all comparing? A lot of people compare great baseball teams to the '27 Yankees, so why wouldn't you bet on the '27 Yanks if you could? Many managers do beat the S&P 500 index, yet the index does beat most fund managers, despite what they say.

Mutual Funds Don't Mean Ruling Stocks Out

The mutual fund craze has more new investors focusing on stock funds than buying individual stocks. Just because funds are promoted from all around you and even if you own one, you can still buy a stock or two that you believe in. Don't let the mutual fund craze scare you away from buying a stock. Yes, it's putting a portion of your investing dollars into one basket, but it's a basket you believe in, plus you don't pay expense costs. Mutual funds can be terrific investment vehicles, but they don't preclude you from buying stock.

fund does not interact with other funds under the same umbrella company. They share printed materials and costs, such as advertising the financial group, but from the perspective of the fund family, each fund is handled separately. In other words, the expense ratio you're paying for "Fund A" will not spill over to pay the manager of "Fund B." Also, the success of one fund does not hinge upon the success of another. Often you will look down the listings of funds in one family and see some winners and losers along the way. Unlike the portfolio within the fund, where the manager can try to dispense of the losers or at lease balance equities that are not doing well with ones that are, the fund family cannot integrate the portfolios of different funds.

NOTE: One advantage of funds being in the same family (as mentioned elsewhere) is that you can save on commissions if you want to sell your shares of one fund and move your money into another in the same fund family. You can also save on the paperwork—and that alone can be a big time-saver!

Fees generally include the following:

Service fees. These fees are used for financial compensation of the planners, analysts, and brokers who assist customers with fund-related questions and provide information and advice regarding the fund. Accounting and legal services may also be included.

Administrative fees. These are the fees associated with office staff, office space, and other fundamentals to running a business, including equipment. Sometimes these funds are absorbed under management fees. Office expenses incurred by a fund also include online support and information, check processing, auditing, record keeping, shareholders' reports, and printed matter.

Management fees. This is the percentage that goes to the fund manager. This can be a flat percentage or one set up to coincide with the growth of the fund based on returns. The bigger the fund gets, in terms of assets, the lower the percentage will generally be.

12b-1 fee. This is a fee used primarily for marketing or advertising the fund. Since there are so many mutual funds on the
market, it is becoming increasingly important for fund families to advertise. Your fee is not just a contribution to the
fund's advertising budget but will hopefully help the fund to
grow—and as the fund grows, there will be more money
available. Therefore, the fund will have greater leverage to
buy more holdings, which can—with a good fund manager—
be to your advantage. In fact, some funds report that
because of advertising, their overall expense ratios have gone
down as the funds have grown. So for those who do not
like the 12b-1 fee, remember that it can work in your favor.

OTHER COSTS

One other "cost," which isn't related to the fund directly but to the
government, is an old standard: taxes. On the plus side, if you lose
money on the fund you won't be paying capital gains tax, but that's
hardly a reason to celebrate. If you see a profit, you will pay taxes
on dividends or on capital gains distributions paid to you while
owning shares of the fund, or on your profits (capital gains) from
selling your shares of the fund. You may also be subject to state
taxes, depending on the state in which you reside.

You may also see capital gains based on the trading done by
the fund manager, even though you haven't sold any of your shares.
These can hit you for taxes. Buying funds late in the year is ill-
advised because you can be hit for higher taxes as the fund is just
about to distribute their capital gains.

More on this can be found in the tax section in Chapter
Eighteen.

EARNING MONEY IN MUTUAL FUNDS

Now that you are aware of how operating costs and commissions will eat into your profits, the big question is *How do you
make money in mutual funds?*

Don't Churn Yourself

Whereas unscrupulous brokers can make trades for the sake of running up commissions—or "churning" as it is called—you can (unintentionally) do the same thing to yourself. If you make constant changes in your portfolio you may (1) not be giving your investments an adequate amount of time to produce results, and (2) be paying a lot more in commissions.

Obviously, selling off shares of your mutual fund at a higher Net Asset Value (NAV) per share than that at which you purchased the fund will net you a profit. The fund acts as a single unit, and the total return is based on all the stocks, bonds, and other securities held. Therefore, if certain stocks do very well within the portfolio while others don't, you cannot simply sell off the lucrative investments or get rid of the losers. You have no say in the individual investments, but you can sell off your shares of the fund as a whole. There can be profits made, however, in the form of capital gains when the fund manager sells off a security. While funds are constantly reinvesting money, you can actually see money from the fund as you hold onto it. Income funds will dispense income from dividends paid by stocks within the portfolio or interest paid by bonds in a bond or balanced fund. If you are seeking a steady flow of income from a mutual fund, this may be the route to go.

Despite operating costs and commissions, there have been some tremendous results from mutual funds in recent years. How long the trend will continue depends on a number of factors led by the economy, the stock market, and the number of effective fund managers, among other things.

KEEPING TRACK

Financial publications, national newspapers, and local newspapers are all places to keep tabs on your mutual funds. Add to that the Financial News Network and online services, and it's likely that you can find all the important information on your mutual fund on a daily basis.

First and foremost, make sure you know EXACTLY what symbol your fund goes by and don't forget the letter following the fund, being the A, B, C, D issue. The letters primarily refer to the type of load, front load, back load, no load, etc. It's amazing how many people have realized, after several days or weeks, that they either can't find their fund or have been following the wrong fund.

Once you have found your fund, you need to understand the letters and numbers that make up the mutual fund listings. Among the many symbols and numbers you will see included the name of the fund family, the name of the specific fund, and the fund's objective

(OBJ), which will be listed such as CV (convertible fund), LG (large-cap growth), or GL (government, long-term bond fund).

The NAV (Net Asset Value) is the current price per share of the fund, or the price at which the fund is selling shares. By multiplying the number of shares you own by that price per share you can tell the current value of your fund. By comparing this to the total at which you bought the mutual fund, you will know how your fund is doing. If you purchased a fund from Aim, for example, at $9 per share and bought 2000 shares, then your initial investment would have been $18,000. If the fund is now at $11, then your value in the fund is now $22,000 or a $4,000 profit (if it's a no-load fund, less operating costs and capital gains tax).

Next the listing will have changes, or the movement of the fund, by either the day, week, or YTD percent (which is year-to-date total percentage, including reinvested dividends and capital gains). All of this will give you an idea of which direction the fund is going. This is how you can follow your fund, but it is NOT how to choose a fund; to choose a fund you need the one-, three-, five-, and/or even ten-year totals and more information. Chasing daily returns is ill-advised in stocks or mutuals.

Some listings will include "Down Market" or "Bear Market," which will indicate how the fund has performed during the down-turns in the market. Again, this is information you'll want when looking to purchase a fund.

A volatility ranking will tell you how much of a roller-coaster ride you can expect. Such a rating is the "beta" of the mutual fund. This is not generally found in daily listings but on comparison listings of funds over time. This can ease your mind on a day-to-day basis—you see sudden drops and then realize that this fund will have its share of peaks and valleys on route to (hopefully) showing solid gains.

MUTUAL FUND VOLATILITY

Mutual funds, as a rule, are not as volatile as a single stock because they are made up of a number of stocks. Even in a market crash some of the stocks will stay afloat, although the fund's per share price will drop. The balance tends to offset losers with winners, particularly since the market has always fared well over time. The more

Timing

NOTE: Find out when a fund last paid a distribution. You don't want to buy shares of that fund two days prior to their next distribution or you will be hit with a taxable capital gain. Mutual fund distributions can be monthly on income-producing funds, or semi-annually or even annually. It all depends on how the fund is set up.

aggressive the fund (the more risky), the more volatile the fund will be. Don't be fooled by short-term pluses and minuses. Once you have looked at the track record of a mutual fund and have seen that the fund you've chosen has performed well over one, three, and five years, you should anticipate investing for at least three to five years.

Greater risk means greater volatility. It also means you need more perseverance, as most funds will recover. If, however, your fund is experiencing volatility because of a change in managers or the direction the fund is taking, then you may want to investigate more thoroughly who is at the helm of the ship and what direction the mutual fund is not taking. There are several reasons a fund may be volatile: fluctuations in the stock market; changing interest rates (particularly pertaining to bonds); foreign currency rates; and fund management. Also, a fund that is actively buying and selling more heavily will often be more volatile. Look to see if similar funds, in the same category, are also experiencing similar volatility. Returning to the notion that a rising tide raises all ships, you may simply find that the volatility of your fund is typical for that type of fund at the present time. If, however, your fund is acting differently from similar funds, look more closely at the management.

In general, whatever the reason, short-term volatility is not at all uncommon for mutual funds. While you can lose money, the odds are strongly in your favor that the fund will bounce back if you hold onto it over time, particularly if it is a domestic-based equity fund.

LITE READING: THE ANNUAL REPORTS

Whether it's annual or semi-annual, a mutual fund's report is your update on how the fund is performing. Yes, it's often dry reading and you may require a cup of black coffee to read it (*don't wait for the movie to come out*), but nonetheless you should find a quiet place to look over this document.

Among the most significant information within the report are the holdings of the fund. It's important to look over this list carefully to determine whether or not the fund manager is "style drifting." In other words, a fund that is supposed to be buying large-cap stocks may suddenly be investing in several smaller companies. It's more likely, however, that the fund may have drifted in the other direction because, as noted earlier, small companies tend to grow—and they move from small-caps to mid- or even large-caps while still sitting in the same mutual funds. Naturally, if the fund is doing well you'll be less concerned. It's amazing how your perspective changes when looking at the holdings based on the fund's performance. What looks like a brilliant move by the fund manager in a fund that has seen a 30 percent rise doesn't look nearly as good in a fund that has seen a 10 percent drop. Some questions may arise: Is the fund satisfying my level of risk or is it becoming too aggressive or too conservative for me? Is the fund lacking in diversification by moving more strongly into similar stocks? The holdings will also tell you which companies the fund believes are strong. Look them over, and see if you agree. You may not know all of the companies held, but investigate a few.

Looking at the portfolio holdings, you want to find:

1. *Familiar names.* "Familiar" means for that type of fund. A household name like Coca-Cola won't show up in a small-cap fund, but you are looking for smaller companies that belong in that fund. NOTE: Just because you own a fund doesn't mean you no longer have to follow the activities of companies and their stocks. If you see holdings in your fund that you don't like, you can look at other funds that have shares of stocks that you feel are more promising.
2. *Portfolio concentration.* Besides showing what is in the portfolio, the annual (or semi-annual) report will tell you how much, or what percentage, the fund is investing in each area.
3. *Performance.* Not surprisingly, for the funds that perform well this information sometimes jumps off the page, while it's harder to decipher in a fund that is not performing well.

You should know how the fund has performed in the short and long term. How the fund has performed against a specific index should also be included for purposes of comparison. There should

Mid-Caps Could Be Growing

One of the best (though more daring) ways to make sure you own a blue-chip stock or two, besides investing in the S&P Index fund, is to find a mid-cap fund or a few mid-cap stocks that you believe in and get them before they emerge into the big blue-chippers with higher prices. "Buy low" is a popular philosophy throughout the investment world. Now add to that "buy mid." A mid-cap value fund might find you some good deals on the future giants.

also be an explanation of WHY the fund has performed well or poorly. Which factors have made an impact on the fund? What management has been doing and some indication of what they are planning to do should be included.

The bottom line is that after reading the annual report you should feel either confident in holding onto the fund or determined to sell your shares. If you are left feeling unsettled as to what you should do (because you do not feel you have adequate information or the report is not easily discernable), then you should look in *Morningstar*, *Kiplingers*, the *Wall Street Journal*, or other sources to see if they discuss your fund. You should also call the fund or fund family and let them know you have some questions; after all, you are paying an operating fee that includes service charges, so let them serve you by providing some answers. If a fund does not help make you feel comfortable, then it's not the right investment for you. Remember, it's your money!

CHAPTER SEVEN

Equity
Funds

SO MANY CHOICES

The hottest and most talked about mutual funds on the market are the equity or (stock) funds. These are primarily made up of individual stocks purchased (at least 75 or 80 percent). Your potential profit is the result of having a fund manager who has accumulated more winners than losers in the funds and more shares of the winners. The stocks comprising the fund are most often common stocks, and the fund managers purchase them based on potential earnings of companies, while looking at the issuer's management, track record, and financial condition. They also look at how the company fares in the overall industry in which it sits. In other words, in an industry such as health, they are looking to see if a company is one of the leaders in its field or lagging behind its competitors.

When looking at an equity fund (or any fund), you want to know the overall goal. Is it long-term growth or short-term aggressive growth? (Both are explained in the next section). Before purchasing a fund you should ask to look at a listing of the stocks currently owned so you can see if the fund managers are indeed following the plan of action they have listed as their goal. The remainder of this chapter explores some of the many types of equity funds.

In an age where we now have to choose between at least five types of Coca-Cola—*classic, diet, cherry, caffeine free, caffeine free diet*, and so on—it should not be surprising that there are a wealth of categories available when selecting a mutual fund. As the market continues to grow, more and more types of funds are created, which adds further confusion.

GROWTH FUNDS

A growth fund is less concerned with the current price of a stock and more concerned that the sales and earnings of the company will grow (then the resulting stock will rise). The idea is not the traditional "buy low, sell high," but buy at whatever price and watch the company build momentum, get on a roll, and grow. Growth investors seek out companies that have tremendous potential based perhaps on new products or services not being offered elsewhere or excellent management. In recent years growth funds have outperformed value funds, but that has not been the case in

the past. Long-term growth funds look to capitalize on larger, steadily growing companies like Microsoft, while aggressive growth funds, listed next, involve smaller companies that are taking off fast, like Amazon.com.

AGGRESSIVE GROWTH FUNDS

These are the funds that generate the most press, because when they are going well they are going *very* well. Some of these have, of late, produced tremendous results. For example, the UltraOTC Pro Fund saw a return of 185.3 percent in 1998. However, investors should know that in this volatile category things can turn around very fast. Aggressive growth funds look for companies poised to grow in the short term, which is why they are riskier investments. You'll find many of the recent aggressive growth funds on the NASDAQ, such as Starbucks, Intel, and Home Depot.

GROWTH AND INCOME FUNDS

You might also choose to go with a fund that specifically seeks out companies that not only are expected to grow but also have a stock that will pay dividends. Such a fund provides steady income, which is attractive to anyone who likes to maintain cash flow even during major dips in the market. A growth and income fund can also work very well for an individual who may be retiring but still wants to have money in the market. Such a fund will provide cash toward living expenses while allowing the investor to maintain some capital. There are also straight income funds, which are more conservative by nature, seeking as their primary objective to pay you dividends from consistently well-performing (usually major) companies. One of the nicest aspects of an income fund is that the companies that pay dividends, hence those in the portfolio, are usually not affected greatly by downturns in the market.

VALUE FUNDS

A value mutual fund invests in stocks that are undervalued. These are companies that—for one reason or another—are struggling, and

Portfolios and Asset Allocation: Start Simple and Build

Financial planners balk at them, because it defeats their purpose, but the bottom line of starting off with an index fund is very common and a good way to step into the mutual fund arena. The S&P 500, a large cap stock fund, and a bond fund might be all you need to begin with. (S&P 40 percent, large-cap stock 40 percent, bond fund 20 percent.) Then work from your capital gains and buy some mid-cap value and mid-cap growth funds. Don't be afraid to start conservatively and build slowly.

The Four Best-Known Indices

Standard & Poor's 500 (S&P 500). Focuses on major companies and major growth companies such as Microsoft, Pfizer, Coca-Cola, and so on.

The Dow Jones. Includes thirty blue-chip stocks: General Electric, IBM, and twenty-eight of the other biggest companies in the United States.

The NASDAQ. Represents the high-tech and Internet stocks, many of which have been soaring in the past couple of years, like Intel.

Russell 2000. Features small-cap and momentum stocks. This is where the fund managers often find the "hot" up and comers. The Russell 2000 is newer and is not yet as widely known as the other three.

the stock prices are low while the actual value of the company may be much higher. Sometimes it's a matter of too much market competition; in other cases it's a company that is lagging behind in the latest technology or has not done anything of major impact of late. However, if the P/E ratio and book value of the stocks in the portfolio are good, the fund can be worthwhile. Value investors are saying that if a company is worth $40 per share and they can buy it at $20 per share, they want to take the stock at that lower (value) price. Although in recent years value funds have been outperformed by growth funds, they adhere to the old adage "buy low, sell high." The stock valued at $40 but selling at $20 allows you more room for error, even if the stock should not reach the $40 mark. At $30 per share you would still be coming out ahead.

SECTOR FUNDS

Sector funds diversify, but only in one sector. Rather than spread your investment around between various types of industries, they choose stocks pertaining to one particular industry, such as oil, health, utilities, or technology stocks. They let you play a variety of stocks in one arena. Naturally, the risk is in whether or not the time is right for that particular market. Thus the risk is higher. Tech stocks in recent years would have been an excellent choice for a sector fund as some have seen huge returns. Certain industries, such as utilities or companies in the food industry, will be less volatile and more consistent than others that are more cyclical. The idea behind buying a sector fund is often, not unlike market timing, selecting an industry that you foresee taking off in the next few years. For example, the new health-related technology has people looking at stocks pertaining to companies that are doing new and innovative things in the medical area. Internet sector funds may also generate more attention, but be careful that an overabundance of Internet providers doesn't bring prices back down to earth. A sector fund can give you a bumpy ride if you are planning to be there for the long haul. Often such a fund works best as part of a larger portfolio that diversifies across industries and sectors.

INTERNATIONAL AND GLOBAL FUNDS

When you see categories of funds such as Europe or Japan, these are not fancy names for a style of investing but literately funds investing overseas in one of, or a wide mix of, the global markets. Many international funds spread your investment around, buying into markets worldwide, while others look at the economic potential of one country. International specialized funds have not fared well over the past three or even five years. This doesn't mean there are not some winners, primarily being the European funds in recent years. Overall, however, the big gains have not been in this area of late.

Usually not the place for a beginning investor, these can be risky funds because of the high volatility of many overseas markets. Unless you are quite familiar with a foreign market—perhaps having spent time in that country or part of the world and knowing something about the future economics of the country—these funds may be best left for the more daring investors. Besides, other funds may already be investing a small portion into overseas investments, thus dabbling in the arena and letting you have some foreign diversification.

Changes in currency and politics make it hard to assess, even for fund managers, what the future investing climate will be on a global basis. All of this "negativity" is not to say that an investor may not do well with an international fund. If you look at a market such as Asia or Brazil and have time to wait for it to turn around, you might get into a fund at a very low price (or get a great discount on a closed-end fund, which we describe later in this chapter).

INDEX FUNDS

From 1987 through 1997 the S&P 500 index performed better than 81 percent of the general equity funds, even if many have claimed otherwise. (After all, 81 percent of the people on Wall Street, including pretzel vendors, will *claim* they can beat the S&P).

While Index funds seem like an easy way out, they are also an easy way to stick with a successful benchmark that everyone uses. They allow you to be in various sectors and to invest in both growth

Index Funds

An index fund is a Mutual Fund that invests in all stocks upon which a market index is based. By investing in every stock in the index, the index fund closely mirrors the performance of the index itself.

and value stocks, giving you maximum diversification. If the S&P 500 is the standard by which funds go up against, then why not go with it? After all your goal is to make money. Index funds will have lower costs since there are not a lot of transactions going on. Also, there is not an amount going to the management of the fund, as they are not managed funds.

BALANCED FUNDS

Balanced funds derive capital gains from a mixed bag of investments primarily consisting of stocks and bonds. This is ideal for those investors who do not want to allocate their own portfolios. Balanced funds provide maximum diversity and allow their managers to balance more volatile investments with safer, low-risk investments such as bonds. They are usually designed for the more-conservative investor who does not want to go too heavily into equities. Naturally, since this fund can have a wide range of investments, it is important to look over the fund's portfolio and get an idea of what makes up the "balance" in your balanced fund. The combination of good returns (category average of 13.1 percent for ten-year returns from 1988 through 1998) plus nice yields make these funds worthy of your attention.

SOCIALLY RESPONSIBLE FUNDS

"Socially responsible" depends largely on the fund manager's definition of social responsibility. Some funds steer clear of products that use animal testing; many do not invest in companies involved with the defense industry, guns, or tobacco; others concern themselves with child labor issues. Some funds use all of the above or other criteria. You then need to match that with what you consider to be socially responsible and find funds that are earning money. They are out there, but they require that you take time to look beyond the marketing and the numbers of a company.

Several funds are trying to make an effort to seek out the less socially offensive aspects of business and society in general. Dreyfus Third Century Fund and PAX World are two of the most successful, best-known funds in this area. They are looking for protection of the environment and natural resources, occupational health and safety, life supportive goods and services, and companies that do not sell liquor, firearms, or tobacco products.

The intentions are good and the funds are profitable. Exactly how closely any of these funds stick to their overall criteria is hard to judge, even while making a concerted effort. While a company may clearly not be manufacturing weapons, they may be inadvertently polluting the environment.

THE DOMINI 400 SOCIAL INDEX

The Domini 400 Social Index is the result of the efforts of Amy Domini, an author and a money manager for private clients for a Boston firm. Reviewing the investments of her own church in the 1970s, she found the church was investing in companies that made weapons and realized that they, like most of us, did not know all the branches, divisions, and practices of major companies. She set out to enhance the public's awareness of the practices and policies of large corporations.

In 1990 Amy Domini started the Domini 400 as a way of screening four hundred stocks with socially redeeming features. Companies in her 400 listing must have a clean record when it comes to the environment, provide fair treatment to women and minorities, and not be involved with alcohol, tobacco, gambling, or manufacturing weapons.

While this is a very broad description of "socially acceptable," the Domini 400 has fared slightly above the S&P 500 over three- and five-year periods. The Domini Social Equity Fund, which uses the Domini 400 as a guide, has returned more than 17 percent in recent years.

Nonetheless, Domini gets both praise and tough criticism for her efforts. For everyone who believes that she's taking a step in the right direction, making an effort toward enlightening the public as to which companies are practicing which "vices" so to speak, there are others who find either fault with some of her criteria or find additional criteria to eliminate companies on her index. There will always be a level of debate.

All in all, social awareness is an important issue, and the Domini Index is making a case for it. Perhaps it will spill over into

Starting with an Index Fund

Investing in a large-cap Index fund is a good idea for new investors because you are investing in solid "bell-weather" companies that are well-established and secure. In this manner, your portfolio can start off by mirroring the stock market, and although there will be downswings, if you are patient, the market will rise and your Index fund will show solid returns. Following the large-cap fund, you might then invest a lesser amount of money in a small-cap fund, giving you more diversity and potentially high returns at a greater risk. A 70 percent-30 percent split, perhaps $3,500 in a large-cap Index fund and $1,500 in a small-cap Index fund, may be a good way to step into the mutual fund buying market before branching out.

Total Returns

When trying to determine how well your mutual fund is doing, you will look at the fund's total returns. The total return, however, is broken down into three parts, which include:

- Dividends, which is income that is paid by the investments in the fund

- Capital Gains, which are net gains from the sale of a stock, bond or other security within the mutual fund

- Share Price Changes, which reflect the overall price of the fund

other areas. Perhaps consumers will simply stop supporting companies that have questionable track records in their hiring policies or in their manufacturing of certain products. Just as there has been an anti-fur movement, people could stop buying products such as sneakers from companies with overseas child laborers or could stop using a leading Internet provider where teenagers regularly discuss sex in chat rooms and pornography is rampant. Social responsibility runs deep if you allow it to. Where one draws the line is a personal decision.

The "socially responsible" funds have met a growing demand by the public for companies to "get their act together." The trend toward this type of investing is expected to grow in the future with the baby boomers and post–baby boomer generations looking at more than just the bottom line of financial figures and investing with their minds and their consciences.

LARGE-CAP, MID-CAP, AND SMALL-CAP FUNDS

In the world of mutual funds, *cap* is another word for capital or size of the company. Large-cap are the major corporations; small-cap are the smaller, often growing companies; and mid-cap are somewhere in between. Naturally, the larger, more established companies will present less risk and are, therefore, a safer investment. Small-cap stocks can take off and often have fared better (although not in 1998 and into 1999), but there is a greater risk since these companies are trying to establish themselves. While some small-caps have become huge quickly, others have moved along slowly or vanished into oblivion.

Small-caps can sometimes be deceiving because a company that starts out small and continues to grow is ultimately no longer a small-cap company. Yet it still may remain in the fund. After all, why throw out your ace pitcher even though he's no longer a little league player? E-Trade was a small-cap company found in many small-cap funds, but as it grew and brought the funds high returns, fund managers enjoyed reaping the rewards (as did those investing in the fund), so it stayed.

Investing in different types of cap funds primarily serves to diversify your investments. You don't want all of the same sized companies because their success does go in cycles. In 1998, large-cap funds sitting with Coca-Cola, General Electric, IBM, and other giant companies performed better than the small-cap mutual funds. One of the possible reasons is the tremendous growth in investing to a much wider sector of the population. No longer are the "yuppies" and Wall Streeters the only ones seeking out stocks and funds. As more and more people get into the stock market and buy into funds from their home PCs, they may be comfortable buying the larger companies with which they are familiar. There's nothing wrong with this. After all, unless you've taken the time to sufficiently study some new, small-but-growing plumbing supply company, you too might lean toward the more familiar Wal-Mart or Disney. Some small-cap companies, such as those in the technical sector, are also very well-known to a very literate computer population, which is why a company like Intel or Dell Computer can also shine. As the newer online investors become more savvy, they too will branch out from safer, more familiar territory and explore the many growing companies.

MEGA FUNDS

In a land where we always strive for something bigger, this is a fund that buys into other funds. Like a bigger fish eating smaller fish, it looks at the smaller funds and lets you diversify your diversification. As the number of mutual funds grows by leaps and bounds, you may see more mega funds buying mutual funds much the way mutual funds select from the thousands of stocks at their disposal.

ASSET ALLOCATION FUND

Not unlike a balanced fund, an asset allocation fund maximizes diversification. The fund is managed to encompass a broad range of investment vehicles and asset classes. If managed correctly, an asset allocation fund will center around a mix of stocks, bonds, and short-term instruments and distribute the percentage of holdings in each area according to which is providing better returns. Whereas a balanced fund tries to maintain a balance between stocks and bonds,

Index Funds = Lower Costs

One of the advantages of going with an Index fund for your mutual fund investment is that you won't pay as much in expenses. Index funds are run by computers so money is not spent on paying a fund manager or research analysts.

Ten Reasons to Invest in Mutual Funds

1. Diversification will lessen the risk factor.

2. There's a wide range of fund choices to fit every possible need.

3. You're able to stretch your investment further through more purchasing power.

4. A professional manages your investment.

5. It is easy to buy and sell funds via phone or the Internet.

(continued)

an asset allocation fund (depending on market conditions) can be 75 percent stocks one year and (should the economy be experiencing a bear market) 75 percent bonds the next year. Factoring in each type of investment, the fund manager has a wide range of choices across asset groups. In a broad sense, this is a manner of "market timing." These fund managers have more leeway, as they are not locked into a set percentage allocated to one type of investment.

CLOSED-END MUTUAL FUNDS

As opposed to being another category of fund, closed-end funds are a broader grouping of mutual funds that include several fund categories that you can buy into. They are unique, however, in several respects.

While most mutual funds are open-end, meaning they will continue offering shares as long as they have buyers, closed-end mutual funds have a fixed amount of shares that they can sell to investors. A closed-end fund, or CEF, is publicly traded. An initial public offering (IPO), like the offering to introduce a new stock to the public, is where the CEF begins. The shares then trade like stocks on the American or New York Stock Exchange. The NAV is the price of the fund, like open mutual funds, which is based on the holdings in the portfolio.

Closed-end funds differ from their open-end counterparts in that by selling a specific number of shares they do not keep growing indefinitely as more investors put money into the fund. Like open-end funds, they have a fund manager who buys and sells stocks, but they remain within the structure and limits of the fund dictated by how many shares there are to sell and at what price.

Another distinct feature of closed-end funds is that, unlike an open-end fund where you buy or sell your shares with the fund directly, with a CEF you buy and sell shares with other investors. If there is a greater demand for the shares, the market price will rise and you will make a profit. This is called a premium. The market price, less the NAV, will give you your premium earned. You can also sell a CEF at a lower price. In this regard, the buying and selling of CEFs is similar to that of the bond market.

Since closed-end funds require you either to know when there is an initial public offering or to have a seller from which you can buy, they are bought through brokerage houses, meaning there will be a commission. There are brokers who specialize in closed-end mutual funds.

Here are some categories of closed-end funds

Diversified stock funds. Essentially growth funds, these funds invest in a variety of industries. In this category you'll find large- and small-cap funds, blue-chip funds, and so on.
Sector funds. Like open-end funds, they also invest in one specific industry.
International or global funds. As implied by the name, these funds invest in markets worldwide. Many funds pertaining to individual countries are closed-end funds allowing a certain amount of investing in that foreign market.
Dual purpose funds. These funds sell some shares for capital appreciation and others to provide income.

There are other types of closed-end mutual funds, and, as you can see, the categories are similar to their open-end brothers and sisters, only the shares are limited. You can get some good discounts on closed-end funds. You can also get in on the ground floor of what becomes an open-end fund, as many do move in that direction at some point.

Ten Reasons to Invest in Mutual Funds

6. There's simplified record keeping, as opposed to charting numerous individual equities and bonds.

7. They are easy to follow through numerous media sources.

8. They are relatively liquid, allowing you to get your money in a short amount of time and with no penalties.

9. You can do the investing yourself through no-loads without the need of a broker or having to pay a commission.

10. There are potentially high returns on your investment.

CHAPTER EIGHT

Choosing, Buying, and Selling Mutual Funds

So, you're ready to buy a mutual fund. The first thing you need to know is how the price is set. The net assets value (NAV) of the fund is the first price you need to be aware of. It is essentially calculated by taking the net asset of the fund and dividing that by the number of outstanding shares. Therefore, if you had a fund with $1 million in net assets and 105,000 outstanding shares, the NAV would be 9.52. That gives you a number by which to gauge the fund, based on everything the fund owns minus its liabilities.

The price at which you can buy shares of the fund, the public offering price (POP), can be the same or higher depending on whether there is a load or not on the fund. A no-load fund will not have a higher POP, while a loaded fund might see the same 9.52 listed at 9.77 to include the load.

At this point you are buying shares in a similar manner to how you buy shares of individual stocks. Therefore, if you wanted 300 shares of this no-load fund at 9.52 per share it would cost you $2,856. Often funds are bought in round numbers for the sake of easier bookkeeping on your part, meaning you might enter a fund with a minimum purchase of $5000 (some are higher and many are lower). Therefore, you would invest $5,000 and have 525 shares ($5,000 divided by 9.52). The loaded fund would simply either cost you more per share, or if you bought $5000 worth, you would have to deduct the .25 load, giving you slightly fewer shares.

COMFORT AND HISTORY

Investment gurus will agree that part of choosing a fund is feeling comfortable and part is examining the history of that mutual fund. To choose your mutual fund, it's a matter of matching your goals, risk level, time frame, and the amount of money you have to invest with the fund category that suits your needs and comfort level. Even if you know you could be investing in a high-risk aggressive growth fund, you may find yourself staying up worrying at night if you do so. Therefore, it's not the fund for you. The material in this or other books on mutual funds can only serve to enlighten you regarding what funds are about and how they operate. The latest up-to-date reports on "hot" funds can make you aware of what someone else is doing with his or her money. What's right for you is what you believe will help you reach your goals and, from doing your homework, what you believe the future holds.

As for selecting a fund family, it is often suggested that you look for one that has been around a while, unless you're going with an emerging industry such as tech stocks, where the newer fund families may all have been around for about the same length of time. The more-established fund families can show you ten-year returns, which you can compare against comparable funds in other fund families that have been around a while. They can also give you an indication of how the fund has fared during the bear markets and how long it took them to recover. Naturally some of this will depend on the fund manager, but you have a better chance of finding a fund manager with ten years' experience at the helm of a fund at an older, more-established company. Look at the ten-year returns and see if the same fund manager was there over that time period. If you look at ten-year returns and see that the current manager has only been on board for three years, those ten-year returns won't mean as much. It's like looking at the last ten years of a baseball team that only acquired its superstars in the past three years; it makes a big difference.

Judging past performance of a fund can be more tricky than it might seem by glancing at five- and ten-year returns. Sectors or industries that are in vogue during one period may not be during the next. For example, if technology stocks returns were to drop to a modest return over the next three years, looking back in five years at their ten- and even five-year total returns is going to show a distorted picture because of how well they are doing now. One spectacular year of 90 percent growth, followed by four years of 10 percent growth, is still going to average 26 percent growth per year, which would not be a good indicator of how that fund is performing at the end of Year 5, when you are looking to buy it. Also, a sector that has not fared well over a stretch of time may be on the upswing due to new products, consumer needs, or public awareness (as with the socially responsible stocks). This won't show up in past performance. The same holds true for the large- and small-cap companies. A fund that invests in small companies will not see large returns when the trend leans toward the large corporations, as it has done in the late 1990s. But if that trend is about to change in 2001, it is not reflected. The best you can do is look at each measure of past performance, read up on future expectations and try to make an informed decision. Remember—long-term five- and ten-year returns *are* important, but they are only part of the larger picture.

One other note is that you should compare the mutual fund you're interested in with other comparable funds. If the fund you like had a 10 percent return last year and other similar funds were also around 10 percent, then the fund is performing as expected. However, if the fund is bringing in 10 percent, and comparable funds in the same category are bringing in 12 percent and 15 percent, then you can do better without changing your goals or choosing a more (or less) risky fund by simply finding another fund in the same category.

Once you finally make a decision, expect to be in the fund for at least one year, and usually five or more. Mutual funds are not generally thought of as a short-term investment.

THE PROSPECTUS: THE MUTUAL FUND BIBLE

In a highly competitive fund market, some funds are actually trying to soften the legalese in which the fund's prospectus is written. However, some are still very hard to decipher. The problem is that while the important information is in there somewhere, it can be hard to find in the midst of a wealth of legal jargon. Therefore, it's to your advantage to read the prospectus with an eye for specific areas of importance.

A few of the important details you should review include:

The fund's objective. The fund should have a clear statement of what the objective is. Is it aggressive growth? Current income? While it may be far more clear-cut in bond funds, it's not always as obvious when reading the prospectus of a stock fund. If the objective is unclear, the mutual fund manager has more leeway. It also means your intentions for choosing that particular fund may not be carried out. If the fund objective is not clear, either seek out a fund that is more clearly defined, ask someone in the fund's investment information department, or follow the old rule of thumb: do your homework. Look up the fund's current holdings.

The investment risks. The mutual fund prospectus should discuss the level of risks the fund will take in conjunction with their objective. Stock funds should discuss the types of stocks they are buying. Are they talking about speculation? Are they telling you about the volatility of particular stocks? Look at the warnings they're giving you. Are they telling you about the currency and political risks involved with their international holdings?" In short, the fund should discuss some of the risks associated with its portfolio. As an investor you should also be aware of the risks of investing in stocks, bonds, and money market funds from reading this book and other sources.

Investment breakdown. The fund should clearly lay out the percentage of holdings they are committed to in each fund group. They should say, for example, that the management is required to hold at least 70 percent of U.S. bonds, or 80 percent in common stocks, or no more than 20 percent in international investments. The breakdown and parameters of the fund give you an idea where your money will be invested. Other types of investments, such as cash instruments, may also be included.

Costs and fees. A fee table should outline all the fees associated with that fund. Read them carefully and make sure you are left with no surprises. Operating costs, loads, and any other fees should all be included.

Financial history. A prospectus will also give you the history of that mutual fund. The financial information should provide the per-share results for the life of the fund—or for funds that have been around for a long time, at least the past ten-year history. You can gauge the annual total return of the fund on an annual basis. You can also look at the year-end net asset values, the fund's expense ratio, and any other information that will help you gauge how the fund has performed over

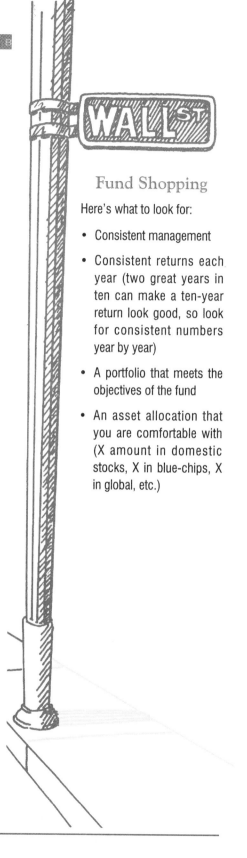

Fund Shopping

Here's what to look for:

- Consistent management

- Consistent returns each year (two great years in ten can make a ten-year return look good, so look for consistent numbers year by year)

- A portfolio that meets the objectives of the fund

- An asset allocation that you are comfortable with (X amount in domestic stocks, X in blue-chips, X in global, etc.)

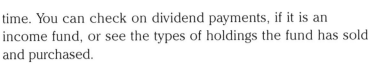

time. You can check on dividend payments, if it is an income fund, or see the types of holdings the fund has sold and purchased.

In the end, the prospectus should answer all of your questions and concerns about a particular fund. There may be a lot of extraneous verbiage for the sake of "legally covering themselves," and some marketing hype, but the bottom line is that the information you need should all be included in the prospectus. Obtaining a prospectus, by the way, should be as easy as calling the fund's toll-free number.

MAKE YOUR OWN MUTUAL FUND PROFILE

From the prospectus or from one of the leading financial magazines (or from both), you should be able to construct an accurate profile of the fund. This is simply discerning the key features of the fund for your own good. Many of the leading financial magazines do this all the time, but rather than waiting for them to highlight the fund you're interested in, you can do it yourself. An example of such a profile follows:

Name: ABCD Fictitious Investment Fund
Symbol: ABCDIF
Category: Small-cap, aggressive growth
Assets: $21.5 million
Expense ratio: 2 percent
Load fund?: No
Minimum investment: $500
Fund manager: James B. James
Tenure: 3 years

The fund generally has a minimum of 70 percent of its assets in small-cap companies, with market capitalization under $250 million. 10 percent of the investments may be in foreign securities.

Composition as of 4/15/99:
Domestic stocks: 87 percent
Foreign securities: 8 percent
Cash: 5 percent

Sector breakdown:
Technologies: 41.3 percent
Financials: 19.7 percent
Services: 21.5 percent
Retail: 10.0 percent
Health: 7.5 percent

Add to this the three-month rate of return plus one-, three-, and five-year rate of returns and you have a basic idea of what can be put together to profile a specific mutual fund. You can then examine the individual segments. You might, for example, want to look more closely at the track record of the fund manager. If the direction and category of the fund appeals to you, you may then look at the specific stocks held by the fund to see their P/E ration and performance in recent months and recent years. Essentially, the prospectus will help you determine your level of interest in the fund. Building a profile, or reading a profile in one of the leading financial publications, will allow you to pull out, and organize, the vital information and determine what additional details you may want to learn about the fund.

STRATEGIES

You can use similar strategies with mutual funds as you do when playing the market and buying individual stocks. One strategy that can work well with mutual funds is dollar-cost averaging. Essentially, this is where you invest a fixed sum of money into the mutual fund on a regular basis regardless of where the market stands. Retirement plans and 401(k) plans are generally built on this principle, except they have restrictions on the withdrawal end. Following a regular investment schedule, whether it's weekly, monthly, or bimonthly, you are not trying to time the stocks in the fund's portfolio. Frequently an investor will decide to have the same amount of money automatically withdrawn from his or her account and invested into the

It's OKAY to Take the Boring Route

Bravado versus boring, old-fashioned practicality. It's not hip to be a fund manager buying the big, stable corporate stocks—it's not exciting enough or daring. You won't be the talk of the town—that role will go to the fund manager who finds some burgeoning young small-cap companies that soar to new heights. The reality is, a fund manager is only as good as the success of his or her fund.

Many of the success stories of 1998 came from the big companies, the ones that the "fashionable" fund managers steered clear of. And what does this mean? It means you should select a fund manager who's not out to dazzle his or her peers, but one who goes with the investments that work best, even if they are considered more conservative or traditional.

mutual fund on a consistent weekly, or monthly, basis—not unlike a 401(k) or retirement plan. Over time, a fixed amount invested regularly, as opposed to buying a fixed number of shares, will reduce your average cost per share over time. In essence you are buying more shares when the prices are low and fewer shares when the prices are high, all by putting in the same amount.

Dollar-cost averaging also eliminates the popular "timing the market" game played by the professionals—sometimes for better and sometimes for worse. Market timing is essentially trying to determine the peaks and valleys of the market and buy and sell accordingly. This is usually not advised for beginning investors. The volatility of the market in recent years has made this method particularly difficult. Fund managers, however, spend a great deal of time trying to time the market—with varying results. The part of dollar-cost averaging that can be difficult emotionally is that by investing on a regular basis you will also be investing during bear markets. Direct deposit makes this a little easier. It's also easier with mutual funds, where you know that a good fund manager should be setting up the portfolio with stocks that will best recover from a market downturn, rather than with one stock, which could take a longer time to rebound.

MUTUAL FUND FAMILIES

Dreyfus, Fidelity, Schwab, etc. There are numerous mutual fund families to choose from. They are essentially brokerage houses. They serve as an umbrella for a number of funds, and they offer various other financial services. Depending on the financial institution the mutual fund selection can be very large; fund families generally offer a wide variety of funds in each broad category to match differing goals. One advantage to staying within a particular fund family is that it is easier to switch funds, and there is not usually an associated cost or fee.

On the next page are some mutual fund families. These are just some of the numerous fund families, based on overall size. This does not mean that a small fund family with five funds may not have three of the most successful funds of the year. Some small fund companies have some hugely successful funds. We simply couldn't list them all.

Advantus	1-800-665-6005
Aim	1-800-347-4246
Alliance	1-800-227-4618
American Century	1-800-345-2021
American Funds	1-800-421-4120
BlackRock	1-800-441-7762
Delaware Investments	1-800-523-4640
Dreyfus	1-800-373-9387
Eaton Vance	1-800-225-6265
Evergreen	1-800-343-2898
Federated	1-800-341-7400
Fidelity	1-800-544-8888
Franklin	1-800-342-5236
Hancock	1-800-225-5291
IDS	1-800-437-3133
Invesco	1-800-525-8085
Kemper	1-800-621-1048
Merrill Lynch	1-800-637-3863
MFS	1-800-637-2929
Morgan Stanley Dean Witter	1-800-869-6397
Oppenheimer	1-800-525-7048
PBHG	1-800-433-0051
Phoenix	1-800-243-4361
Pioneer	1-800-225-6292
Prudential	1-800-225-1852
Putnam	1-800-225-1581
Schwab	1-800-435-4000
Scudder	1-800-225-2470
Smith Barney	1-800-451-2010
Stagecoach	1-800-222-8222
Strong	1-800-368-1030
Templeton	1-800-292-9293
T. Rowe Price	1-800-638-5660
USAA	1-800-382-8722
Vanguard	1-800-851-4999
Van Kempen	1-800-341-2911

Mutual Fund Tax Surprises

A mutual fund that sees a large number of transactions can hit you with a greater tax bite, as you are taxed on each capital gain within that fund. Therefore, it's to your advantage to look at the turnover ratio of the fund. A ratio of only 10 percent means only 10 percent of the securities in the fund's portfolio have been traded over the past year. Conversely a high ratio of 90 means that 90 percent of the portfolio has been turned over.

Money Market Mutual Funds

The rage when they were first introduced in the late 1970s, money market mutual funds are still popular because they offer a steady yield and are low-risk funds. They are "share-based," meaning they offer a rate of $1 per share. This means simply that the number of shares you buy is the number of dollars you spend.

Like other mutual funds, there is a fund manager running the show and a management fee, although usually this is kept relatively low. Money market mutual funds invest in short-term, high-quality obligations. These, also known as "commercial paper," include CDs, treasury bills, bankers' acceptances, and other like funds, and provide the shareholders with the income accrued. Since they are dealing with safe investments, these funds have become a handy alternative to bank accounts with slightly higher yields.

Many money market accounts offer check-writing privileges, although you usually (not unlike checking accounts) need to maintain a minimum balance in the account. You can also sell off shares if you choose, usually as easily as with other mutual funds—a phone call.

Not unlike the bond mutual fund managers, the money market fund managers keep a close eye on the interest rates and try to buy and sell in conjunction with (inversely related to) whether interest rates are rising or falling.

In a money market mutual fund, the portfolio, by law, is not allowed to have long-term securities, so everything in the portfolio will reach maturity in a short time frame. There are other restrictions put on money market fund managers, including those that do not let them invest heavily in one company or even one market. They must therefore diversify widely, which gives you more security. It is also to your advantage to have the fund manager handling the paperwork. Short-term notes come due frequently, so if you were on your own, you would have to handle the paperwork and renew or reinvest. This is all part and parcel of the money market fund, which allows you access to a wider range of securities than you could buy on your own.

You can also get tax-free money market mutual funds, which invest in municipalities (in shorter terms than bond funds). Generally they offer slightly lower yields than their taxable counterparts.

However, if you have high state income taxes, these might be more beneficial. You have to look at the returns and compare them with the profit you would retain after paying taxes on the taxable fund.

The bottom line is that these are very safe funds, often called *capital preservation funds* because they essentially preserve the capital amount for you. They are for the investor who wants interest on a regular basis, whether it lands in your pocket or is reinvested, which is generally the case. Money market mutual funds are a step between money in the bank and taking a plunge into the other fund markets. Often people will hold onto a money market account to use as their checking account while investing elsewhere, using this as their safety cushion. If you have short-term goals or long-term goals coming up soon, this is a place to set aside funds and not have to worry about the volatility of the market.

This is a safe haven for investors. Often new investors and conservative investors will have a higher percentage of their investment portfolio tucked away in a money market account. There's nothing wrong with this, as it boils down to a comfort level. In recent years, money markets are only paying around 5 percent, but with inflation being very low, this is not necessarily that bad. After all, higher inflation and a higher yield still leave you with the same amount.

Money market mutual funds are also often a safe place to keep money that is earmarked for investing while you are waiting to find the value stock you've been seeking or the right fund. This allows you a higher interest rate, liquidity, and a place to move your funds when coming into and out of your other investments. Many fund families will have money market accounts that you can open and use exactly for that purpose. One person described his money market fund as like having a netting in your sofa for catching all the loose change that falls out before you decide which pocket to put it in.

NOTE: The advantage to using such an account as a checking account is that your money is being more actively managed and you are seeing higher yields than you would in the bank.

CHAPTER NINE

Bonds: Basics in Brief

While they are certainly not the trendy, glamorous topic of discussion at financial forums and social gatherings the way mutual funds are, bonds play an extremely significant part in the economy of the United States—and, for that matter, the world. Bonds are necessary to enhance economic development, helping cities, towns, and counties as well as companies and corporations to grow. They are fundamental at the federal as well as the local level.

Bonds are used to help fund everything from waste removal to corporate expansion to potentially lowering the mortgage on a beautiful new home. They are integral to the success and growing needs of large corporations and can provide the financial surge a small start-up company needs. Parks, schools, libraries, and public areas are most often partly, if not solely, backed by bonds.

But what exactly are bonds?

Good question. Bonds are essentially a manner in which you loan a company, municipality, or the government (or a foreign government) money to be paid back at a set date in the future. For lending them the money, the borrower (or issuer of the bond) agrees to pay you a rate of interest. Bonds are sold in specific increments and can be bought on a short-term basis (up to five years), intermediate-term basis (generally seven to ten years), or a long-term basis (usually around twenty to thirty years). Longer-term bonds will pay higher yields (they've averaged higher than six percent over the last fifty years) than short-term bonds. They will, over the time you hold them, fluctuate more with changes in interest rates, which primarily matters to you if you are trying to sell a bond (more on this later).

A bond will have a date of final maturity, which is the date at which the bond will return your principal, or initial investment. Some types of bonds can be called earlier, which means that the lender pays you back at an earlier date. A $5,000 bond is therefore worth $5,000 upon maturity as long as the issuer does not default on the payment. The interest you receive while holding the bond is your "perk," so to speak, for lending the money. Interest is usually paid semi-annually or annually, and it compounds at different rates.

Bonds can be bought directly as new issues from the government, from a municipality, or from a company. They can also be

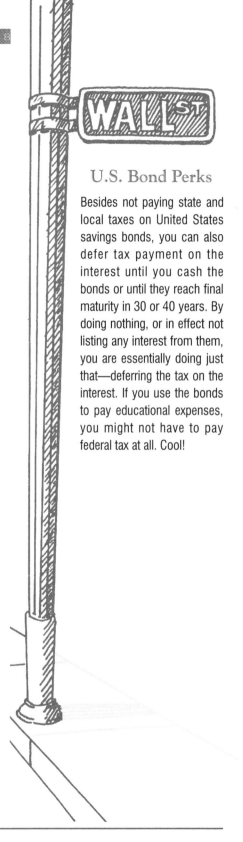

bought from bond traders, brokers, or dealers (as they're called) on the secondary market. The bond market will dictate how easily you can buy or sell and at what price.

As a bond holder, unlike a stock holder, you are not taking part in the success or failure of the company. Shares of stock will rise and fall in conjunction with how the company is doing. In the case of bonds, you will receive interest on your loan (from the bond issuer) and get your principal back at the date of maturity, regardless of how well a company is doing—unless, of course, they go bankrupt. Bonds are therefore referred to as "fixed income" investments because you know how much you will get back unless you sell, and then the price will need to be determined based on the market.

As a general rule, bonds are considered less risky than stocks and are therefore considered a more conservative investment, particularly when you discuss U.S. government bonds. Bonds also provide a higher rate of interest than you'll receive from a bank account or CD, and this, along with a steady flow of income, usually makes them attractive, "safe" investments.

There are drawbacks and risks inherent to bonds, which will also be discussed in more detail later. The most basic is that an issuer may default. You can also lose money in bonds if you are forced to sell for purposes of liquidation when interest rates are high. As returns go, you will not see the type of high returns from bond investments that you can see from (more risky) equity mutual funds or from a "hot" stock.

BUYING AND SELLING

Bonds are almost always purchased through brokers and brokerage houses. All the major brokerage houses handle bonds and can get you the best bond rates. They sell bonds that are already on the market and inform you about new issues. This is true for corporate and municipal bonds as well certain types of government bonds, such as treasury bonds. The government also sells treasury bonds through the Treasury Department and savings bonds which brokers do not handle. Savings bonds can also be purchased through some banks. Ask at your bank if you are interested in buying a savings bond.

U.S. Bond Perks

Besides not paying state and local taxes on United States savings bonds, you can also defer tax payment on the interest until you cash the bonds or until they reach final maturity in 30 or 40 years. By doing nothing, or in effect not listing any interest from them, you are essentially doing just that—deferring the tax on the interest. If you use the bonds to pay educational expenses, you might not have to pay federal tax at all. Cool!

Bonds Online

BONDS ONLINE will provide daily quotes on U.S. Treasury notes, bonds and bills. Quotes are available by 5:00 PM EST.

If you own a bond with a fixed interest rate and plan to hold it to maturity, you need not worry about the fluctuations in the interest rate unless you are forced to sell. If you are looking to sell a bond, then it's important that you follow the interest rates. Interest rates vary based on a number of factors, including the inflation rate, exchange rates, economic conditions, supply and demand of credit, and so on. You need not be concerned with all the factors that make up the current rate of interest, but simply how that rate affects the bond market—and your bond(s) in particular.

The simplest rule of thumb to remember when dealing in the bond market is that bond prices will react the opposite way to interest rates. Lower interest rates will mean higher bond prices, and higher interest rates will mean lower bond prices. The phrase "you're only as good as those around you" might explain how this works. A marvelous young actor is less sought out when the cast around him is full of headliners. Inversely, the same talented actor shines when performing with a groups of amateurs. The bond market works the same way. Your bond paying 8 percent is sought out when interest rates drop and other bonds are paying 6 percent. However, when interest rates rise, and they are all paying 10 percent, suddenly your bond is not sought out and is therefore harder to sell and less valuable. Therefore, the old concept of supply and demand will be a major factor in your selling a bond.

Since the rate is generally locked in when you purchase it, the bond becomes more or less valuable as the interest rate moves. The bond's current yield (the current percent of interest you are receiving) versus the rising and falling interest rate will determine the bond's volatility. Shorter-term bonds will come due more quickly and be less affected by the movement of the interest rate. They will also pay lower yields. Generally, short-term bonds are less than five years to maturity. Longer-term bonds will be subject to greater interest rate fluctuation because there is more time until your bond matures. Therefore, bonds with longer maturities offer higher yields than shorter-term bonds because they are subject to a greater degree of risk in the bond market. Long-term bonds are considered to be those that mature in twelve years or more.

THREE TYPES OF INTEREST

Like everything else, there are varieties on the theme. Interest is usually thought of—and most commonly in the form of—a *fixed interest rate,* meaning you will see interest paid consistently at the same rate.

You can also have interest paid at what is called a *floating rate.* The floating rate will vary, which means the rate will change with the swings in the economy.

Zero coupon bonds pay no ongoing interest. In their favor, they are sold at a deep discount and redeemed at full value. They are therefore building up, through compounding interest, to their face value, which is the value stated on the bond to be paid at maturity.

YIELDS: RIGHT OF WAY

There are two types of yields that you need to be most aware of with a bond: current yield and yield-to-maturity. *Current yield* is the yield you receive annually based on the dollar amount you paid for the bond. A $2,000 bond bought at par value (at $2,000), receiving 6 percent interest would be a current yield of 6 percent. The current yield will differ if you buy the bond at a price that is higher or lower than par. For example, if you bought a $2,000 bond with a rate of 6 percent at $1,800, you are paying less than par. Your yield would be 6.67 percent. Take the $2,000 x .06 (interest rate) and you'll get 120. Now divide that by $1800, which you paid for the bond: .67 or 67 percent. Add that to the current interest of 6 percent to account for the $200 premium.

Yield-to-maturity is generally considered the more meaningful number to look at. It is the total amount you will see as a return on the bond from when you buy it until it reaches maturity. This includes interest over the life of the bond plus any gain or loss you may have based on whether or not you purchased the bond above or below par, excluding taxes. Taking the term of the bond, the cost at which you purchased it, and the yield into account, your broker will be able to calculate the yield-to-maturity. Usually this calculation will factor in the coupons or interest payments being reinvested at

the same rate. Yield-to-maturity will make it easier to compare various bonds. Unlike stocks, which are bought at a specific price per share, various factors will come into play when buying a bond, including term of maturity, rate of interest, price you paid for the bond, and so on. The idea is to find out how well the bond will perform *for you*.

BOND CALL

As noted in the introduction, bonds can be "called." A *call* means the bonds are recalled when the issuer wants to issue new bonds at a lower interest rate. A bond that can be called will have what is known as a "call provision," letting you know exactly when the issuer can, if they so choose, call in their bond. A fifteen-year bond might say, for example, that it is callable after eight years. A called bond usually means that if you choose to reinvest in another bond, it will generally be at a lower rate. Naturally, as a potential "call" date approaches, such a bond becomes harder to sell.

Since the idea of having your bond plucked from you when it's looking good doesn't seem particularly attractive, the issuers of callable bonds will usually offer a higher yield as an inducement for you to purchase them. However, that's not—on its own—going to sell you on a callable bond. Therefore, the issuer will generally give you more than the face value amount of the bond when it's called as a bonus. The potential higher rate or "premium," should the bond be called is what allows callable bonds to sell on the secondary market. How are a few terms you should know:

The call option. The term used whereby the issuer has the right to call the bond. It must be clear to you as the purchaser.

Call risk. The risk you take that your investment will be redeemed by the issuer.

Yield-to-call. Like yield-to-maturity in that it is a gauge of how much you will earn from that bond until it is called. When buying a call feature you will want to get the yield-to-call in case the bond is called, and the yield-to-maturity, which is the final maturity in case the bond is not called.

BOND RISKS

As is the case with all investments, there is some degree of risk involved. There are several types of risks, some discussed earlier in the book, that pertain to bonds. Here is a list of the most significant risks and how they affect the bond market.

CREDIT RISK

This is the risk that the company issuing the bond will default and you will lose your principal investment. This is why bonds are rated (see "Bond Ratings" in the next section). Government bonds won't have this risk and therefore need not be graded because they are simply "safe" investments. As a potential investor you need to compare the risk and the yield, or return, you will get from different grades of bonds. If, for example, you will do almost as well with a tax-exempt municipal bond after taxes than you will do with a lower-grade bond, take the safer route. Buying riskier bonds, or lower-grade bonds, is only worthwhile if you will potentially see returns that merit taking that credit risk.

INTEREST RATE RISK

If you are holding the bond to maturity this is not significant, since by not selling you are not particularly affected by changing interest rates. However, if you are selling a bond, you need to concern yourself with the rate of interest which—as mentioned earlier—ties in with the yield of the bond.

The longer the maturity of the bond, the more volatile the price will be with a change in yield. You will better manage interest rate risk by buying shorter maturities and rolling them over. However, if you are looking for higher returns over a longer period of time, then you will want to go with the longer-term bond and hope you do not have to sell it. Many financial brokers talk a great deal about the interest fluctuations on bonds. This is because they are in the business of buying and selling them. Many bond owners, however, tuck bonds away for years and enjoy the income generated. Therefore, before worrying greatly about the interest rate fluctuations making your bond more or less valuable in the secondary market, decide what your plan is. Are you buying bonds to sell them or to hold them to maturity? If you consider yourself financially sound, and are

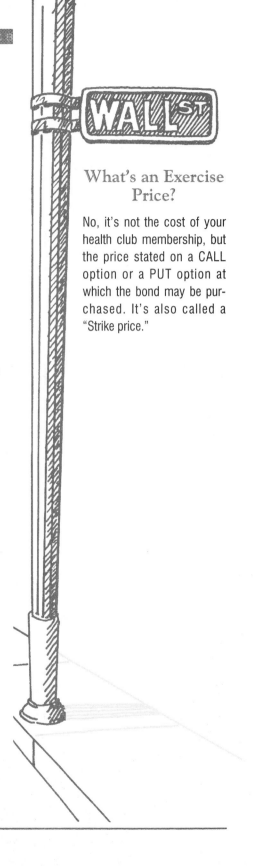

What's an Exercise Price?

No, it's not the cost of your health club membership, but the price stated on a CALL option or a PUT option at which the bond may be purchased. It's also called a "Strike price."

Floating Bond Rates

A floating rate bond security provides an interest rate that varies from time to time and is usually based on some benchmark interest rate. Floaters can be appealing when interest rates are low as they ought to reset at higher levels as rates rise.

simply looking to purchase a long-term bond for a future goal, with all intentions of holding it to maturity (and subsequently enjoying the higher yield), then by all means go with your plan. Even if you are forced to sell a fifteen-year bond twelve years toward maturity and take a loss on the price, you will have still enjoyed higher yields than you would have with the short-term bonds.

NOTE: Buy bonds based on your needs and financial situation. Don't fall victim to what we term "what if" risk, which is planning to buy a bond with the intention of holding it to maturity, and then altering your plans because brokers (who buy and sell) are saying, "But what if you need to sell the bond?" If you are buying with the intention of entering the secondary sellers market, that is your choice as an investor. BUT, buying defensively "just in case" you need to sell is defensive buying, and in the long run you may regret your decision. If you want to stay more liquid try laddering, but don't change a plan that is right for you because someone has made you fearful. Only you can best evaluate your own financial situation.

INCOME RISK

This is the risk that (1) should you sell, you won't get the full value or par, and (2) inflation will surpass the rate of income you are receiving from the bond (or inflation risk.) If you are reinvesting your interest income, you also will see less income. However, you will be building your investments.

The best way to manage income risk is to, once again, stagger or ladder your bonds so that you can pick up the higher interest rates along the way (as well as the lower ones). Inflation risk is also combated by simply looking to re-evaluate your asset allocation and possibly move to an investment that is higher than the inflation rate until the rate drops. If you already have an income-producing bond paying a rate of 3.9 percent and inflation has gone up to 4.1 percent, you can reinvest the income in a higher-yield (perhaps slightly riskier) vehicle. An equity fund will more likely beat the inflation rate.

CALL RISK

As explained previously, this is the risk of the bond being called by the issuer prior to maturity.

BOND RATINGS

Corporate bonds and some municipal bonds are rated by financial analysts at Standard & Poor's (S&P) and Moody's, among others. They are rated to give you an idea of how sound the issuer of the bond actually is as a company, municipality, or corporation. The ratings are, therefore, a report card of sorts on the company issuing the bond. Analysts look at the track record and financial situation of the company, the rate of income, and the degree of risk associated with the bond. All of this is put together and the bonds are graded.

A high rating, or grade, of AAA or Aaa, depending on which rating system you are looking at, is the highest quality bond. This means you are dealing with a sound financial corporation or municipality. Generally bonds of AAA, AA, A, or BBB (Aaa, Aa, A, or Bbb in Moody's system) are considered high-quality bonds. BB or B bonds are more questionable, because the companies are lacking some of the characteristics of the top-level corporations. Anything below B, such as C- or D-level bonds, are considered low-grade or "junk" bonds. Obviously they are investments in companies that have a much greater chance of defaulting on the bond. These companies, however, may also be new emerging entities that at some point in time may be the next Disney. If you pick the right rising company, a "junk" or high-yield bond can be very successful. BUT the risks are high.

Bond ratings from an issuer can change over time. A company issuing BBB bonds may become a much more stable fixture as a largely successful company, and their bonds may be A-rated next time they are graded. Like report cards, bonds are graded periodically, and depending on the stability of the company—among other factors—the grade of a bond can change. It's a good idea to keep tabs on the grades of the bonds you own for the purpose of potential resale as it will affect the bond's marketability.

ZERO COUPON BONDS

Zero coupon bonds can be issued by companies, government agencies, or municipalities. Known as "zeros," these bonds do not pay interest periodically as most bonds do. Instead they are purchased at a discount and pay you a higher rate (both interest and principal)

The Four Most Popular Types of Bonds

1. Corporate Bonds – This is where you invest in a corporation by purchasing a bond issued by a company which can be a small start up company or a huge company such as IBM.

2. Government Bonds – Including treasuries and savings bonds, these are bonds issued by and backed by the full faith of the United States Government.

3. Municipal Bonds – These are bonds issued by municipalities including local governments.

4. Mortgage Bonds – Not government bonds, these are bonds generally bought through a government agency that deals in the real estate market. They are bonds issued by mortgage lenders.

Ups and Downs

Sometimes stocks and bonds will follow a similar route, but this it is not always the case. Bond values will often increase in value when the market goes through a major downturn. For example, in August 1987, when the S&P Index showed a four-month drop of 21.42 percent, the Lehman Brothers Intermediate Government/Corporate Bonds Index rose by nearly 3 percent. Similarly, in 1990, from July until October the S&P dropped 14.10 percent while the same bond index rose again by nearly 3 percent. Investors will lean toward the safer bond market when the stock market goes south. It's a safe place to hang out until the stock market "rights" itself.

when they reach maturity. In other words, it's like lending someone $100 and having them tell you that they'll give you an extra $50 on a specific date when they pay you back, but they will give you nothing in between.

The interest rate is locked in when you buy the zero coupon bond at a discount rate. For example, if you wanted to buy a five-year $10,000 "zero" in a municipal bond, it might cost you $7,500, and in five years you would get the full $10,000. The longer the bond has until it reaches maturity, the deeper the discount will be. "Zeros" are the best example of what compound interest is all about. For example, a twenty-year zero coupon bond with a face value of $20,000 could be purchased at a discount for around $7,000. Since the bond is not paying out annual or semi-annual dividends, the interest continues to compound and it will earn the other $13,000. The interest rate will determine how much you will need to pay to purchase such a bond, but the compounding is what makes the discount so deep.

Like many other bonds, "zeros" are also callable, meaning you may receive the money you invested and the interest accrued to a particular point when the bond is called, and then have to find another place to reinvest the money, probably at a lower rate. Government "zeros," however, are not callable.

Other "zeros" may be convertible, meaning that the bond can be converted to common stock in the same corporation. If there is a "put" feature included, you can sell the "zero" back to the issuer. You can also sell your "zero" on the secondary market, and like other bonds, the market value will vary depending on the prevailing interest rate based on the economic conditions at the moment. Generally, however, you don't buy zero coupon bonds for liquidity.

As for taxes, despite the fact that you are not seeing any interest payments, you need to report the amount increased each year as the bond grows.

READING BOND PRICES

So you want to sell a bond or buy one on the bond market. First, you need to know the latest in bond prices. For this information you can go online, to a financial newspaper such as the *Wall Street*

Journal or *Barron's*, or to the financial section of *USA Today* or your local paper. Bond prices do fluctuate, so the price you see quoted may change several times throughout the next business day.

Since there are far too many bonds to list, 1.5 million in just the municipal bond market alone, there is no complete listing found. This would also not be practical as many bond holders are hanging onto their bonds until maturity. Therefore, the listings you will see are benchmarks from which you can determine what a fair price would be. Interest rates play a role on bonds in a broad sense, and therefore fixed income securities, as a rule, will be affected similarly.

In the bond listings you will find key information for treasury, municipal, corporate, and mortgage bonds. The numbers you will see listed may vary in format from paper to paper, but will essentially look like the following:

Rate 6½ percent. This is the yield that the bond is paying.

Maturity March, 06. This is the date of final maturity—in this case, March of 2006.

Bid 103:12. This mean a buyer is offering a bid of $1033.75 on a $1,000 bond or a profit of just over 3 percent to the bond holder who bought the bond at par, or face value ($1,000).

Ask 104.0. This is the seller's lowest asking price, or in this case $1040.00.

You may then also see the Ask/yield, which gives you the yield-to-maturity based on the asking price. This means how much the buyer will earn on the investment based on interest rate plus how much he or she paid for the bond. A buyer who bought the bond at more than the face value will be receiving a lower yield-to-maturity. The opposite is true if the bond was purchased at a discount, which means it was purchased for less than par.

Bond trading is brisk, so the price you see in the paper is likely to change by the time you make your decision to buy or sell. The price will also be affected by which broker can get you the best price on a particular bond. Don't forget that the dealers set their prices allowing for a spread, or some money for themselves, on the transaction.

Who Buys "Zeros"?

If you are looking to save money for college tuition, "zeros" are a popular vehicle. They are also used for retirement purposes. In short, if you have a goal set several years in the future and are not looking for interest along the way, you can purchase such a bond to be due at the appropriate time, or have several due at various times (laddering). These bonds allow you to strategically plan ahead. If, for example, you have $20,000 to put into zero coupon bonds at 8 percent, in twenty years you would have more than $100,000. If you can spread it out so that the bonds come due at various intervals over two or more years, it can also be beneficial from a tax perspective

CHAPTER TEN

Bond
Mutual Funds

In the overall scheme of things, bond mutual funds:

1. Are generally less risky than stock mutual funds.
2. Generally do not yield the same high rates of return as stock mutual funds.

Like stock funds, bond funds buy bonds in bulk quantity. They are also categorized into different bond groupings depending on the types of bonds they buy. One of the nicest features about a bond fund is liquidity. When you purchase a single bond, your money is tied into the bond until maturity. You can sell the bond, but sometimes bonds can be more difficult to sell because they trade in the bond market. In a bond fund, buying and selling the bonds is the job of the fund manager, which takes many of the complications associated with understanding bonds away from you. Your concern becomes the overall success of the fund.

Bond fund managers, like equity fund managers, do the research and homework to stay abreast of the bond market, which is good because bonds aren't as "sexy" as stocks (the yields are lower and the investments are more conservative), and it's not always as easy to get all the latest information on the bond market.

For someone seeking income from a mutual fund, a bond fund, thanks to interest, can provide a monthly check. Such a dividend can be especially welcome to someone who is retiring, or simply as income support. It is comforting to get a steady income when the stock or bond market is down. If you are not looking for a dividend check, the money can be reinvested into the fund. Since a bond fund is buying as many as hundreds of bonds with all different dates of maturity, there is always a bond paying a dividend and very often one coming due and being reinvested. Like stock funds, the diversification is something you could not accomplish on your own without a great deal of money and a lot of research—not to mention that individually you would pay more to buy each individual bond, where in a fund you are saving money and only paying the operating fees and load fees when applicable.

One notable difference that is less positive about bond funds, when compared with bonds, is that unless the company goes bankrupt, you will see your capital preserved in a bond, and in a U.S. government bond you will always see your capital retained. Since a bond fund is operating as a mutual fund with an overall net asset value (NAV), the fund price could drop and you could lose some of your initial investment. Your principal is not secured in a bond fund.

The value of the bonds in the portfolio will fluctuate until they reach maturity, based inversely on the interest rate (see Chapter Nine). This means bonds in the fund may be sold at less than their value. However, the number of winners have beaten losers by a healthy amount in recent years. Again, be reminded that bond funds do not see returns that are as high as stock funds. As of the end of 1998, one-, three-, and five-year bond funds were averaging between 5 and 6 percent growth (domestic bonds), while one-, three-, and five-year domestic equity (stock) mutual funds were averaging between 12 and 19 percent.

TYPES OF BOND FUNDS

While looking through bond funds, you will notice the three primary types of bonds represented: corporate, government, and municipal. International bond funds also exist.

As is the case with stock funds, there are different levels of risk associated with different types of bond funds. Inversely, the greater the risk, when dealing with junk bonds for example, the greater the potential returns, and vice versa—when dealing with low-risk government bond funds, the rate of return is relatively low.

MUNICIPAL BOND FUNDS

These are bond funds that invest in either intermediate or long-term municipal bonds. Such money is often allocated to worthwhile projects such as building new roads, repairing older ones, upgrading sewer systems, and other projects that both produce revenue and add to the community. An incentive of such "munis," as they're often called, is that they generally offer you income that is not taxed. The tax-free bond funds, while paying lower yields, are often paying as much or more than many taxable bond funds because you are not paying those ugly federal—and in many cases, state—taxes. Municipal bond funds can be national, investing in municipalities

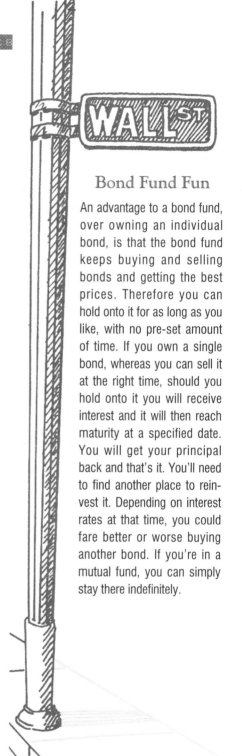

Bond Fund Fun

An advantage to a bond fund, over owning an individual bond, is that the bond fund keeps buying and selling bonds and getting the best prices. Therefore you can hold onto it for as long as you like, with no pre-set amount of time. If you own a single bond, whereas you can sell it at the right time, should you hold onto it you will receive interest and it will then reach maturity at a specified date. You will get your principal back and that's it. You'll need to find another place to reinvest it. Depending on interest rates at that time, you could fare better or worse buying another bond. If you're in a mutual fund, you can simply stay there indefinitely.

nationwide; statewide, investing in specific state municipalities; or local, investing in local municipalities. If you are in a state with high taxes you may find these funds to be appealing because you avoid such taxes. Crossing state lines, however, may require you to pay taxes. In other words you may be taxed if you buy a municipal bond from another state.

One potential concern when investing in municipal bond funds is there are states where the economy is not doing well. A national bond fund will diversify geographically, so you will have holdings in some states that are doing well economically as well as in some states that are not doing as well economically.

There are also municipal bonds that are lower-graded munis. They have higher volatility than other munis and higher yields. A few in a portfolio can potentially enhance the yields without hurting the portfolio too much if one goes sour. The more muni-junk, or high-yield low graders, the riskier the fund.

YIELD TO MATURITY

UNITED STATES GOVERNMENT BOND FUNDS

You want low risk? Invest in the government. Despite high deficits and being owed money by countries that are no longer on the globe, the United States government has never defaulted, and there is no risk in the securities in a government bond fund. These funds hold treasury securities, bonds, and notes, as opposed to savings bonds. There is some volatility because the fund managers do trade on the market, but for the most part, this is a very safe route, and many people will use a government bond fund to balance out other funds they hold. Since there are not as many choices in regard to government bonds and since the risks are significantly lower, many investors do not bother looking for such a fund, but simply purchase their own government investment vehicles, particularly from the government directly, since it is so easy to do.

CORPORATE BOND FUNDS

The majority of the holdings in this type of fund are, as the name implies, in corporations. Like the equity funds, there are a variety of types of corporate funds, and they differ depending on the corporations from whom they are purchasing bonds and the length of the holdings. Bond funds buying high-grade (or highly rated) bonds from major corporations are safer on the fundamental risk scale than other corporate bond funds and will generally produce slightly better returns than the government bond funds. Investment-grade funds have produced 6 to 7 percent returns over the past three to five years and nearly 10 percent returns for the twenty-year period through 1998. These are the equivalent of the stock funds holding blue-chippers and other stocks of long-established companies. However, some of these funds "cheat" a little, although legally, being able to own a small percentage of lower-grade bonds to balance out their portfolio and—if they pick the right ones—enhance the numbers slightly. As is the case with most funds, there is some flexibility beyond the category in which the fund falls.

The other side of this equation are bond funds buying bonds from a corporation that is newer (perhaps going through a transition) and is issuing bonds that are below investment grade. These junk bonds produce a high-yield fund that can be more volatile than many equity funds. The risk of the company backing this bond is higher and, therefore, the yield is also higher to compensate. In short, junk bond funds mirror junk bonds (which are high-risk bonds), only that you have more of them. By diversifying you are lowering your risk somewhat. A good fund manager is especially important when dealing in an area such as a high-yield bond fund. While the interest rates remain low, junk bond funds can enjoy growing closer to double-digit returns. However, if the economy takes a downturn, the possibility of default on these bonds becomes more real. Therefore, if you are thinking "high-yield bond fund," pay close attention to the current interest rate and listen to economic forecasts for the future.

UNIT INVESTMENT FUNDS

A unit investment fund is a type of bond fund that has municipal bonds in the portfolio. Unlike most mutual funds, however, a UIF is not a managed fund but maintains a steady portfolio. It is a bond mutual fund with municipal bonds, and they don't trade them, they just hold onto the same bonds in the fund. There is a prospectus, which details any costs and expenses inherent to the fund.

More for Your Money

Could you buy 100 bonds through your brokerage house? If they were $2,000 bonds, you'd need to spend $200,000. However, for $2,500 you can buy into a Bond Mutual Fund that handles 100 bonds and get a piece of the action for a lot less money.

Turn up the Volume on Those Bonds!

Volume means, simply, how active the bond was in terms of trading. This will give you an idea of the demand for a bond if you are looking to buy or sell.

OTHER FUNDS

These are just a few of the most common bond funds out there. You can also find global bond funds investing in markets worldwide, convertible bond funds, and closed-end bond funds. These funds will often be listed as short-term, intermediate, or long-term, giving you a choice. Often the longer-term bonds will fluctuate more and be more risky because of changes in the interest rate, while paying off higher yields. However, the default risk level will still depend ultimately on the type of corporate or municipal bond you own shares in.

PICKING BOND FUNDS

There are four key factors when it comes to picking bond funds:

1. Are they picking bonds with long or short maturities?
2. What quality bonds are they selecting?
3. Are you in the market for taxable or nontaxable bonds?
4. Who is doing the picking?

Yes, you also want to know the track record of the fund. But it's important that you first satisfy your own needs, which fall into the four categories listed here.

Bonds with longer maturities and bonds of a lower grade, or lesser quality, are more risky, which taps into your risk/tolerance equation as mentioned several times throughout this book. Risk/tolerance is always a key factor in your investment selection process, and although bonds are generally perceived as a less risky alternative to equity investments, there are risks in the bond market and in bond funds. Since bond funds do not hold onto most of their bonds until maturity, longer-term bonds will have more time to fluctuate and therefore be more risky. If the bond were being held until its final maturity, these changing rates would not matter

The taxable-nontaxable question reflects primarily on municipal bonds. Why in the world would anyone want a taxable bond if you can own one and pay no taxes? A 12 percent yield on a "junkier" bond, after taxes, still earns you more than a 5 percent yield on a tax-free bond. However, when the yields are closer you need to do the math (see Chapter Nine to figure this out). Also, if you are buying the bond fund in a tax-free vehicle such as part of your IRA, why purchase a tax-free fund? You are already not paying taxes, so it's a useless advantage. Go with taxable bonds (or a bond fund) in a tax-free retirement vehicle.

As for management, it means once again evaluating how the fund is run. Bond funds generally have fewer operating costs than equity funds. However, they generally have fewer high payoffs.

Many people select bond funds to round out an equity fund portfolio, with perhaps two stock funds and two bond funds, or one balanced fund and one bond fund. Often the inclusion of a bond fund is to have a conservative safeguard in the portfolio.

Someone who is primarily investing in bond funds, however, may—just like the equity fund player—allocate a certain amount to safer bond funds while putting the rest toward the lower-grade or riskier funds. The higher-yield funds do have their share of successes, and with the right fund manager, like a good equity fund, they can be profitable. Unlike owning one "junk" bond, a high-yield fund will balance out the portfolio carefully so that if one or two of the issuers actually default, you will still be fine, having a great deal of diversification in that area.

Like all other areas of investing, bond funds offer higher rewards for higher risk. And, while there are many funds to choose from, it's also to your advantage to understand more about bonds in general. Therefore, you should look over Chapter Nine in this book and familiarize yourself with the basics of bonds before moving into bond funds.

CHAPTER ELEVEN

Corporate Bonds

nlike buying shares of stock, which means you own a piece—be it a small piece—of a company, buying corporate bonds (or "corporates" as they're also known) means you are lending the company some money for a specified amount of time and at a specific rate of interest. While corporate bonds are more risky than government or municipal bonds, long-term corporate bonds, over the past fifty years, have outperformed their government and municipal counterparts. Unlike the United States government, however, companies can—and do—go bankrupt, which can turn your well-intentioned bond certificates into wallpaper (although with book entries there are no more valueless certificates to plaster on the walls). Woolworth's is an example of one of the few "larger" companies that went bankrupt in recent years. Therefore, the risk of default comes into play with corporate bonds. The rating system, listed earlier, will guide you to the more secure bonds issued by the more stable companies.

Corporates are generally issued in multiples of either $1,000 or $5,000. While your money is put to use for anything from new office facilities to new technology and equipment, you are paid interest annually or semi-annually. Corporate bonds pay higher yields at maturity than various other bonds (of course, the income you receive is taxable at both the federal and state level).

If you plan to hold onto the bond until it reaches maturity, and are receiving a good rate or return for doing so, you should not worry about selling in the secondary market. The only ways in which you will not see your principal returned upon maturity is if the bond is called, has a sinking-fund provision, or the company defaults. Here is a bit more about those terms.

Bond calls. A bond that can be called (as mentioned earlier), needs to provide you with the call provision, so you know at what time the issuer can call the bond should it choose. The problem with a bond being called is that to reinvest you are usually looking at lower rates. Since the "call" will cause the mathematics to differ, your yield-to-maturity won't be the same if the bond is called.

Sinking-fund provision. This means essentially that earnings within the company are being used to retire a certain

Buying Corporate Bonds

Here's what you should look at:

1. *The background of the company*. Look for financial security, look at earnings, and so on—much in the same way you would look at a company when buying stock. Growth potential isn't as important, however, since you won't see the direct results as you might with a stock.

2. *The rating of the bond*. This is VERY important. Check Moody's, Standard & Poor's, Duff and Phelps, or Fitch, who all offer bond ratings. Look for at least BBB- or Bbb-rated bonds.

3. *The date of maturity*. Are you looking at a short-term bond (one to four years), medium term bond (five to twelve years), or long-term bond (more than twelve years)?

4. *The call provisions*. You'd like to hold onto a bond paying a high interest rate for a while or at least have a reasonably higher "call rate" (or premium) should the bond be called.

5. *The future plans of the company*. See if the company is overextending itself. Buyouts, takeovers and other activities can bring stock prices up while lowering the value of the bond because of the amount of debt the company now takes on.

number of bonds annually. The bonds will indicate that they have such a feature and they are usually chosen randomly. Unlike a "call" provision, you may not see anything above the face value when the issuer retires the bond. On the other hand, these bonds are lower in their risk of default because the company is actively using money to repay their outstanding debt.

There are a few other reasons why bonds can be called early, and those are written into the bond provisions when you purchase them. As is the case when you buy any investment, you need to read everything carefully when buying bonds. There are numerous possibilities when it comes to bonds and bond provisions. Read all bond provisions very carefully before purchasing.

NOTE: There are also bonds with *put* features, which is a bond that gives *you* the right to "call" it at a certain time, or basically redeem it for your principal prior to the bond's maturity. The yield on this type of bond will be lower. It may be worth buying when you are looking for a safe investment during a time when interest rates are low. This way, when rates go up, you can get rid of it without having to try to sell it. Also a put feature gives you greater liquidity if you need to sell the bond. You don't have to look for a buyer.

CORPORATE BOND CATEGORIES

DEBENTURES

This term is used for unsecured bonds, backed only by the company's general credit. This is the heading that most corporate bonds fall under. These bonds are the reason people look closely at the bond grading, or ratings system of Standard & Poor's or Moody's.

GUARANTEED BONDS

These are bonds backed by a larger or parent company, which will cover the principal if the bond from its subsidiary company is not able to pay. This type of bond can allow an investor to purchase a bond from a smaller, perhaps growing, company at a good rate

Best Bond Returns

Although government bonds have been consistent and treasury bills do not "lose" money, the best total returns for bonds over the past fifty years has come from Long Term Corporate Bonds.

and with less credit risk, since the company is under the umbrella of the larger corporation, which has more established credit.

COLLATERAL TRUST BONDS

These bonds are backed by collateral from the issuing company. Naturally the collateral, as is the case with a loan, must be valued at an amount equal in value to that of the bond. The advantage to this type of corporate bond is that should the company go out of business, your bond is secured against the assets of the company. Secured bonds, however, pay a lower rate of interest.

MORTGAGE BONDS

These bonds are generally issued by utilities. They are types of collateral bonds that are backed by real estate or similar property. There are a host of complexities that follow such bonds; look into these before purchasing such a bond. For all bonds, read the security's offering statement or prospectus.

CONVERTIBLE BONDS

These bonds can be converted into shares of stock in the company in which you purchased the bond. Essentially the company is saying that instead of us paying you by check or in money at the maturity of the bond, they pay you by converting your bonds to shares of stock. They allow you, if you so choose, to cash in at some point on the success of the company. Otherwise you can keep the bond and continue to get the interest on a semi-annual basis. The interest is usually a little bit lower on such a bond because they are offering you the chance at higher returns if the stock is successful.

Convertible bond rates, should you choose to sell, are treated much more like stocks since their value hinges upon their market value, and that value hinges upon their convertibility into stock. In other words, if the stock is rising and the bond is worth more, you can either convert it or sell the bond at a higher rate. If you are looking at a convertible bond, look at how the stock of the company is doing. For the most part, convertible bonds are somewhere between stocks and bonds in the wide world of risk. People often avoid them because they can be confusing.

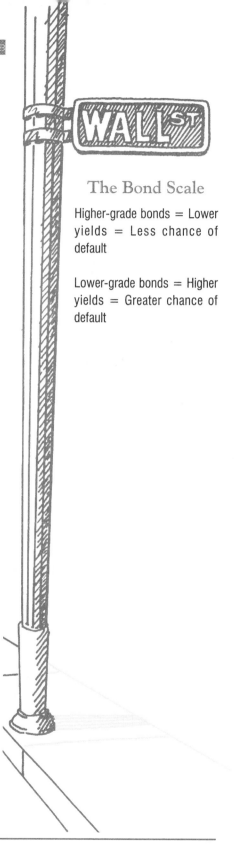

The Bond Scale

Higher-grade bonds = Lower yields = Less chance of default

Lower-grade bonds = Higher yields = Greater chance of default

THOSE CORPORATE "JUNK" BONDS

These are bonds that didn't make the grade. They are bonds graded below BBB, or Bbb (depending on where you are looking). They are issued by companies that are growing or reorganizing, or for whatever reason are considered a more risky investment in terms of the possibility of defaulting on the bond. Often these bonds are issued when companies are merging and have debts to pay in such a transaction. They are used as a method of financing such acquisitions.

The bottom line is that these so-called "junk bonds" are risky investments. Known in the financial world by their official name, "high-yield bonds," these bonds can provide a higher rate of return or higher yield than most other bonds. The risks include a risk of default and a risk of the market value of such a bond dropping quickly. Since the companies that issue these bonds are not as secure as those issuing high-grade bonds, their stock prices may drop, bringing the market value of the bond down with it. This will mean that trading such a bond will become very difficult, and therefore you have no liquidity.

Sometimes a company begins by issuing lower-grade high-yield bonds and does well, with their sales numbers going up. Eventually this company reaches a level where they can issue higher-grade bonds. This means in the short term that you can see high yields from their original low-grade bonds. It also means that they will call the bonds as soon as they are able to issue bonds at a lower yield.

If you see a company with great potential that has not yet hit its stride, perhaps you will want to take a shot at a high-yield bond from that company. If you are not that daring, you might opt for a high-yield bond mutual fund, which diversifies so that you are not tossing all your eggs into one high-risk basket. In this manner, if one company defaults you are still invested in others in the fund, some of which may prosper.

BOOK ENTRIES AND REGISTERED BONDS

So what do you actually receive when you buy a corporate bond?

Essentially there are two forms of corporate bonds: "Book-entry bonds" and "registered bonds." Book-entry bonds are bonds where there is no certificate forwarded to the bond owner. Instead all of the bond information is recorded in the investor's account by the brokerage house. This is becoming more in vogue because of the rapid manner in which bonds are now traded via technology through brokerage houses. It also eliminates the physical need for bond certificates to be moved from place to place as they are bought and sold. With registered bonds, you—as the investor—are issued a certificate with your name on it. Naturally, the sheer volume of trading lends itself to book-based bonds in the electronic and technological age.

THE MARKET

The corporate bond market is huge. Corporate bonds are issued at an astonishing rate by major corporations in various industries, including industrials, rails, and public utilities. In fact, the market value of outstanding corporate bonds in the United States is in the neighborhood of $2.5 trillion. On a daily basis, billions of dollars in bonds are traded, and the number keeps increasing. Those who thought bonds were losing popularity should check the numbers. In 1980 less than $50 billion was issued in corporate bonds. By 1995 the number was over $160 billion, and by 1997 it was nearly $600 billion. So if you think bonds aren't what they used to be, guess again.

There are two places you can look for buying and selling corporate bonds. One is, oddly enough, the New York Stock Exchange (NYSE), where the debt issues of major corporations are traded daily. Corporate bonds are also traded by bond dealers and brokers, or on the OTC (over-the-counter) market. The combined OTC market and NYSE bond market trade at nearly $10 billion daily.

The larger of the two markets, the OTC, places a current value on the bond, should you wish to sell, and depending on numerous economic factors (including the interest rate), the bond will be priced at more, the same, or less than the amount at which you purchased it. Bond dealers and brokers buy and sell bonds based on those current rates. The OTC investment minimum is usually at least $5,000 to make the trading worthwhile to the brokers. Short-term bonds of up to four years, medium-term five- to twelve-year bonds, and long-term bonds of twelve or more years are all briskly dealt.

Bearer Bonds

Bearer bonds are the old system whereby bonds were issued with coupons. The coupon could be redeemed by whomever was holding it for the interest. The problem was that the coupons, with no names on them, were essentially like cash and could easily be stolen. Bond owners could actually sell these on their own which also created difficulties. Thus, as of 1982 the issuance of any new bearer bonds bit the dust with a government reform act. Some, however, are still in circulation.

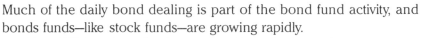

Much of the daily bond dealing is part of the bond fund activity, and bonds funds—like stock funds—are growing rapidly.

The OTC bond market is not actually a single market or exchange like the NYSE. It is the sum total of the bond brokers and dealers across the country. You can easily sell a bond before it matures because the market is so large.

A bond is not sold for a set amount as a stock would be, having a price per share listed. The amount is set by economic factors, and the price will be higher or lower as the selling market dictates. Bond traders sell for more than the price of the bond and make their money off what is called "the spread," which is like a markup. Thanks to global technology, the ease of selling a bond today defies the common myth that bonds are not liquid investments. In fact, bond traders should be able to immediately quote a price for a specific bond, and since the market is so vast, you will always be able to sell if you so choose.

Bond dealers can act as agents or they can play the role of bond sellers as they often do through their brokerage house. As bond sellers, they purchase large amounts of bonds and resell them at a slightly higher cost. This can be risky if the bond is not selling and the brokers are sitting with it. However, bond dealers are versed in where the market stands as well as which types of bonds to buy, and when. They are also well-versed in selling bonds. NOTE: Don't buy a bond simply because it's the only one the broker has on hand.

Numerous municipal bonds are also sold on the OTC market through bond dealers. Besides the corporate bond market, there are billions of dollars worth of municipal bonds, as well as institutional bonds, sold.

CHAPTER TWELVE

United States Government Bonds

Bond Tip

Bond tip: If you are buying a bond, buy late in the month to take advantage of the month's interest, and if you are cashing in, cash in early in the month.

One of the safest, low-risk forms of investing is in U.S. government bonds. Popular with your parents, and even your grandparents, U.S. savings bonds have been one of the benchmarks of investing since the "war bonds" of the 1940s helped support the military in World War II. Besides being a patriotic gesture, buying government bonds can provide a solid base in your portfolio and has tax advantages as well. It's no surprise that more than 55 million Americans now hold nearly $200 billion in U.S. savings bonds. Some are third-generation bond owners while others are buying savings bonds to round out the more conservative end of their portfolios.

Backed by the full faith and credit of the U.S. government, these bonds are as safe as any investment you can find. Government bonds can be purchased directly from the Treasury Department:

The Bureau of the Public Debt
Division of Customer Services
Washington, DC 20239
202-874-4000

By purchasing them directly you do not have to pay a broker fee.

THE NAME IS BOND, U.S. SAVINGS BOND

There are different types of U.S. savings bonds to choose from. You can obtain EE, HH, or the new I Bonds. There are other bonds still in circulation, such as the H bonds, which were issued up until 1979 (you may still have one thanks to a gift from your parents or even grandparents). The latest bonds vary in terms, and it's to your advantage to learn about government bonds before purchasing them. Many people do not bother to learn about government bonds, making the assumption that there's nothing to know, or that *you just buy them and hold onto them*. While that is part of the scenario, you should know about things like semi-annual interest, which you will be receiving, and about cashing the bonds in. You should also be aware of the length of time until the bond reaches original maturity and final maturity.

Some savings bond terms to keep in mind include:

Original maturity. This is the maximum time it will take the bond to reach face value at the guaranteed interest rate.

Extended maturity. This is the period after your bond reaches original maturity. This is a ten year period unless it's the last period until final maturity.

Final maturity. At this point the bond will no longer earn interest. You should redeem them at this point or you can roll them over into HH bonds. You have up to one year past final maturity in which you can do a rollover into an HH bond.

SOMETHING NEW: I BONDS

The new I bonds are the first new government bonds issued in nearly twenty years. Similar to the EE Bonds, the I is called an *accrual bond*, which means the interest is always added to the value of the bond. It is not paid out to the bond owner, but added to the bond. These bonds are purchased at face value, or original maturity, and have a total life of thirty years, at which point they will no longer pay interest. The interest rate is made up of two parts. The first part is a fixed rate, which is assigned when you buy it and stays with the bond for the life of the bond. The second part is an inflation-adjusted portion, which is tied to the consumer price index (which goes up or down every six months). That is added to the fixed rate every six months. The variable part of the bond is tied to inflation, hence the I name.

I bonds can be purchased in denominations of either $50, $100, $200, $500, $1,000, $5,000, or $10,000. They are purchased at face value, meaning a $500 bond costs $500. You can purchase up to $30,000 in I bonds, which is twice as much as you can purchase in EE bonds. Banks, savings and loans, and credit unions can all sell the new I bonds. However, not all banks, savings and loans, or credit unions participate in bond selling, so you should call before visiting them.

You need to hold onto an I bond for at least six months before redeeming it. After that you can cash it at any financial institution that handles bonds. However, if you cash it before five years, you will lose three months of interest.

Savings Bonds/ Treasury Bonds

The two fundamental differences between savings bonds and treasury bonds are:

1. Savings bonds allow you to defer the tax on interest for the life of the bond which could be thirty or forty years if that is the final maturity date. With Treasury bonds you receive semi-annual interest and have to report the interest annually.

2. Treasury bonds can be sold or purchased on the secondary market through brokers, meaning you can buy one at a discount or sell and make money. This is not the case with a U.S. Savings Bond which you can only purchase from the government and cannot be resold.

The Rules

Keep in mind that a bond is subject to the rules in effect when you purchase it. Since the government has changed bond rules periodically, make sure you familiarize yourself with the current rules of purchase. Request a buyer's guide from the Federal Reserve Bank or U.S. Treasury.

The I bonds, by the way, feature pictures of a variety of famous people including Helen Keller, Dr. Martin Luther King, Jr., and Albert Einstein on the actual bond.

BOND PERFORMANCES

Bond performances are tied to different things. You will need to factor these in when deciding between different bonds. The EE bond is tied to the five-year treasury yield. The I bond is tied to inflation and the fixed rate. So it becomes a matter of whether you feel the five-year treasury yield is going to outpace the combination of inflation and the fixed rate. Thus far, when the fixed rate is 3.25 percent or higher for the new I bonds, they have slightly outperformed the EEs. Every May and November, both rates are reset—other than the fixed part of the I bond. So it's unsure which will be the better bond to buy at a given time. The low inflation of late has been part of the I bond's initial success.

So, what is an HH bond, and where can you get one? As it turns out, you cannot buy the HH bond for cash. It is a "rollover" vehicle from EE or the older E bonds. The HH bond pays a fixed ten-year rate of 4 percent that is on a 20 year bond. You might choose this bond if you have an E or EE bond with a lot of interest that has grown on the bond. Rather than getting hit with a lot of interest income (for tax purposes), by rolling over the bond into the "HH" you can defer reporting that interest until you cash the HH bond in. Thus, you get twenty years of deferred interest. The new I bond cannot be exchanged for an HH bond. In other words, it is a bond to which you can roll over your older bonds and save deferring taxes if your tax rate is high.

Savings bonds are unique in that they act independently of the stock market. Therefore when the market is dropping or there is a great deal of volatility, people can choose to move to savings bonds. There is also no secondary savings bond market. Therefore, the bonds won't vary and have a higher or lower market value. Once you've bought it, you are the owner of the bond. It is a nonmarketable security, and you need not worry about the value of your investment—there's no market risk. It is also therefore a low-maintenance security since there's nothing

you can do with it. The only catch is knowing when to cash savings bonds in for optimal results.

Daniel Pederson, the former supervisor of the savings bond division of the Federal Reserve Bank and now owner of the Savings Bond Informer, a consumer bond information service based in Detroit, Michigan, explains that Americans forfeit more than $150 million a year by cashing their bonds at the wrong time.

"Most people who own bonds know very little about the bonds that they have," says Pederson. "People need to know the different maturities of their bonds as well as other important details, including when they should cash them in."

Since most bonds increase only twice a year, if you don't cash them in at the right time you can forfeit up to six months of interest per bond. Nothing on the bond tells you when that bond increases. It's not necessarily on the year and on the six-month anniversary of the date you purchased the bond. The Federal Reserve Bank has tables and charts showing when your bond will increase in value. This is more critical to determine with bonds you already hold. Bonds purchased as of May 1997, however, increase in value monthly and not semi-annually (at the first of the month), so whereas you could still lose money by cashing the bond in late in the month, it would only be up to thirty or thirty-one days—and not several months—worth of interest.

KEEPING TRACK

As is the case with all bonds, it's important to keep track of your savings bonds. It's important to know which are earning a lower rate, so that if you are cashing in some of the bonds, you will cash those and hold onto the ones earning you more interest. U.S. savings bonds will generally issue between 4 percent and 6 percent in interest and, depending on the bond, will stop earning interest at a specified time (usually in thirty years). There are some exceptions to the rule. The popular EE bonds issued between March 1993 and April 1995, because of a special retroactive "catch-up" clause, will issue 10 percent on their fifth year.

Guaranteed rates of interest are the minimum rates you can receive on that bond during a particular extension period. In other

Final Maturity: When Does the Bond Stop Paying Interest?

For the HH bond it's twenty years; for the EE and I bonds it's thirty years; for a savings note it's thirty years; and for any remaining H bonds, it's thirty years. For those holding the old E bonds, it's either thirty or forty years, depending on when it was issued.

Selling a Treasury?

The quickest and most efficient way to sell treasury bonds is through your own broker/dealer. The Treasury Department will not sell them for you nor will they buy them back. They are not in the retail market business. Unlike savings bonds, which have no secondary market, treasuries do, so they can be marketed.

words, if you purchased a particular series in May of 1995 with a 7.5 percent guaranteed rate, then it would remain that way until the end of the extension period, which would be May of 2005. If the guaranteed interest rate at that point was 6.7 percent, then that would be locked in as the minimum for the next extension period. *"Guaranteed" on savings bonds that you already hold did not mean guaranteed minimum forever, but for that extension period of every ten years.* Often people think that when they buy a bond the rate at which they buy it is good for the entire life of the bond. It is good only until the bond reaches its first maturity.

When buying long-term savings bonds, it's a good idea to keep records in a safe place. You need to have a record of when you bought the bonds and for how long they are paying interest. Although it sounds obvious, you don't need a bond sitting around that was given to you when you graduated high school at eighteen if you are fifty-five years old. The thirty-year anniversary means that you have held that bond for seven extra years without redeeming it. There are more than $3 million worth of bonds that fit such a scenario in the United States. Some people believe that if you hold a bond forever it will forever earn interest, while others who perhaps know that that isn't the case apparently don't clean out their dresser drawers or closets very often.

The tendency for many people is to follow stocks closely because there is no final date at which you must sell them, leaving them open-end. There is also much more attention paid to stocks in the media. Bonds, however, do not grab the headlines, and because there is a maturity date, or a final date when (unless the bond is called) you will receive your principal, many people just tuck a bond away and forget about it (particularly savings bonds, because there is no secondary market). The reality is, however, that if you cash them at the right time you can then move the money into a more lucrative investment.

For more information you can go to the *Bond Informer* newsletter, a consumer-oriented site at www.bondinformer.com, or look at the government site at www.publicdebt.tres.gov. *Bond Informer* approaches the area of bond investing from the consumer angle. The government site gives you their specific bond information. There's also a new government project called Easy Saver, where you

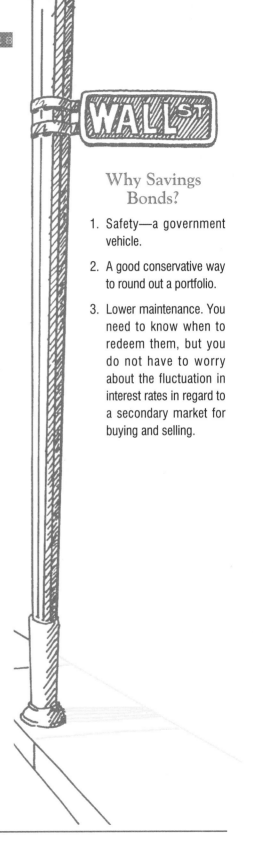

can sign up to have money automatically taken out of your savings or checking account and have the bond mailed to you. Look at www.easysaver.gov or call 877-811-8273 for information. They are also in the process of putting together a means for direct online purchases of government bonds.

For bond education and detailed reports on your bonds, you can contact the *Bond Informer* at 1-800-927-1901. For a detailed look at U.S. savings bonds, the book *Savings Bonds: When to Hold, When to Fold, and Everything In-Between* by Daniel Pederson (Sage Creek Press) should cover all your needs.

NOTE: Savings bonds, and now certain municipal bonds, are considered registered securities in that only the people named on the bonds can negotiate the bonds. This means if you lose a bond you can file a lost bond claim form and the government will research it free of charge and replace the bond certificate free of charge.

TREASURY BONDS

Treasury bonds are issued in denominations of anywhere from $1,000 on up. Every six months you will receive interest and you can, if you so choose, through Treasury Direct, have the interest from your bond deposited directly into your bank account or money market fund. They are, like U.S. savings bonds, as safe an investment as you'll find. They are backed by the full faith and credit of the U.S. government, which is as good as your investment security will get.

You can buy treasury bonds directly from the Federal Reserve Bank or from the Bureau of Public Debt. Quarterly auctions are held, and you can put in a noncompetitive bid, meaning you will get the bond at whatever the current rate is. You can also buy through a brokerage house, but you will pay a commission.

Beyond purchasing from the government, you can buy or sell treasury bonds on the bond market (which you can't do with savings bonds). Like other bonds, it's a matter of buying and/or selling at the right market price, which varies based on economic factors. The market for treasury bonds is enormous, so there's always a buyer or seller, but not necessarily at the price you want.

Why Savings Bonds?

1. Safety—a government vehicle.

2. A good conservative way to round out a portfolio.

3. Lower maintenance. You need to know when to redeem them, but you do not have to worry about the fluctuation in interest rates in regard to a secondary market for buying and selling.

Savings Bond Tax Advantages

Some advantages over CDs and money market funds include the fact that the interest you earn on the savings bond is deferred, meaning you don't have to report it until you cash the bond in, which gives you control over when you want to report that interest. Therefore, if you have a low-income year, you can take the income in that year instead of having the interest tacked onto your income each year. Also, the interest is subject to only federal taxes and not to state and local taxes (as CDs and money market funds are). This is especially advantageous if you are living in a state with high state income taxes.

Treasury bonds are not callable, and you can have them for a long time, such as thirty years. If you already own bonds and locked in a good rate before the current rates dropped, you have been enjoying better returns than anything you will get today. Rates on long-term treasury bonds have been in the 5 percent to 6 percent range of late. With inflation low, it's not a bad investment, especially since you do not pay federal or state taxes on the interest income. This makes your yield equal to that of slightly higher-yield investments where you are paying taxes, especially in states with high state taxes. You will, of course, pay capital gains tax should you sell the bond and make a profit.

Treasury bills and treasury notes are also ways in which you can invest in the United States government. Both are very safe investments with specific parameters.

CHAPTER THIRTEEN

Municipal Bonds

GO Bonds

A tax-free bond that is safe in terms of credit quality and with a high yield would be a AAA or AA General Obligation (GO) bond. GOs are defined as municipal bonds backed by the full faith and credit of the municipality issuing the bonds.

Munis, as they're called, are very popular for their tax-free advantages. States, cities, towns, municipalities, and government entities issue them, and they are used to build schools, parks, and numerous other important aspects of our communities. And for lending money to help with such worthy ventures, you not only receive interest on your loan, but your bond is usually exempt from federal—and often state—taxes. The last part is what catches people's attention, since most other investments have Uncle Sam camped on your doorstep waiting to take a bite.

The yields on municipal bonds generally won't pay as high as those of their corporate counterparts. However, when you consider the yield after the taxes are paid from the corporate bond, the munis often don't look too bad, particularly in a state with high state taxes. You need to report tax-exempt interest on tax returns, but it is just for record-keeping purposes.

When comparing taxable and tax-free bonds, begin with the tax bracket in which you file. If, for example you are in the 36 percent tax bracket and you are investing $15,000, you can look at the taxable and tax-free bonds and their yields. If the tax-free bond yields 5 percent, you'd earn $750. If the taxable bond is 7.5 percent, you would earn $1,125, but after paying taxes at the 36 percent rate, you'd pay $405 in taxes and end up with only $720. Therefore, a higher yield in a taxable fund may be less practical for your purposes than a lower yield in a tax-free fund. Here's a formula to help you decide.

Step 1: Subtract your federal income tax rate from 1.00.
For example, if your rate is 36 percent you would put 1.00 –36=.64.
Step 2: Divide the yield from the tax-free municipal bond you are considering by your answer to Step 1. If, for example the yield is 5.0 percent, divide that by .64. You get 7.81 percent.

In this case if you are comparing this tax-exempt municipal bond (or any other tax-exempt investment) you would need to find a taxable investment yielding at least a yield of 7.81 percent to come out ahead.

If you are living in a state with state taxes you need to add them in as well. Here's how:

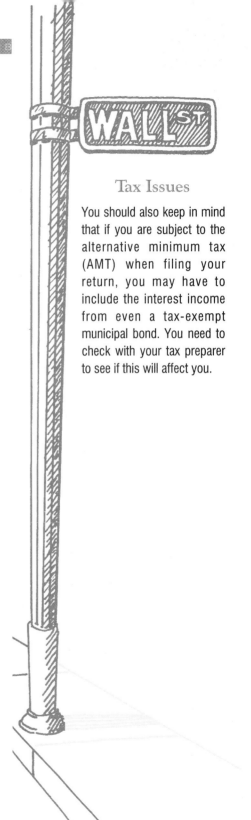

Step 1: Subtract your federal income tax from 1.00 as you did above: 1.00 −.36=.64.

Step 2: Multiply your state tax rate by your results to Step 1: .64 x 7.2 = 4.61.

Step 3: Add the federal tax rate to your answer: 36 percent + 4.61 = 40.61.

Step 4: Subtract your combined tax rate from 1.00: 1.00 −.4061 = .5939.

Step 5: Multiply your answer to Step 4 by the tax-exempt rate of the municipal bond you wish to purchase (we'll use 5 percent for the example): 5 divided by .5939 = 8.42 percent.

Therefore, you need an investment with an interest rate of 8.42 percent to improve upon your 5 percent tax-free investment.

Tax-exempt municipal bonds make sense most of the time. However, if you have a tax-exempt retirement plan, which includes IRAs, you should not be looking to include such bonds since you are already not being taxed in the plan.

Not unlike corporate bonds, many municipal bonds are also rated, and those with the highest ratings rival only the government bonds in their degree of low risk. The bonds are graded in much the same manner as corporate bonds by companies like Standard & Poor's (S&P), Moody's, and other investment services. They use AAA (S&P) or Aaa (Moody's) as the top grade. Usually you will look for bonds of at least BBB or Bbb to invest in. Naturally, as is the case with corporate bonds, the lower the grade the higher the risk. To ensure safety, you can get your investment secured, or in this case insured, so that you cannot lose your principal and interest due.

Municipal bonds will cost you $5,000 or a multiple of $5,000. Yields will vary, like other bonds, based on the interest rates. Actual prices for traded bonds will be listed in the financial pages. Prices will vary based on the size of the order of bonds traded and the market. Like other bonds, you can sell a muni on the secondary market and, depending on the current rate, receive a higher rate than that at which you bought the bond. If you sell a municipal bond, however, and show a capital gain, the "taxman" will cometh.

Tax Issues

You should also keep in mind that if you are subject to the alternative minimum tax (AMT) when filing your return, you may have to include the interest income from even a tax-exempt municipal bond. You need to check with your tax preparer to see if this will affect you.

Why Municipals?

You can choose to invest in the economy of a specific location or region.

You receive steady income from yields.

They are usually graded, providing you with a fair assessment of their risk of default.

They are usually a safe investment.

They are often free from federal—and often state—taxes.

You can sell them in the market before maturity for a capital gain.

TYPES OF MUNICIPAL BONDS

To follow are all the primary types of municipal bonds that you are likely to find.

Revenue bonds. These are bonds usually issued to fund a specific project, generally for the public, such as a bridge, an airport, or a highway. The revenue collected from tolls, charges, or in some manner from the project will be used to pay interest to bond holders. You may also hold a "moral obligation bond." This is essentially a revenue bond where if revenues fall short and, although there is no legal obligation, the state wants to honor the moral pledge to uphold their own reputation—and because they want to issue bonds successfully in the future.

General obligation bonds. If the issuer has the power to tax, they can back up the interest payments on the bond by taxation. Known as "gos," these bonds are "voter approved," and the principal is backed by the full faith and credit of the issuer.

Taxable municipal bonds. Why would anyone want a taxable muni if nontaxables exist? Simple: They have a higher yield more comparable to corporate bonds, generally without much risk. Such bonds can be issued to help fund an underfunded pension plan for a municipality or to help build a ballpark for the local baseball or football team.
Private activity bonds. If a bond is used for both public and private activities, it is called a private activity bond.
Put bonds. These are bonds with some built-in liquidity. They allow you to redeem the bond at par value on a specific date prior to its reaching maturity. This is particularly good if you are following the interest rates. Should you see bonds issued at higher interest rates you can cash in this bond and buy a replacement at the higher rate.
Floating and variable-rate municipal bonds. If it appears that the rate of interest will be on the rise, then these are good investments because they will—as the name implies—vary the interest rates accordingly. Naturally there's a greater interest risk involved with such bonds.

BUYING MUNICIPAL BONDS

When you buy a muni the bond will be registered in your name. This means your name appears as purchaser and is on the issuer's books. As is the case with corporates, there is what is known as "book entry" whereby you receive confirmation that you have purchased the bond via a written record of the transaction from your brokerage firm or your bank. The bonds are protected against theft or loss. Also, you will be notified if the bond is called.

If you are looking to find prices to buy municipal bonds that are being traded, you can usually find them in the financial section of a major paper or in a financial publication. Municipal brokers can then give you their own price quotes. The current market price will vary often, so if you are looking to buy (or sell for that matter), you need to stay on top of the current market price.

RESALE

There is a big secondary, over-the-counter, market for munis, including banks and securities dealers that are registered to sell them. As with other types of bonds you can buy and sell munis for higher or lower rates. Dealers make their money on the spread between what the bond is selling for (the market price) and what they are making on it. Basically, dealers sell at net cost and profit on the "mark-up." Since there is not a secondary municipal bonds exchange, there are more than two thousand securities dealers and banks that are registered to buy or sell municipal bonds over-the-counter.

SOME BOND STRATEGIES

Bond fund managers and strategists have various methods to their reinvesting madness. The idea is to take a bond that matures and reinvest that maturity into another bond. You can, however, elaborate on that basic premise by diversifying your bond investments or portfolio. Diversification is always a good way to help minimize fundamental risk, particularly if you diversify between higher- and lower-grade bonds. You might diversify between government bonds (for their added safety) and corporate bonds, including some with high yields. Adding in municipal bonds might take a bite out of taxes

Municipal Notes

A short-term municipal bond is called a municipal note. These bonds are generally issued for one year or less. Since the time frame is short, like zero coupon bonds (which are much longer), the interest is paid on maturity. Often such bonds are issued so that the issuer can cover short-term cash needs, meet unanticipated deficits, or begin raising capital for long-term projects.

Individual Bonds Versus Bond Mutual Funds

Advantages to an individual bond include:

1. No expenses to a fund (although bond fund operating expenses are generally low).
2. A greater guarantee of principal with high-grade bonds since bond funds can lose money.

Advantages to buying shares of a bond fund include:

1. Greater diversification.
2. It's easier to sell shares of a bond fund than a bond itself.
3. You can spend less money to become involved in the bond market.

if you are afraid of moving into the next tax bracket or if, like so many investors, you want to ease your tax burden.

One manner of diversification is laddering. With laddering, you choose short-, intermediate-, and long-term bonds and stagger them so that they reach maturity at various times. You might have an equal number of bonds that mature in two, four, six, eight, and ten years. By doing this you reduce your interest rate risk by having the more volatile long-term bonds as well as the short-term bonds. This won't affect you if you do not need to sell the bond and can hold it to maturity as planned.

Laddering also allows you greater liquidity without having to worry about selling, since there will be bonds coming due more often. For this reason you should also not be forced to sell a long-term bond, thus making their volatility even less significant and lessening your interest rate risk. Laddering involves good bookkeeping on your part because you have to keep reinvesting regularly—again, like dollar-cost averaging.

The "barbell strategy" says to leave out the intermediate bonds and go with the short- and long-term models. It is another way to diversify and cover your bases as you do with laddering. It allows you to be more liquid with short-term bonds and also balance the volatility of long-term bonds.

"Bond swapping" is where you sell off a bond and immediately buy another, or "swap" your bond so to speak. This can be done if you are looking to change maturities, move to a higher-grade bond, or sell at a loss to offset capital gains for tax purposes.

MORE BOND BUYING?

While the stock market sees consistent gains for long-term players, the volatility can be too much for some investors. During particularly volatile periods, where the market experiences significant declines, more investors look to the bond market. Also, as more people are reinvesting money coming from plans like 401(k)s and pension plans, bonds become attractive places in which to invest. They offer income and greater security than equities.

According to a recent study by American Century Investors, the onset of retirement was cause for 48 percent of investors to increase their fixed income holdings while a higher-rate investment would prompt 31 percent of respondents to purchase more bond products. The "bond attitude survey" conducted by the forty-year-old investment firm also determined that if stock prices declined by 10 to 20 percent, 21 percent of respondents would add more bonds to their portfolio.

While adding bonds to the portfolio has typically been thought of as a conservative move, there are other reasons why it is gaining momentum. Today, with baby boomers approaching their fifties and seeing higher levels of income, the bond market is looking brighter as a place to avoid paying higher taxes. Municipal bonds and municipal bond funds are generating attention with this very investment-conscious and savvy level of investor. Baby boomer bracket watchers are keeping an eye on their tax bracket and looking more closely at municipal bonds. They provide a way to manage tax risk within the area of bonds or while allocating your overall investments. Many equity investors are looking to put a percentage of their portfolio into bonds, and tax-exempt bonds are inviting.

On the other side of the equation are a larger number of retirement plans than ever before, with IRAs and 401(k)s also being utilized by the higher-income baby boomer set. This points to a segment of their portfolios going to taxable, generally corporate, bond funds. The low-expense costs are making these funds even more attractive, with some seeing 8 and 9 percent yields against 0.25 percent in expenses.

Suffice to say, the future of the bond market looks promising, particularly with inflation being low.

CHAPTER FOURTEEN

Retirement Plans and Other Safe Investments

401(k) and Spreading Taxes out

Once you retire you can take the money out of your 401(k) plan at the age of 59½ or greater in one lump sum. You can pay the taxes over the next five years, averaging the total amount out to ease your tax burden. If you were born before 1937 you can spread the tax payments out over ten years.

It's never too early to plan for your retirement or to set your sights on other future goals. As life expectancy increases, there are more years to enjoy, so it's to your benefit to plan accordingly. There are various popular options that provide comfortable investment opportunities. Some, like 401(k) plans are retirement plans set up by employers, while others, like IRAs, are retirement plans that you set up for yourself. These plans will work as a vehicle for various types of investments.

Along with, and included in, retirement plans are other investment options besides stocks, mutual funds, and bonds. CDs, for example, may not be generating the same excitement as the hottest stocks and mutual funds, but they serve very important purposes. They are short-term cash instruments that work for a conservative investor looking simply to keep some money in a safe place. Treasury instruments like T-bills (Treasury bills) provide an extremely safe haven for investors who are looking for a cash instrument and no fear that the "company"—or in this case the country—will go under.

But there's more. The real-estate market provides various opportunities, including some for new investors who may not be financially ready to plunk down money for an office building.

Collectibles is a fun way in which people can also find themselves both investing and enjoying a hobby. In short, there are a number of very diverse ways in which a person can invest his or her money, ranging from the safer cash investments to backing an off-Broadway show. In this chapter we explore some of these investment opportunities.

401(K) PLANS

For nearly twenty years, one of the most significant investing tools has been the 401(k) plan. Not actually an investment but a vehicle to invest within, the 401(k) is designed to help you save money (and build money) for retirement. The plan is set up by your employer and works in a manner similar to that of a mutual fund. These plans are becoming more and more common in major companies. The money is pooled and invested in stocks, bonds, mutual funds, or other types of investments. Usually the money is taken via salary reductions directly from your paycheck and goes directly into your 401(k) account. If such a plan is offered where you work, there is no reason not to jump at the opportunity. Putting the money in a plan earmarks it for your retirement, and you don't have to pay taxes on it as the money grows. AND, employers generally put in a contribution as well, which can be 10, 25, or even 50 percent of the amount you are contributing.

A 401(k) plan can be set up by an employer in a number of different manners, with some going into effect immediately and others kicking in after you've worked in the company for six months or even a year. Currently, as of 1999, you can contribute up to $10,000 of your salary to your 401(k) plan in a given year.

The big difference between a 401(k) and buying your own mutual funds is that you are not penalized if you sell your shares in a mutual fund, although you can lose money. In a 401(k), you must maintain the account until you are 59½ years old, or you will face a penalty upon early withdrawal.

Similar to mutual funds, your investment in a 401(k) is diversified, and you generally have several options as to where you want the contribution invested. Furthermore, you can change the percentage of money you want in a particular area. Plans generally invest in general growth funds, equity funds, money market accounts, and sometimes in shares of stock in your own company.

When you change jobs, by your own choice or by the decision of your company, you can have your 401(k) plan directly transferred to the new employer if they also offer such a retirement plan. By having the 401(k) rolled over by direct trustee to direct trustee, known as a trustee-to-trustee transfer, you will not have the money in your possession or personal account and will avoid paying taxes on it. By law, employers have to allow you to roll the money over. If you roll over the money yourself, the company will issue you a check for the money, less 20 percent, which they hold onto as insurance that you will roll it over into another 401(k) or into an IRA (discussed in the next section). You have to roll the money over in sixty days or you'll be hit with taxes and penalties, and you'll have to replace the 20 percent your company withheld. Play it safe and do a trustee-to-trustee transfer if at all possible, or you will pay a lot in taxes. Otherwise, the clock is ticking. If you are not starting a

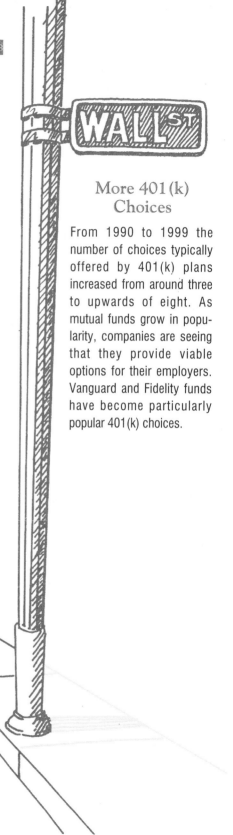

More 401(k) Choices

From 1990 to 1999 the number of choices typically offered by 401(k) plans increased from around three to upwards of eight. As mutual funds grow in popularity, companies are seeing that they provide viable options for their employers. Vanguard and Fidelity funds have become particularly popular 401(k) choices.

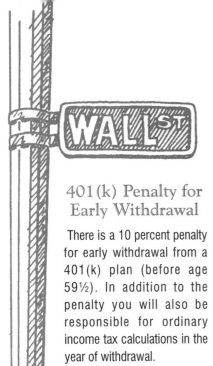

401(k) Penalty for Early Withdrawal

There is a 10 percent penalty for early withdrawal from a 401(k) plan (before age 59½). In addition to the penalty you will also be responsible for ordinary income tax calculations in the year of withdrawal.

new job or are joining a company that does not have a 401(k) plan, roll yours over into an IRA.

Again, there is no reason not to start a retirement plan through a 401(k). The fact that your employer is making even a 10 percent contribution (10 percent of what you put in) means you are already seeing a 10 percent growth on your investment, plus whatever the plan accrues over time. It is a simple solution to retirement planning that you do not have to set up yourself. You do, however, need to keep tabs on where your 401(k) money is being invested. Too many people just make a choice and "let it ride." You can be more or less conservative about your 401(k) depending on what is going on in the market. Since you are in a retirement plan—whether it is a 401(k) or an IRA—for the long haul, you need not worry too much about the days, weeks, or even months when the stock market is down. In fact, drops in the market can play into your favor as you continue to put money into the plan through payroll deductions. This will allow you (through dollar-cost averaging) to be buying more shares of the stock or mutual fund when the rate is lower. In the long term, of course, the market will go up and you'll be doing fine.

Since a 401(k) plan is a long-term retirement vehicle, it's important that you remember your long-term goals and stick to them. Don't be easily swayed by some hot stock or mutual fund. Focus on the long term and, as you approach retirement, maintain a solid assessment of how much money you will have when you retire and how much income will be coming in. Determine how much you will need, and remember that the 401(k) will most likely *not* be your only place to turn for retirement income. Besides Social Security benefits, you may have a pension plan, as well as other savings. Many retirees find that they have other investments such as stocks or bonds that are providing income, while others find part-time jobs for income and to be busy—which is investing in yourself.

With the 401(k) you can take your money out in one lump sum, which will mean paying taxes at one time. You can take the money out over time, spreading tax payments out, or roll the 401(k) into an IRA. Like an IRA, at seventy you must start taking money out or face penalties. However, if you are still working at seventy, you can keep the money in the plan and keep contributing.

All in all, the 401(k) plan is an excellent opportunity to build for your retirement and do so at the level you feel most comfortable. As one financial analyst put it, "No matter what I say or suggest, the bottom line is that the individual has to be able to sleep comfortably at night." Therefore, it goes back to risk/tolerance. First, be proactive and don't just forget about the money in your retirement plan, and second, determine what level of risk is okay for your 401(k).

For people working in nonprofit organizations such as schools or hospitals, a 403(b) plan may be available, which works similarly to a 401(k). Such plans generally have fewer investment options, but they are also tax-deferred and similar in their makeup. Government workers may be offered a 457 plan, which is also similar in principle to a 401(k) or 403(b), with some additional restrictions.

IRAs

The most popular retirement plan of the last decade has certainly been the IRA, or Individual Retirement Account. Now sporting two varieties, IRAs offer you a safe tax-favored way for your money to grow for your retirement years.

TRADITIONAL IRAs

The traditional IRA allows you to contribute up to $2,000 per year, with a non-working spouse contributing up to an additional $2,000. A couple filing a joint tax return may put up to $4,000 into two separate IRA accounts, the only stipulation being that the amount being put into either account not exceed $2,000. If you are receiving alimony you also qualify to make an IRA contribution. All or a portion of your contributions may be tax-deductible, depending on your adjusted gross income (AGI) and whether or not you partici-pate in a qualified retirement plan. You'll have to look over the tax

Get More From Your 401(k)

Most 401(k) plans offer several choices including a range of asset classes from which you can choose. It's to your advan-tage to spread your assets out. If your company's plan is not offering enough choices you should talk to your plan admin-istrator. It's in the best interest of the company to have a plan that will attract a wide range of employees at various salary levels since the government has "discrimination tests" to make sure all employees are represented.

IRA Candidate

An ideal candidate for an IRA is someone who doesn't have a company retirement plan and whose earnings fall below the IRA ceiling. If your earnings are too high to "qualify" under IRA guidelines, you can still invest in an IRA although you can't deduct your contribution.

tables closely to determine the tax advantages a traditional IRA will have for you.

While you will be able to deduct all or part of your contributions into a traditional IRA, once there are earnings, they will compound annually, tax-free. Thus your account will grow more rapidly than if taxes were deducted. If you have many years ahead for your IRA account to grow until retirement, it is worthwhile to watch your money grow without taxation.

Of course, like anything else, IRAs have their rules, and a traditional IRA says once you put money in for retirement, it is there until you are 59½ years old. This essentially ensures that you are indeed putting the money away for retirement purposes (even if you keep on working past 59½). If you withdraw money prior to 59½, you will be penalized unless you qualify for one of a few exceptions, including first-time home-buying expenses, substantial medical costs, qualifying higher education expenses, or ongoing disabilities. All of these need to be validated.

Once you are past 59½ years of age you can withdraw the money as you see fit until you are 70½, at which point the government starts putting minimums on how much you need to withdraw annually. When you do withdraw the money you will pay income taxes on the investment earnings based on your tax bracket. The long period of tax-deferred income, however, still outweighs this taxation. Also, it is very often the case that the income level for someone in their sixties, and perhaps semi-retired, is lower than it was in their forties, so they will fall into a lower tax bracket. Since the government changes the rules from time to time, and the methods of taxation in the United States are under a great deal of criticism, some experts feel that if you can defer tax payment now for another twenty years, why not do so. After all, tax laws could certainly change by the second decade of the twenty-first century.

As for actually starting your IRA, you can choose to start one through a bank, brokerage house, or mutual fund depending on where you want your money to be invested. Traditionally banks offer fewer options than brokerage houses for where your IRA investment can go, usually sticking with the safer options such as a CD. Brokerage houses offer a wider range of options should you choose to be more savvy with your IRA investment, or you can play it safe

The Comfort Zone

Norman
Retired
Age: 68

For Norman, the main concern is maintaining a series of investments that he has held for several years that pay a steady income. "I have moved the money I accrued in my retirement plan into income-producing vehicles," he explains. "The stocks I have all pay steady dividends, and I have a few bonds to round it out. Between the dividends, interest, social security, and a few dollars made from some part-time entertaining as a comedian, I have reached a secure, comfortable place. I also have some money tucked away in the bank. It doesn't earn a lot of money, but it makes me feel good knowing that it is there."

Norman retired from a career as a salesman in a small family-owned company. Although there was no 401(k) plan, he was able to build up money for retirement in an IRA. He stopped working to pursue entertaining in his late fifties but the money invested in dividend-paying stocks plus the bank accounts were able to keep him living comfortably until the IRA came due. Now, with the added money, he still plays the market occasionally. "Once you know you have enough income to keep you living comfortably, there's nothing wrong with playing the market a little bit. I'm not married and don't have children, so my financial responsibilities are limited to pretty much just taking care of myself. I enjoy finding a stock now and then to follow. I have a good broker who generally lets me know if he thinks I've selected a bad choice," he says.

As the population lives longer, there is certainly no reason to stop investing at sixty-five, since you may have another twenty years ahead. While many people feel this is the time to be very conservative, if you do find you have extra money beyond that which meets your needs, why not enjoy investing it and following your investments? Being active is important—and investing and following your investments, as Norman is doing, is one way of keeping active.

with a money market fund. Mutual funds are, by definition, (usually) riskier than a CD or money market account. Essentially, within the IRA you need to do some investing homework if you want to get the most out of the account. The long time frame of an IRA makes equities or equity funds more attractive for some investors. Like other investments you can move your investments around within the IRA and suit your level of comfort in regard to risk.

Too many people put money into an IRA and forget that they can still work with that investment. There is often a feeling that once the money is in an IRA, because you cannot take it out until age 59½, you also can't touch it. That is not the case. There's nothing wrong with being proactive with the money you are investing within the IRA. In fact, you should be.

ROTH IRAS

As noted earlier, there are two types of IRAs. Thus far, we've discussed the traditional IRA. There is also a Roth IRA, named for legislation formulated by Senator William Roth. This relatively new IRA offers no tax deductions when you contribute at the same $2,000 annual ceiling. BUT (and this is the good part), *upon withdrawal you will not be taxed*. In fact, there are very few regulations when it comes to withdrawing the money from a Roth IRA. The money must be in the plan until you are at least 59½. However, the money can be withdrawn after five years, penalty-free, if you are disabled, if you use the distribution to pay up to $10,000 of the qualifying first-time home-buying expense, or if the distribution is to another beneficiary following the death of the account owner. If you do not need to take the money out, however (unlike a traditional IRA where at age 70½ the government says you must start making minimum withdrawals or face a penalty), you can leave the money in the Roth IRA with no minimum distributions upon withdrawal. This can even allow for a large tax-free benefit to pass directly to your heirs if you so choose.

Whereas your tax bracket (and whether or not you are invested in an employee sponsored retirement plan, SEP IRA, or Keogh) will determine whether or not you can make the appropriate deductions for a traditional IRA, for a Roth IRA your income will determine your eligibility. This income structuring began with the advent of the new Roth IRA in 1998 and is subject to change, so you must ask about your eligibility when you decide to investigate a Roth IRA. As of 1999 the Roth is phased out as adjusted gross income (AGI) rises above $95,000 and $110,000 on a single return and between $150,000 and $160,000 on a joint return.

Assuming you are eligible for both traditional and Roth IRAs, the biggest determining factor is whether it is to your benefit to take a deduction now and have to pay the taxes on withdrawing the money or to take no deduction at present and not have to worry about taxation or minimum deductions upon withdrawing the money later. The determination of whether to invest in or roll over your money from a traditional IRA to a Roth is based on your own financial situation. Many experts agree that taking the tax hit on the $2,000 now is far better than taking it on the much larger sum later on.

The two IRAs have given Web sites and financial magazines a whole new area on which to write volumes. The question is, *Which IRA Is Right For You?* Once again there is no definitive answer without looking at your own personal financial situation. Nonetheless, Web sites have calculators and fancy ten-page sections devoted to figuring out the answer to this question, which is now posed to rival the age-old question, *What is the meaning of life?* It shouldn't be all that complicated. AND a good accountant should be able to help you figure it all out in less time than it takes to download and evaluate the methods of calculations.

To make matters worse, questionnaires will ask you questions such as *What tax bracket will you be in thirty years from now?* This is an interesting question, considering the entire tax system could be revamped three times over by then. You will be asked questions like *At what age will you need the money?* and *How much income will you need at age sixty-five?* Again, you are being asked to predict the future.

The bottom line is that no matter how much you calculate, you cannot know for sure what the next thirty years have in store in terms of taxes, the rate of inflation, the cost of living, your own health, and the stability of your job. While it is to your advantage to

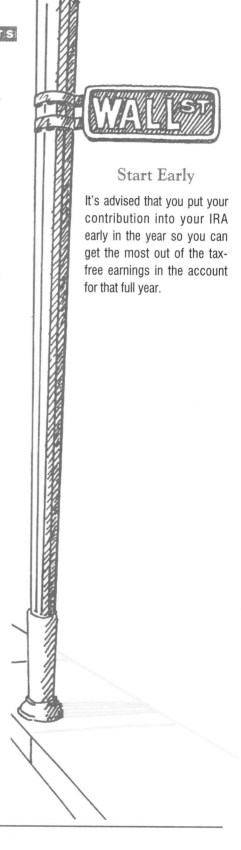

Start Early

It's advised that you put your contribution into your IRA early in the year so you can get the most out of the tax-free earnings in the account for that full year.

401(k) Loans

Consider other sources first, but if you do borrow from you 401(k) be sure you intend to stay with the company for awhile. If you leave for any reason, you may have to pay back the loan immediately. If you can't, you will owe income taxes on the balance of he loan. Plus, you will have to pay a 10 percent penalty.

put money away for your retirement years, the decision to choose the traditional or the Roth IRA is not as tough as it is made out to be. Either way you will have saved money for your retirement years. If you qualify for both plans, the simple equation, as stated earlier, is whether it's to your benefit to take tax deductions now or whether you can afford not to and have benefits later on. Thus, figure out basic, approximate numbers with your accountant, consider other factors in your life, make an overall assessment of your future as you'd like it to be, and pick one. Since your future is not a certainty, go with your best assumption.

CERTIFICATES OF DEPOSIT (CDs)

Unlike a 401(k) or an IRA, which are vehicles in which to place investments for retirement, a CD is a cash investment unto itself.

Through a bank or credit union you can purchase a CD for three months, six months, a year, or several years. Insured by the FDIC, these popular places to store your money have no risk. You can spend a few hundred or a few thousand dollars on a CD—banks usually set minimums. CDs secure an interest rate when you initially purchase them. Yields on CDs, while not matching those of the stock market, will generally run between 4 and 5 percent, which matches many bonds. Rates are calculated by banks based on the interest rates, the supply and demand for loans and other economic factors. Interest can be paid out to you periodically on longer-term CDs or paid to you all at once on shorter-term CDs (a three-month CD will pay upon maturity). Interest can, and often is, reinvested. You should also take note of how interest is paid out. You'll see interest compounded daily, weekly, monthly, and so on. This is as important as locking in a good interest rate. Since banks are no longer regulated, and can pay the interest that they set up, it's important that you lock in a good rate. While CDs are not bringing home the high returns they were in the 1980s, the rates are competitive, so you should shop around—read the ads and financial listings and check online for the best interest rate. There are numerous variations on the theme, as banks enjoy coming up with new ideas to bring in your business. Some will even, after a few months, give you a higher rate of interest, while others will let you customize, or choose, the terms of the CD.

The one drawback of a CD is liquidity. If you need to cash in your CD early you will be penalized. It's often suggested that you divide your money up over several CDs purchased at different times and, therefore, with different maturities. This system of "laddering" will lock in better (and worse) interest rates, but will allow you to have CDs maturing at various times, should you need the cash. This does require good record keeping, especially if you are reinvesting once the CDs come due.

U.S. TREASURY BILLS

In the 1980s, T-bills—as U.S. treasury bills are known—were paying double digit-returns. Needless to say, they were very popular investments. Today, T-bills are not paying tremendous returns, but they are still very safe; like government bonds, they are backed by the full faith and credit of the United States government. Treasury bills are sold at government auctions every Monday. The government sets the yield price, which in recent years has been around 5 percent.

But how do they work? When you purchase a T-bill, through your bank or directly through the federal government, you immediately get a check for the amount at which the bill is paying interest. Therefore if you buy a $5,000 T-bill at 5 percent, you will receive a check for $250, or 5 percent, about a week after you've invested. If it's a 26-week T-bill you will then have a chance to renew at twenty-six weeks or get the $5,000 investment back. Every time you renew you get the interest check immediately, which is your "discount."

T-bills are good investments because they are safe and cannot be taxed at the local or state level, making them preferable if you live in a state that has high state taxes. Of late the rates have been low, but they have kept pace with most cash instruments. Your money, however, is not liquid, which often discourages people from long-term T-bills.

One of the positive aspects of T-bills is that you get all your interest immediately, so while your principal is tied up for either thirteen, twenty-six, or fifty-two weeks, you can take the money earned and put that into another investment. For instance, if you buy a 26-week T-bill at $10,000 and the rate is 6 percent, you will receive a check for $600 (your 6 percent) a week after making the investment.

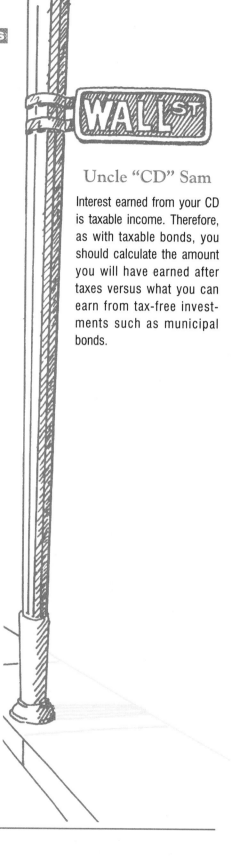

Uncle "CD" Sam

Interest earned from your CD is taxable income. Therefore, as with taxable bonds, you should calculate the amount you will have earned after taxes versus what you can earn from tax-free investments such as municipal bonds.

Retirement Inventory in Brief

The most important pre-retirement steps you can take include:

1. Taking inventory of your holdings, including all assets (car, home,etc.), IRA's, retirement plans, savings bonds, stock holdings, real estate investments and so on.
2. Determine what you will be getting in terms of income including Social Security and all payouts from plans from which you will be taking money out.
3. Determine what you will need for living expenses.
4. Determine which investments to cash in, such as savings bonds.
5. Determine which investments you can make to best cover the difference, if any, between what income you are generating and your anticipated living expenses or to earn additional income.

Then in twenty-six weeks you will receive your $10,000 back, or you can reinvest to start the process again for another twenty-six weeks. This allows you the opportunity to put the $600 into an investment that might earn you additional money over the same six months. T-bills are simple. You pay $10,000 and get 6 percent interest up front. That's all you get. When the twenty-six weeks are up (or fifty-two weeks) you get your $10,000 back. That's it. It can be less than $10,000 and the rate doesn't have to be 6 percent.

Until 1998, T-bills were sold in minimums of $10,000, which put them out of reach for many investors. Now they can be had for as little as $1,000 and purchased in increments of $1,000.

You can sell T-bills and notes based on the interest rate. If you have a long-term note with, for example, an 8 percent rate and other notes are paying 5 percent, you might want to sell it. Your $10,000 note could be worth $12,000 on the market. It's all a matter of supply and demand, and a high-yield note in a low-yield market is valuable. Of course, it can also go the other way. Your 5 percent bill could be worth far less if everyone else is able to buy bills at 8 percent. If you hold to maturity, however, you will get your initial investment or principal back. Unfortunately, you will be reinvesting at a lower rate. Rates on the short-term T-bills, however, do not change that drastically.

Since there are no longer actual "certificates" issued, U.S. securities are issued in what is known as "book form," which means they are issued by electronic entries. Interest is paid into a treasury direct account, which you open when you purchase a U.S. treasury security from the Federal Reserve Bank. A broker can also purchase a U.S. treasury for you and set up your treasury direct account, but for this you will pay at least $50.00 for a service that you can easily do yourself. Call the Federal Reserve Bank closest to you and ask to set up an account.

Treasury notes come in either the two- and five-year variety, which are auctioned the last business day of the month, or the three- and ten-year notes, which are auctioned quarterly. For notes over five years the minimum investment is $1,000, but for five years or less the minimum is $5,000. You can purchase treasury notes from the U.S. government that range from one to ten years. They are exempt from state and local taxes, which can make them appealing, and they are also safe investments backed by the full faith and credit of the U.S. government. The shorter-term notes, usually under four years, are sold for $5,000 or more, with the longer-term notes, four to ten years, selling for $1,000+. Treasury notes have longer terms (one to ten years) than T-bills. They pay interest semi-annually, whereas T-bills pay all your interest in one lump sum. The other advantage of treasury notes *was*, until last year, that they cost less than T-bills (T-bills had a $10,000 minimum), but T-bills can now be purchased for various amounts.

The United States Treasury is also well-known for—among other things—savings bonds, which are discussed in Chapter Twelve. They are longer-term securities that can pay interest for thirty or forty years.

CHAPTER FIFTEEN

Real Estate

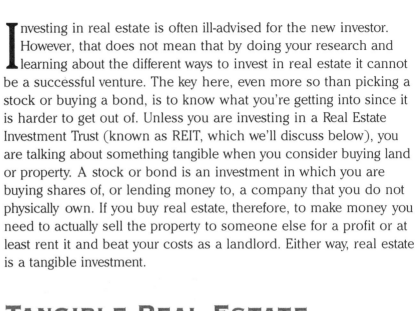

Investing in real estate is often ill-advised for the new investor. However, that does not mean that by doing your research and learning about the different ways to invest in real estate it cannot be a successful venture. The key here, even more so than picking a stock or buying a bond, is to know what you're getting into since it is harder to get out of. Unless you are investing in a Real Estate Investment Trust (known as REIT, which we'll discuss below), you are talking about something tangible when you consider buying land or property. A stock or bond is an investment in which you are buying shares of, or lending money to, a company that you do not physically own. If you buy real estate, therefore, to make money you need to actually sell the property to someone else for a profit or at least rent it and beat your costs as a landlord. Either way, real estate is a tangible investment.

TANGIBLE REAL ESTATE

If you are considering making a real-estate purchase for rental purposes, you will choose between either commercial or residential property. You need to assess your own financial situation first, as this is not the most liquid investment. It's important to determine how much money you will need up front, how much money you can borrow, and what the terms will be. Investment capital is the first item on your agenda. If you do not have it you'll need to borrow it. For a new investor, borrowing for the purpose of buying real estate is not usually advised unless you are well-versed in the field. Unlike stocks or bonds, you cannot start out with a $100 investment.

Besides the money, there are other aspects to buying real estate for the purpose of renting or selling that involve you as an individual. It's important that you have good management skills and an eye for detail, as there are numerous details involved with any property. You need to be able to maintain the property, which means proper upkeep. You have to factor that into your costs. Unless you are talking about a small summer house and you are very handy, you will need to know how and where to find the right electricians, plumbers, and contractors. Maintaining a property is a major responsibility—it doesn't just exist while you make money off of it, like a stock or bond.

Howdy, landlord!

If there are renters, you are now a landlord, which means you need to communicate effectively with tenants. There will be numerous problems that will arise in any rental situation, and how you handle them is important to maintaining the property without having to pour a lot of money into it. The movie *Money Pit*, with Tom Hanks and Shelley Long, is worthwhile viewing prior to purchasing a property; it's an extreme reminder (and mediocre movie) of how rough it could be. It's far easier to make the effort to maintain a property when it's your primary place of residence. However, you'll have to do as much—if not more work—when it's to protect an investment. If an investment cuts too deeply into your time, you may be losing income by losing time in which you can earn money elsewhere. If you are spending hours maintaining a property, you are cutting into your income-earning time and losing money in the process. One of the reasons people choose stocks, bonds, and mutual funds is that other than tracking them, you do not need to do too much work to maintain your investment.

If you are purchasing a commercial or residential property with the idea of renting it out or selling it in the future, you need to consider the following:

- Is this a prime location? The old saying "location, location, location" still means everything in real estate.
- Has this property been rented successfully before?
- How old is the property?
- Has it been thoroughly inspected and given a clean bill of health? You may need to arrange for this yourself, including electricity, plumbing, foundation, roofing, etc. Everything must comply with local safety ordinances.
- How much renovation and work needs to be put into this property? This will follow, in part, from the inspections. Changing the interior to fit your business needs or rental needs (such as if you are making a one-family house into a two-family rental) is an important cost factor.
- What are the zoning laws in the area? This is particularly important if you are opening a new type of business in a commercial property.

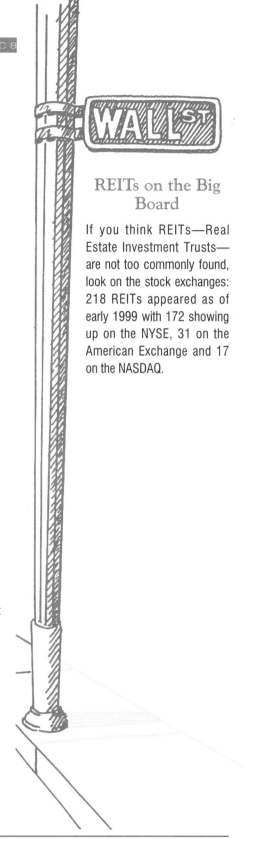

REITs on the Big Board

If you think REITs—Real Estate Investment Trusts—are not too commonly found, look on the stock exchanges: 218 REITs appeared as of early 1999 with 172 showing up on the NYSE, 31 on the American Exchange and 17 on the NASDAQ.

- What is the crime rate? How safe is the neighborhood?
- What is the accessibility to and from the property (roads)? Whereas you may want to rent out the perfect little hideaway as a "summer retreat," a business will need to be accessible.
- How much will you need to spend to maintain the property? Do you need gardeners? Will there need to be a janitor on the premises at all times? Upkeep is important when evaluating the potential resale, as well as rental value, of the property.
- What is the economic state of the area? Even a business with the best intentions cannot survive if everyone in the area is being downsized and moving elsewhere.
- What plans are being made for the future of the area? Is a new highway coming through that would help your business by high visibility? Or is a new highway coming through that would ruin the rental value of your secluded, quiet villa?
- How much insurance will you need? What are the rates for that property in conjunction with the purposes of your investment? A day care center will have you paying very high insurance to safeguard that the children do not injure themselves because of your faulty stairway. Various businesses will have various needs. You also need to be insured if you are renting for residential purposes.
- What property taxes are applicable? What can be deducted?

If this list hasn't scared you and you are still reading this section, then perhaps, just perhaps, you are real-estate-buying material. Not unlike investing in stocks, there is an issue of timing when it comes to investing in real estate—even more so. The stock market will, over time, always end up ahead. Real estate should as well. However, the economic climate can change, and since, as mentioned earlier, you need a buyer, this can be risky.

A couple who bought a beautiful house in upstate New York, after watching their children grow up and go off to college, decided they did not need such a big house any longer. Eleven years had passed. Since property values go up, why shouldn't their house be worth more money? Well, the house, with some additions, *was* worth more money. The book value said it had increased in value.

However, the house next to this particular house was empty. The bank had foreclosed on it and the structure had sat empty with the grass on the front and back lawns uncut for a long time. Furthermore, one of the local industries that was important to the economics of the area was laying off workers. To make a long story short, the couple saw their asking price dropping because a house with an empty property next door, in an area that people were moving out of, was not as desirable despite the "book value." The moral to the story is that the "value" of your property is only as good as the old supply and demand.

A modest one-bedroom apartment in midtown Manhattan, because it's close to everything, can sell for more than a nine-room house on a three-acre property just outside Kansas City. Not that there is anything wrong with the suburbs of KC; it's simply that the supply and demand dictates the value. The same holds true for renting your property. There are numerous factors involved when it comes to real estate as an investment.

One of the best things a potential real-estate investor can do is look for an area that is marked for revitalization. Carefully looking at what is happening on the local political scene can help you determine in which direction an area is headed. See what significant changes are being made. A major theme park opening up might mean it's advantageous to buy the family restaurant down the road, or transform a property into such a place. Perhaps you find out that a major New York City-based company is buying property in Tenafly, New Jersey, for their corporate headquarters. Is there property for sale in that area? It might be valuable with the influx of twenty thousand people every day. Places where people are moving to or are coming to for some reason are places you want to look for commercial property. People bring money into an area.

The same holds true to an extent with residential property. However, the needs are different. Families buying homes are concerned about things like shopping, good schools, transportation, and so on. Think about a property from the perspective of *If I were going to be living here, would this area have what I need?* Sometimes a highly commercial area cannot be built into a residential community as well.

There are numerous factors to consider when buying real estate for the sake of renting or reselling. The bottom line is that you need to do A LOT OF HOMEWORK!

REITs

A REIT, or Real Estate Investment Trust (pronounced REET), offers investors a way to invest in commercial real estate in much the same manner as they would invest in the stock market. It is the difference of public versus private or indirect versus direct investing in real estate. In short, it lets you invest in real estate without having to actually buy property or land. There are over two hundred REITs to choose from, and shares of REITs are traded much like shares of stock. In fact, you can find REITs listed on the stock exchanges.

Less popular than stocks, funds, and even bonds, REITs are not new, having been established more than thirty years ago as the "safe" way to get into the real-estate market. They are more attractive than buying real estate because, unlike buying property, your investment is more liquid; selling off the shares are the same as selling off shares of a fund or a stock. And, since you don't actually own the real estate, you do not have the headaches attached with other forms of real-estate investing. On the other hand, if you are looking to own real estate, a REIT does not give you ownership rights.

REITs do, in fact, share the characteristics of both stocks and mutual funds. They are publicly traded companies, so owning shares is similar to owning shares of stocks. On the other hand,

HELP THIS WAY

REITs, which were created from an act of Congress in 1960, were created to follow the paradigm of the investment companies, or mutual funds. Because most small investors could not invest directly in income-producing real estate, this would allow them to pool their investment resources. A REIT is, therefore, like a mutual fund and is called a "pass through" security, passing through the income from the property to the shareholders. The income is not taxed at the corporate level, but at the investor level provided they pass their profits through.

Unlike mutuals that purchase stocks in companies that manufacture products, REITs purchase mortgages, rental properties, properties for resale, and so on. They are dealing in the real-estate market, so there is a wide variety of real-estate a REIT can be involved in purchasing. REIT legislation actually does not mean that a REIT must own properties but that it earns income off of real-estate investments. These investments usually take one of two forms: either buying properties and investing in the equity (*equity REITs*), or by investing in commercial mortgages that help to provide financing for someone to acquire buildings (*mortgage REITs*). In the latter, the income comes from the interest on those mortgages. Of course, like everything else, there's always one option that fits in the gray area in between. In this case that's known as a *hybrid REIT*, which does a little of each.

REITs both buy and manage properties. There are laws that govern the buying and selling of properties and that keep REITs from being in the property brokerage business. REITs are designed to serve as investment vehicles. They pass income through to shareholders and end up with no retained earnings. Therefore they always have to go back to capital markets to finance their growth. Unlike a company such as Microsoft, which grows through internally generated funds, a REIT cannot retain earnings to grow.

What does all this mean to you?

It means that REITs can be attractive investments. But, as with any other investment, *you must do your homework.*

NAREIT, the National Association of Real Estate Investment Trusts (with a Web site at www.nareit.com) offers a great deal of information on REITs. (NAREIT can also provide you with information by calling 1-800-3NAREIT). Brokerage houses also have REIT information. Many of the REITs themselves have Web sites as well. Since they are not as common as corporate stocks and mutual funds, however, *you need to speak with people educated in this area,* which will eliminate a lot of brokers, some of whom will try to fake their knowledge in the area while others will try to steer you into an area in which they are more comfortable dealing

The companies themselves will give you financial reports and other information. REITs in the NAREIT index (which is not an index in which you can actively invest, yet) will provide you with detailed information.

Best Credit Cards

Now you can go Online to search for the best credit card deals. Bank Rate Monitor lists competitive card rates from banks throughout the United States.

WHAT TO LOOK FOR WHEN COMPARING REITs

Look at the following:

1. *Dividend yield.* Review how much they offer when paying dividends and how that compares to the price of the stock. Dividend yield is the dividend paid per share divided by the price of the stock. So if the price goes down, the dividend yield goes up. Dividends as of early 1999 were averaging around 8 percent for REITs.
2. *Earnings growth.* Look at the FFO, or funds from operations, which is an indicator of how rapidly the company is growing. The FFO, as defined by NAREIT, is net income (computed in accordance with generally accepted accounting principles) excluding gains or losses from sales of property or debt restructuring, and adding back depreciation of real estate.
3. *Types of investments held.* Identify what properties they are investing in. REITs can invest in office buildings, shopping malls, and retail locations; residential property, including apartment complexes, hotels, and resorts; health care facilities; and various other forms of real estate.
4. *Geographic locations.* Check out where they invest. Some REITs invest on a national level and others specialize in regions of the country. Although the economy of late has been strong, that does not mean that every area of the country is doing as well financially. Therefore, many investors like to find REITs that diversify geographically.
5. *Diversification.* There's that word again. Whether it's a REIT that diversifies across state borders or you are buying several REITs with the idea of investing in everything from a small motel to a massive office complex, you should always favor diversification when investing, and that includes investing in REITs.
6. *Management.* Much like buying shares in a mutual fund, you are purchasing an investment that is run by professional management and buys investments in the real-estate market. You

should look at the background of the manager. In this case you'll looking be for, and generally finding, someone with a real-estate background. REIT managers often have extensive experience that may have begun in a private company that later went public as they continued on with the company. Naturally, you'll also look for stability in the leadership. You don't want to see a change in leadership every year.

Just as there are a wide variety of stock and bond choices for your mutual funds, REITs can hold anything from residential properties to shopping malls to mortgages (although less than 10 percent of REITs are mortgage REITs). REITs vary in their investments, but they hold true to the common theme: real estate. For that reason, just as you investigate the company issuing shares of stock, you have to investigate the company behind your REIT. And just as you look at the industry and how it fares when buying a stock, you need to look at the real-estate market and the economic conditions in the area, or areas, where your REIT is doing business.

REITs share prices are quoted on a daily basis. In this way, you follow your investment much as you would a stock or a mutual fund. The FFO is one way to judge how a REIT is doing. It is basically a way of seeing how much profit the REIT is bringing in from operations.

Funds from operation is a measure of REIT earnings. The FFO differs from corporate earnings in that commercial real estate maintains its residual value more so than property does in an office. In other words, after ten years, although there may be some depreciation, an office building essentially still is of value as opposed to office equipment, which after several years has depreciated considerably. The performance of a REIT is often judged by the FFO growth.

You can also get the price multiple ratio of stock price to FFO per share, which would be comparable to the P/E ratio for any other company (the ratio of the stock price to the net income per share).

REITs: A Listing

So where exactly do REITs fall in regard to corporate stocks and various bonds? Good question!

Over the 20-year span from the end of 1978 to the end of 1998, you'll find compound annual rate of return for equity REITs (which is by far the majority) is 14.35 percent. For the S&P 500 during the same stretch of time it was 17.74 percent, and for a bond portfolio it was 11.39 percent. Therefore, the average return over a long period of time is between higher-growth companies and bonds that have no growth but pay dividends. REITs pay large dividends and have some moderate growth. They fall somewhere between the stability of bonds and the volatility of stocks. The same holds true for their level of risk. Like other stocks, they face market risk, and the per share price can fall. For some this lower price can be attractive, particularly because the dividend yield becomes higher.

All in all, if you believe that the time is right to invest in real estate, the best choice for beginning investors are REITs. They provide a cost-effective way to invest in income-producing properties that you otherwise would not have the opportunity (or the capital) to become involved in.

Although they appear on the stock exchanges, REITs do not catch the eye as easily as IBM, DIS (the ticker symbol for Disney), or other well-known companies. Therefore, here is a list of some of the largest public REITs (market cap $1 billion+), courtesy of the National Association of Real Estate Investment Trusts.

Company Name: Alexander Haagen Properties, Inc.
Located: Manhattan Beach, CA
Exchange: Amex
Ticker Symbol: ACH
Segment: Retail
Type of REIT: Equity
Market Cap: $317.5 million

Company Name: AMB Property Corp.
Located: San Francisco, CA
Exchange: NYSE

Ticker Symbol: AMB
Segment: Industrial/office
Type of REIT: Equity
Market Cap: $2 billion

Company Name: Apartment Investment and Management Co.
Located: Denver, CO
Exchange: NYSE
Ticker Symbol: AIV
Segment: Residential
Type of REIT: Equity
Market Cap: $1.6 billion

Company Name: Arden Realty Group, Inc.
Located: Beverly Hills, CA
Exchange: NYSE
Ticker Symbol: ARI
Segment: Industrial/office
Type of REIT: Equity
Market Cap: $1.7 billion

Company Name: Avalon Properties, Inc.
Located: Wilton, CT
Exchange: NYSE
Ticker Symbol: AVN
Segment: Residential
Type of REIT: Equity
Market Cap: $1.3 billion

Company Name: Boston Properties, Inc.
Located: Boston, MA
Exchange: NYSE
Ticker Symbol: BXP
Segment: Industrial/office
Type of REIT: Equity
Market Cap: $2.2 billion

Wide Ranging REITs

NOTE: You can also be invested in a REIT through other sources, including mutual funds, insurance companies, and bank vehicles. Because of the tax structure, or the fact that corporations or trusts that qualify as REITs usually do not pay corporate income tax, they can pass income on to their shareholders. They can also be included in IRAs and other types of pension and retirement plans.

Company Name: BRE Properties, Inc.
Located: San Francisco, CA
Exchange: NYSE
Ticker Symbol: BRE
Segment: Residential
Type of REIT: Equity
Market Cap: $1.2 billion

Company Name: Capstead Mortgage Corporation
Located: Dallas, TX
Exchange: NYSE
Ticker Symbol: CMO
Segment: Mortgage backed
Type of REIT: Mortgage
Market Cap: $1.2 billion

Company Name: CarrAmerica Realty Corp.
Located: Washington, DC
Exchange: NYSE
Ticker Symbol: CRE
Segment: Industrial/office
Type of REIT: Equity
Market Cap: $1.8 billion

Company Name: Cornerstone Properties, Inc.
Located: New York, NY
Exchange: NYSE
Ticker Symbol: CPP
Segment: Industrial/office
Type of REIT: Equity
Market Cap: $1.8 billion

Company Name: Crescent Real Estate Equities, Inc.
Located: Fort Worth, TX
Exchange: NYSE
Ticker Symbol: CEI
Segment: Diversified
Type of REIT: Equity
Market Cap: $4.3 billion

Company Name: Developers Diversified Realty Corp.
Located: Moreland Hills, OH
Exchange: NYSE
Ticker Symbol: DDR
Segment: Retail
Type of REIT: Equity
Market Cap: $1.1 billion

Company Name: Duke Realty Investments, Inc.
Located: Indianapolis, IN
Exchange: NYSE
Ticker Symbol: DRE
Segment: Industrial/office
Type of REIT: Equity
Market Cap: $1.9 billion

Company Name: Equity Office Properties Trust
Located: Chicago, IL
Exchange: NYSE
Ticker Symbol: EOP
Segment: Industrial/office
Type of REIT: Equity
Market Cap: $7.6 billion

Company Name: Equity Residential Properties Trust
Located: Chicago, IL
Exchange: NYSE
Ticker Symbol: EQR
Segment: Residential
Type of REIT: Equity
Market Cap: $4.8 billion

Company Name: FelCor Suite Hotels
Located: Irving, TX
Exchange: NYSE
Ticker Symbol: FCH
Segment: Lodging/resorts
Type of REIT: Equity
Market Cap: $1.4 billion

CD Tips

If the rates are *dropping*, it's to your advantage to buy longer-term CDs. This way the CD won't come due in six months, forcing you to roll it over into a lower-rate CD.

If rates are *rising*, you may want to go with a shorter-term CD and pick up a higher rate to start with on your rollover to a new CD in three or six months. The short-term CD is your way of "buying time" as the rates go up. If you see that rates are continuing to rise, stay with the short ones for a while so you can keep getting the higher rates. Then when they start going down, switch to the previous advice and go to the longer-term CDs.

You should also keep an eye on the Federal Reserve. When they change a key rate that means banks will shortly follow. Economic indicators, including unemployment and the inflation rate, will often indicate what the Federal Reserve will do. In short, stay aware of which way the interest rates appear to be headed.

Company Name: First Industrial Realty Trust
Located: Chicago, IL
Exchange: NYSE
Ticker Symbol: FR
Segment: Industrial
Type of REIT: Equity
Market Cap: $1.3 billion

Company Name: Franchise Finance Corporation of America
Located: Scottsdale, AZ
Exchange: NYSE
Ticker Symbol: FFA
Segment: Retail
Type of REIT: Equity
Market Cap: $1.4 billion

Company Name: General Growth Properties, Inc.
Located: Chicago, IL
Exchange: NYSE
Ticker Symbol: GGP
Segment: Retail
Type of REIT: Equity
Market Cap: $1.3 billion

Company Name: Health and Retirement Properties Trust
Located: Newton, MA
Exchange: NYSE
Ticker Symbol: HRP
Segment: Health care
Type of REIT: Equity
Market Cap: $2.1 billion

Company Name: Health Care Property Investors, Inc.
Located: Newport Beach, CA
Exchange: NYSE
Ticker Symbol: HCP
Segment: Health care
Type of REIT: Equity
Market Cap: $1.1 billion

Company Name: Health Care REIT, Inc.
Located: Toledo, OH
Exchange: NYSE
Ticker Symbol: HCN
Segment: Health care
Type of REIT: Equity
Market Cap: $688.5 million

Company Name: Highwoods Properties, Inc.
Located: Raleigh, NC
Exchange: NYSE
Ticker Symbol: HIW
Segment: Industrial/office
Type of REIT: Equity
Market Cap: $1.8 billion

Company Name: Hospitality Properties Trust
Located: Newton, MA
Exchange: NYSE
Ticker Symbol: HPT
Segment: Lodging/resorts
Type of REIT: Equity
Market Cap: $1.5 billion

Company Name: IndyMac Mortgage Holdings, Inc.
Located: Pasadena, CA
Exchange: NYSE
Ticker Symbol: NDE
Segment: Mortgage backed
Type of REIT: Mortgage
Market Cap: $1.6 billion

Company Name: Kimco Realty Corporation
Located: New Hyde Park, NY
Exchange: NYSE
Ticker Symbol: KIM
Segment: Retail
Type of REIT: Equity
Market Cap: $1.4 billion

Company Name: Liberty Property Trust
Located: Malvern, PA
Exchange: NYSE
Ticker Symbol: LRY
Segment: Industry/office
Type of REIT: Equity
Market Cap: $1.5 billion

Company Name: Mack-Cali Realty Corp.
Located: Cranford, NJ
Exchange: NYSE
Ticker Symbol: CLA
Segment: Industrial/office
Type of REIT: Equity
Market Cap: $2.2 billion

Company Name: The Meditrust Companies
Located: Needham, MA
Exchange: NYSE
Ticker Symbol: MT
Segment: Health Care
Type of REIT: Hybrid
Market Cap: $2.7 billion

Company Name: Nationwide Health Properties, Inc.
Located: Newport Beach, CA
Exchange: NYSE
Ticker Symbol: NHP
Segment: Health Care
Type of REIT: Equity
Market Cap: $1.1 billion

Company Name: New Plan Realty Trust
Located: New York, NY
Exchange: NYSE
Ticker Symbol: NPR
Segment: Retail
Type of REIT: Equity
Market Cap: $1.5 billion

Company Name: Patriot American Hospitality, Inc.
Located: Dallas, TX
Exchange: NYSE
Ticker Symbol: PAH
Segment: Lodging/resorts
Type of REIT: Equity
Market Cap: $3.0 billion

Company Name: Post Properties, Inc.
Located: Atlanta, GA
Exchange: NYSE
Ticker Symbol: PPS
Segment: Residential
Type of REIT: Equity
Market Cap: $1.4 billion

Company Name: Prentiss Properties Trust
Located: Dallas, TX
Exchange: NYSE
Ticker Symbol: PP
Segment: Industrial/office
Type of REIT: Equity
Market Cap: $1.0 billion

Company Name: Public Storage, Inc.
Located: Glendale, CA
Exchange: NYSE
Ticker Symbol: PSA
Segment: Self-storage
Type of REIT: Equity
Market Cap: $3.4 billion

Company Name: Reskcon Associates Realty Corp.
Located: Melville, NY
Exchange: NYSE
Ticker Symbol: RA
Segment: Industrial/office
Type of REIT: Equity
Market Cap: $1.0 billion

Company Name: The Rouse Company
Located: Columbia, MD
Exchange: NYSE
Ticker Symbol: RSE
Segment: Diversified
Type of REIT: Equity
Market Cap: $2.1 billion

Company Name: Security Capital Atlantic
Located: Atlanta, GA
Exchange: NYSE
Ticker Symbol: SCA
Segment: Residential
Type of REIT: Equity
Market Cap: $1.0 billion

Company Name: Security Capital Industrial Trust
Located: Aurora, CO
Exchange: NYSE
Ticker Symbol: SCN
Segment: Industrial/office
Type of REIT: Equity
Market Cap: $3.1 billion

Company Name: Security Capital Pacific Trust
Located: El Paso, TX
Exchange: NYSE
Ticker Symbol: PTR
Segment: Residential
Type of REIT: Equity
Market Cap: $2.2 billion

Company Name: Simon DeBartolo Group, Inc.
Located: Indianapolis, IN
Exchange: NYSE
Ticker Symbol: SPG
Segment: Retail
Type of REIT: Equity

Market Cap: $3.6 billion

Company Name: Sovran Self-Storage
Located: Williamsville, NY
Exchange: NYSE
Ticker Symbol: SSS
Segment: Self-storage
Type of REIT: Equity
Market Cap: $395.8 million

Company Name: Speiker Properties, Inc.
Located: Menlo Park, CA
Exchange: NYSE
Ticker Symbol: SPK
Segment: Industrial/office
Type of REIT: Equity
Market Cap: $2.4 billion

Company Name: Starwood Hotels and Resorts
Located: Phoenix, AZ
Exchange: NYSE
Ticker Symbol: HOT
Segment: Lodging/resorts
Type of REIT: Equity
Market Cap: $10.0 billion

Company Name: Storage USA, Inc.
Located: Columbia, MD
Exchange: NYSE
Ticker Symbol: SUS
Segment: Self-storage
Type of REIT: Equity
Market Cap: $1.1 billion

Company Name: United Dominion Realty Trust, Inc.
Located: Richmond, VA
Exchange: NYSE
Ticker Symbol: UDR

Segment: Residential
Type of REIT: Equity
Market Cap: $1.5 billion

Company Name: Vornado Realty Trust
Located: Saddle Brook, NJ
Exchange: NYSE
Ticker Symbol: VNO
Segment: Diversified
Type of REIT: Equity
Market Cap: $3.1 billion

Company Name: Weingarten Realty Investors
Located: Houston, TX
Exchange: NYSE
Ticker Symbol: WRI
Segment: Retail
Type of REIT: Equity
Market Cap: $1.2 billion

Company Name: Westfield America, Inc.
Located: Los Angeles, CA
Exchange: NYSE
Ticker Symbol: WEA
Segment: Retail
Type of REIT: Equity
Market Cap: $1.3 billion

CHAPTER SIXTEEN

Collectibles

Collectibles Web Sites

There are numerous sites from collectibles dealers, magazines, auction houses, clubs, and so on. Below are a few sites with links and an abundance of information.

www.collectoronline.com: A major site with a collectibles mall featuring numerous dealers and their wares.

www.collectorsnet.com: World Collector's Net, featuring a shopping arcade, news and features about collectibles, a bookstore, price guides, and more.

www.wcd.com: World Collector's Digest has listings of trade shows, research, memorabilia, price guides, and so on.

www.1collector.com: Interactive Collector fills you in on exhibitions around the country, auctions, a dealer directory, and more.

There are thousands of items that fall under the always expanding heading of collectibles. Some, such as rare coins, stamps, baseball cards, and—of course—figurines, have huge followings, while others are more specialized in nature. It is now estimated that nearly half of all Americans are collecting something. Most people collect for the fun of it or with the idea in the back of their mind that "someday this could be of value." The first level of collector involves people with a collection of something they simply enjoy or enjoyed as a child and have maintained an interest in. They add to their collection when the opportunity presents itself. The next level includes more serious or dedicated collectors who are actively collecting as a hobby. They are aware of the value and spend time reading about and being involved with the process of collecting. These two levels encompass the majority of collectors. The reasons why people engage at either level is usually connected to a personal story, which might relate to their childhood or a particular passion— perhaps for history, sports, or a type of craftsmanship.

Collectors at the higher level are looking for items that will potentially be of value in the future. These are individuals looking to buy and later sell when the market is right for a profit. For them, collecting is an investment, as they are thinking about the potential return on their dollar.

Collectibles is now a multibillion-dollar industry. Because it has grown so big and so far-reaching over the years, collectors must now be more discerning and more careful in what they invest.

VINTAGE COLLECTIBLES

These are the items that are valuable because they are no longer being made, or made in the same manner. From old-fashioned golf equipment to items from the Civil War, vintage collectibles are the artifacts from yesteryear, and as they diminish in number their value theoretically rises. We say "theoretically" because if there is no buyer or market for an item then its value is essentially worthless. There is, however, a market for almost everything, and a buyer somewhere in the world for practically any piece of history you can image. From soup cans to antique toilet seats, someone will collect them—and know all about them. In fact, there are more than 1,500 clubs dedicated to a wide variety of vintage collectibles.

One of the problems collectors run up against is that the guidelines for collecting are not monitored in the same manner in which the SEC monitors the "financial world." Authenticity is therefore a prime concern, and finding a reputable, knowledgeable appraiser through a recommendation is important. Even someone who is licensed to appraise can try to low-ball you. Therefore, it is very important for a collector to also collect various opinions and price quotes, whether they be "official" from a dealer or by members of the club or group one belongs to. An appraiser is supposed to give you the true value, while a dealer will tell you (based on supply and demand) what the going market value is from his or her perspective. The market value can change from dealer to dealer, depending on where they are dealing.

Do your homework if you plan to sell collectibles. There is no "big board" with the latest prices. There are, however, plenty of guide books and magazines featuring information and pricing for many types of collectibles.

PRICING

The pricing of vintage collectibles can be tricky. Items are judged by their:

Scarcity, or rarity
Condition
Authenticity

Not in that order. The tricky part is that the value placed on an item from a book, a magazine, or an appraiser can be greatly swayed by two important factors:

1. Supply and demand
2. Sentimentality

The first item is the key. Mark McGwire's seventieth home run ball garnered millions of dollars because it was one of a kind and heavily sought out. The great demand for the ball made the price rise to an extraordinary height.

Most often a collector is seeking out a potentially marketable item at an undervalued price. Shrewd investors look in areas of low

A Word About Online Sites

Online sites can be very valuable for obtaining information about collecting, but be careful. For actually purchasing or selling, it's imperative that you know who is running the site and can check them out carefully.

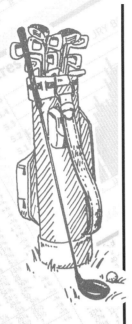

demand for an item that in another area will be of great demand. For example, a gentleman purchased an antique set of golf clubs from a woman at a garage sale for $50. Then, at a golf memorabilia show, he sold the clubs for $400. How does this happen? At the garage sale, the clubs were not in demand. They were simply being sold, perhaps to clear a space in the garage. At the golf show, however, a knowledgeable group of golf collectors knew the value of the clubs and several people wanted them. Thus there was a demand, and up went the price. When you sit in at an auction you can see firsthand how the demand drives an item up. Does this mean that the woman at the garage sale was ripped off? No. It means that she profited on an item that was of no value to her. She did not have the wherewithal, the means, or perhaps the time to take the clubs to a golf show and deal with golf enthusiasts.

Sometimes people will sell off collections at prices below their top market value because they need the money or simply do not want to be bothered storing the items. "Value" comes in many forms. The flip side is someone who turns down a handsome profit because the item is of great sentimentality and the owner cannot part with it.

Another good example of how people "buy low and sell high" in collectibles comes from a man in the Midwest who purchased an old Boston Red Sox jacket for $25 in a store selling old clothes. The store's owner knew the jacket was probably worth more, but in his part of the country, there were no higher bidders. The jacket had been part of a pile of old clothes he had bought for $8. Therefore he was happy to make a profit since no one was beating down his door for the old jacket. The purchaser, however, decided that the next time he made a business trip to Massachusetts, he'd stop by Boston.

Visiting areas around Fenway Park, he easily found that there was a great deal more enthusiasm for the old Sox jacket, which he sold for $300. Sometimes it's a matter of being in the right place.

From an investment standpoint, collectibles are risky and only as liquid as the market allows them to be. A baseball card collection is liquid if you go to a card show and sell it. The current value of the collection as you hold onto it is based on the market price set forth by the dealers and traders. Hobbyists enjoy looking through books to find the value of their collections. Often the values are guided by an organization or graded, such as coins or stamps.

The most important aspects of collecting are:

1. Get a good idea from various sources of the value of the items you are looking to buy or sell.
2. Look for authenticity. This can be difficult with autographs and less commonly marketed items.
3. Keep your collection in a safe place. Unlike many investments that are "book" or computer transactions, collectibles are tangibles which you can touch.
4. Be patient. The longer you hold onto something, the more valuable it (usually) gets.
5. Look for propitious selling opportunities. A ballplayer about to go into the Hall of Fame for his particular sport will see his "stock rise" so to speak. A collectible from the *Titanic*, although always valuable, hit higher numbers during the wave of excitement (pun intended) surrounding the film; non-collectors entered the bidding and drove the price of such items up.
6. Have fun. There are plenty of other investment choices out there, and this one can be highly inconsistent in your rate of return, so at least enjoy collecting.

CONTEMPORARY COLLECTIBLES

As we enter the new century, the modern-day collectible market is growing by leaps and bounds. By 2001 it is expected to be more than a $17 billion industry. The market includes cast art, animation art, and other types of collectibles made in association with current trends, films, sports heroes, and so on. They are essentially items being made for the purpose of collecting. Good investments? Not really. Great as hobbies and for enjoyment? Yes.

Contemporary collectibles, like their vintage counterparts, are not of great value when they are first produced. Like vintage collectibles, they can, and very well may, become valuable over time. A Barbie from 1959 has become rare and grown in value over the years. It

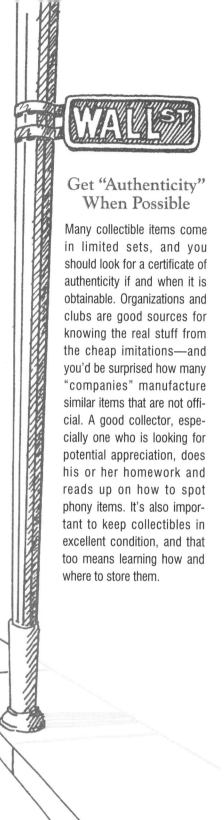

Get "Authenticity" When Possible

Many collectible items come in limited sets, and you should look for a certificate of authenticity if and when it is obtainable. Organizations and clubs are good sources for knowing the real stuff from the cheap imitations—and you'd be surprised how many "companies" manufacture similar items that are not official. A good collector, especially one who is looking for potential appreciation, does his or her homework and reads up on how to spot phony items. It's also important to keep collectibles in excellent condition, and that too means learning how and where to store them.

Galleries and Dealers

Deal with galleries and dealers you are comfortable doing business with and don't be pressured into buying something you do not like or feel is of value—if that's your reason for buying. Also, don't be pressured into selling a piece of art unless you want to—it's yours to enjoy.

has more then forty years of appreciation. It is rare because there are few such dolls in existence anymore; people may have thrown them out, lost them, or damaged them (thanks to little brothers and dogs), and the production itself would have been far less than the mass productions of today. A 1999 special Barbie may someday be valuable, but as a current collectible, it is essentially worth no more than what you paid for it. Of course, if you took the doll to a country where Barbies are not widely marketed, you could possibly get more money for it. Again, it's a matter of supply and demand. For the most part there is no demand here in the United States because the doll is still readily available in the store.

Ideally you would want the 1999 Barbie to be manufactured in a "limited edition." Those are key words when buying contemporary collectibles. Some "limited editions" even come with a letter or certificate telling you how many were issued and what number you have. This may or may not always be 100 percent valid. Another "limited set" may be issued elsewhere and you do not know it. Nonetheless, in a perfect world, this would be one of only five thousand of this Barbie made and you would keep it on a display stand/or in a safe place. After twenty-five years you would then have one of perhaps two thousand copies of this doll that remain in good condition. Let's say that for whatever reason there is a resurgence of Barbie once again in the year 2025. You could therefore sell the doll for $5,000. It has become a vintage collectible.

The idea, from a collectibles and investment standpoint, is to buy something that may, over time, become a rare item that will grow in demand. Baseball card collectors seek out rookie cards of the players whose stocks they believe will go up, knowing that the player can have only one rookie year (and a ton of rookie cards nowadays). Nonetheless, if in twenty years the player makes the Hall of Fame, the card will be worth something. A lot of money? Probably not, since there are numerous cards available and unlike the vintage collectibles, which people have only by the fact that no one threw them out, these items were bought with the intention of saving them as a collectible. In essence, the manufacturers of contemporary collectibles control their future value based on how many items they manufacture.

Other problems arise with this type of collectibles when various companies can manufacture the same version of similar items. The question then becomes a matter of determining which is the "authentic" item. Not only does this question involve copies or imitations, but it can also be a matter of deciding which brand is really more valuable. Is Donruss more valuable than Topps when buying baseball cards?

All of this brings us back to the idea of collecting as a hobby. Yes, you can and may find a contemporary item that is truly limited in quantity, but for the most part contemporary collectibles are for fun. They give people an outlet and provide pleasure. There are thousands of clubs and organizations, plus numerous publications and online sites devoted to collectibles. People seek out items that have a personal significance to them or are simply just pleasing.

ART

The right piece of art can be extremely valuable. However, these items are not easy to come by. Art appreciates over time and by the notoriety of the artist. It is not an area new investors will generally delve into unless they are sitting as heir to a masterpiece.

Most of us buy art because we simply like the painting or sculpture. We may enjoy a particular style or appreciate the work of a specific artist. From an investing standpoint it's very difficult to know, without a background in art, which artist's work will greatly appreciate over the years. Sometimes the best work by a lessor artist will command more attention than the lesser work of a great artist. You may also be able to buy such a work for less money, thus allowing a greater potential appreciation—unless you are talking about a lesser work by Picasso.

If you have a work of art that you believe is valuable, you should have it appraised twice. See if the appraisals match. Look it up in books and do some research on the artist and, if possible, the painting. Limited prints and lithographs can also be valuable, and also more affordable.

Fine Art

Art is essentially like any other collectible, only fine art is on a much higher monetary level. It's a matter of supply and demand, and if you've got the one-of-a-kind work, you'll get the demand to make money from it. Good luck.

CHAPTER SEVENTEEN

Futures and Commodities

CFTC

The Commodity Futures Trading Commission (CFTC) is the governing body of the commodities brokerage firms. All brokerage firms dealing in commodities need to be licensed by CFTC. The industry-wide, self-regulatory association, the National Futures Association, oversees the conduct and standards of everyone involved in the futures market. You can contact them to find out about the licensing of a brokerage house by calling 800-621-3570.

The vast majority of new and even experienced investors do not deal in the areas of futures and commodities. There is a lot to learn before venturing into this area of investing, and it is not an area where new investors should dabble. Investors playing the futures and commodities game are dealing in an adventurous, risky arena that is essentially a whole other world from the more popular stocks, bonds, and mutual funds. Nonetheless, we touch upon—or skim the surface—of this area so that you will have a very basic idea of what futures and commodities are all about.

The futures market deals with commodities that include grains, meats, industrial metals, precious metals, foods, textiles, and even energy sources such as gas and oil. Financial instruments and international currencies, such as the Swiss franc, Japanese yen, and British pound, are also traded in the futures market, which is a continuous auction market featuring buying and selling of all of these commodities at prices that are constantly fluctuating. It is also a market where for every buyer there is a seller, which is different from the stock market, where a company can have numerous unissued shares of stock.

Just as stocks are bought and sold on the stock market, futures have their own futures exchanges. The difference is that with stocks you can sit back and see which direction your stock is heading (and profit over time), while in the futures market, you can lose a fortune in a few minutes—or make one. You must stay on top of the price of your chosen commodity and know that you are dealing in a high-risk business where a change of five cents could wipe you out or make you very rich. In other words, unless you have fairly large sums of money to back up potentially major losses, YOU SHOULD STAY AWAY.

With that said, futures trading is a means of buying and selling contracts for a particular commodity. Sellers, or hedgers, lock in a contract with a buyer at a certain price in an effort to secure that price. They want to be protected against fluctuations in that price and secure a profit margin between their selling price and their purchase costs. A seller, for example, might get a price such as $3.45 a bushel on corn, anticipating the price will change. Therefore, the seller has locked in a certain price ($3.45) for a specified amount of the commodity.

Speculators, which are the investors, are looking to cash in on that contract. They are speculating on the price movement. It's almost as if you purchased a bond at a locked-in rate and other people were taking bets on whether the interest rate went up or down in comparison to the rate you were locked into. Yes, that analogy is stretching the point a bit, but it is roughly what is going on. Futures trading began with corn sellers hedging their corn crop prices while speculators gathered around and tried to guess which way the price would go. The basics haven't changed all that much today, except the numbers are much higher and there is a worldwide market, with electronic channels linking up buyers, sellers, and brokers around the globe, providing the latest prices on a vast assortment of commodities.

Investors buying futures contracts, looking for a price increase, are said to be "buying long," which means they are anticipating the price to rise. Conversely, an investor can do what is called "going short" or selling short, meaning the contract is sold and the profit is realized by purchasing an offsetting contract at a lower price. This is essentially betting that the price will drop.

Today, investors most often buy on margin. Therefore, the numbers only need to fluctuate a little for a great swing in your money, as you are buying and selling based on a much larger dollar amount. You put down a down payment, or margin, on the total price of the contract. In other words, if you want to control 200 ounces of gold and the day you open the contract the price of gold is at $300 an ounce, you can put down a $1000 down payment. Therefore you control the contract. BUT, the contract is for the entire amount, which is 200 ounces at $300, an ounce, or $60,000. Therefore you are playing with much more than your $1,000 investment. You are, by buying the contract, buying the full $60,000 worth. If the price goes up, your account will be credited, but if the price drops you will be hit with a margin call, which means you are responsible for the other $59,000 or whatever amount has been lost as the price dropped. Since your small investment is actually just part of a much larger investment, every cent the price moves reflects a lot more than meets the eye.

The futures market allows you to control a much larger amount of a product without paying a lot of money up front. However, since you are playing with such high stakes, it's important that if you are going to venture into this area, you study up on it and work with experts and/or analysts in the field. It is also a very hands-on area of investing, meaning that you or your analysts must stay on top of the price changes at all times.

The longer you hold onto a futures contract, the more money you will owe as the contract continues with margin requirements, not unlike buying and paying off a new car. The only difference is that in this case you can be stuck with bushels of corn or some other such commodity. Less than 1 percent of commodities contracts are held to their completion by investors. Those that are end up with a warehouse receipt, which is also marketable. The contract and the commodity are ultimately purchased by the companies that need the products, such as food or textile manufacturers or companies that use the specific commodity. You, however, are responsible for that contract, and it gets more and more difficult to sell as the delivery date nears or you pass what is called a "notice."

There are several fees included in commodities dealings, including broker fees, exchange fees, and insurance fees. Many investors look to advisors and analysts to help them in this highly specialized, complex area of investing. Managed accounts are not uncommon, whereby you give an account manager power of attorney to make transactions for you, later confirming all transactions. Other investors maintain control but seek out expert advice since they are dealing in such a risky area of investing.

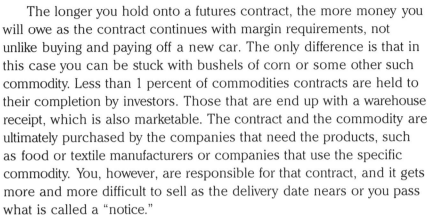

The oldest of the futures exchanges is the Chicago Board of Trade. The London International Futures Exchange, the New York Cotton Exchange, the Chicago Mercantile Exchange, and many others exist throughout the world. Exchanges set the minimum amount that a price can fluctuate, and they can set daily limits. For example, if a $.15 limit is set on a particular commodity price, and the price is $3.45 per bushel, that day the price can only move up or down to $3.60 or $3.30 ($.15 in either direction).

CHAPTER EIGHTEEN

Investing and Taxes

Double Tax Benefits

Company benefit plans, such as a 401(k), allow you to take advantage of tax breaks in two ways. First, you are making a contribution directly from your salary, meaning you are taxed only on the remaining portion of your salary. Secondly, you are not taxed on the savings which are accumulating tax deferred.

Naturally, there's a fly in the ointment when you talk about those high returns that have been seen on fast-rising tech stocks and hot mutual funds. Once again, good old Uncle Sam wants a piece of the action. However, when you stop and think about it, as much as you may dislike paying taxes, it's only in this government of ours that such an economic system exists whereby investments are (even after taxes) providing people with a solid means to meeting their goals and dreams. The idea of doubling your investment in a few years (or less) with the right stock or fund is part and parcel of the strength of the United States economy and capitalism. Therefore, although burdensome (and in need of some reform), taxes are part of a larger system that as a whole is pretty effective.

So much for preaching. The primary areas of concern regarding taxes on investments are:

1. Capital gains tax
2. Tax on interest and dividend income

There are fine details and strategies you can discuss with your accountant regarding both of these areas. The bottom line, however, is that any interest or dividend income generated from your investments, unless you are in a tax-sheltered retirement plan such as a 401(k) or an IRA, will be taxed at your normal rate of return.

Capital gains, from selling your shares of stock, shares of a mutual fund, bonds, and so forth, are either considered short-term capital gains or long-term capital gains. If you held the investment for at least one year, it is considered a long-term capital gain (or loss). Most long-term capital gains are taxed at a maximum of 20 percent. Short-term gains are taxed at your rate of income tax. The profits on items or investments received via inheritance are also considered long-term capital gains.

What many investors fail to think about when they purchase a mutual fund is that all dividends or capital gains within the fund are taxable, even if they are then reinvested. Your statement will show how much your earnings were within that fund during the year, and they should indicate which were capital gains from the sale of a security and which earnings were interest income from dividends.

Zero coupon bonds will also be taxed even though you are not seeing any interest as your investment grows to full maturity. The interest is being reinvested and growing through compound interest. But as a $7,000 purchase in a "zero" grows to its full $20,000 value, you will be taxed each year on the portion of the $13,000 that has been earned.

Another area of confusion comes with treasuries or municipal bonds when they are sold on the secondary market. Once again, these tax-exempt bonds are taxable in this manner. Tax-exemption comes in the area of dividends and interest income and only where specified. For example, if you buy a tax-exempt municipal in another state it may be taxable (and usually is) in your state.

If you should lose money and have a capital loss, you can take up to $3,000 as a deduction and, if your loss was greater than $3,000, spread the remaining amount over several years. For example, if you lost $6,000, you could take a $3,000 deduction for one year and then take another one for the next year as well.

One of the most important concerns regarding taxation is record keeping. The basics of taxes and capital gains are relatively simple regarding the long term versus short term, the 20 percent ceiling on long-term gains, and declaring interest and dividends as income. The problems that arise are often due to dealing with more than one brokerage house, inheriting items, and other manners of having securities that are more complicated than a simple stock purchase at a broker (for which you have statements). If, for example, you transferred your account from one brokerage house to another, the new brokerage house will have a record of when you started dealing with them. If you changed brokers three months ago and you are doing your taxes, how do you report the capital gains on a stock you just sold that you actually owned for three years? It's a long-term capital gain and can be taxed at the 20 percent maximum. BUT, you have to show that you bought it three years ago and not simply look at the statement from the new brokerage house, which may only date back three months.

In short, you need to keep records of the buying and selling of all securities and at what cost. You should carefully file each transaction statement. When you inherit something of "value," get it appraised in writing. Once you have the fair market value, you can

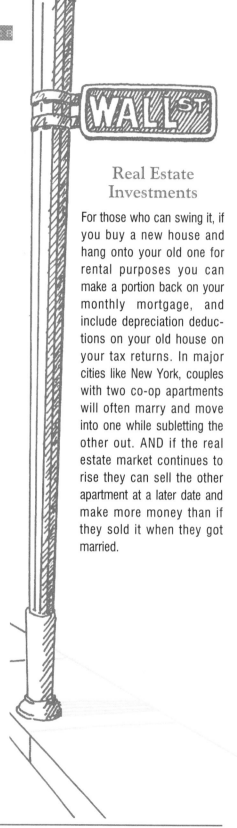

Real Estate Investments

For those who can swing it, if you buy a new house and hang onto your old one for rental purposes you can make a portion back on your monthly mortgage, and include depreciation deductions on your old house on your tax returns. In major cities like New York, couples with two co-op apartments will often marry and move into one while subletting the other out. AND if the real estate market continues to rise they can sell the other apartment at a later date and make more money than if they sold it when they got married.

Did You Know?

That until at least the year 2001, shopping on the Internet will remain tax free thanks to the Internet Tax Freedom Act. Congress and your friends at the Internal Revenue Service may have other plans for your online shopping by January 1 of 2001.

accurately report the capital gain should you sell it. The same holds true when you sell a collectible or artwork. The income must be reported and you should have a written record of the transaction. A paper trail of all transactions is VERY important should you ever be audited. One of the biggest difficulties people run into with the IRS is a lack of backup information. This also means it is your responsibility to make sure your broker is providing you with all the necessary paperwork.

Since taxes are part of almost all aspects of making money, they shouldn't deter you from investing as you so choose. The strategies, as mentioned in Chapters Twelve and Thirteen, suggest that investors help themselves manage tax risk by rounding out portions of their portfolio with tax-free investments. Naturally, in a retirement plan, these investments would be useless since you are already tax-deferred.

CONCLUSION

So, there you have it, a look at some of the most popular manners in which to invest your money. Throughout the entire book we mention risk/tolerance often and maintain the attitude that people must do what is best for meeting their goals and needs. It's important not to think of investing as "gambling" or a means to quick cash.

An area that is not discussed is investing as a family or, for that matter, as a couple. While children generally do not have a say in the family's investments as they grow up, explaining that mommy and daddy own a very very tiny piece of Disney through shares of stock is a way of teaching them about money and, in time, about investing. Investing is a way of building toward a brighter future for your children, as it can open the door to a college education as well as give them some financial backing to pursue their own goals and dreams. It also teaches them by example that saving money can bring you more money.

Couples often find that money is the most significant cause of discord between them. In fact, it is listed in survey after survey as the top reason couples fight or break up. Money can, and is, very easily acquainted with power—and that can spell trouble in a relationship. If one person uses his or her propensity for making a higher income or his or her savings as a means of control, the other party can, and often will, become disenchanted. For other couples, money is a source of pressure or tension, as one party does not feel the other is earning enough. When it comes to investing the problem that often arises is lack of "full disclosure," a situation whereby one party is making investment decisions without telling the other.

The road to harmonious investing in a relationship is an open line of communication, starting with determining your goals and dreams as a couple. If one person has a greater aversion to risk than the other, then this too must be discussed and a compromise needs to be reached. The handling of finances in the home also needs to be addressed. One couple may be satisfied with a situation where one party makes the investment decisions while the other does not get "involved," while another couple converses about all money matters, including investments. It's important that whichever manner a couple takes, it be discussed and established early on in the relationship. Communication and honesty are important in all relationships and especially when it comes to money—which is often at the root of many other problems.

It is therefore worth remembering that although this entire book is focused on investing to make more, there is a lot more to life than earning money. After all, and it has been said many times before, "You can't take it with you." Thus, if you are wealthy and miserable, you need to change your perspective. Many people have a few investments, are "comfortable" financially, and are enjoying life. Factor investing in as one of the many aspects of life.

Good luck, and happy investing.

Resources

DISCOUNT BROKERS

Here is a listing of some of the numerous discount brokers available. Many offer you the opportunity to trade online, while most sport toll-free numbers for easy phone trading. Some online brokers are very popular with those who believe technology rules supreme (and that is a growing segment of the population). However, there are also many "hardliners" who are tired of faceless, nameless technology and want a toll-free number to speak to another human being if necessary. As fast as technology is, when something goes wrong, it's a painfully slow, complicated process to correct it. Most discount brokerage houses offer a choice between online trading AND toll-free numbers.

The following list contains just some of the many popular, easily accessible discount brokers throughout the United States. This list includes brokers with toll-free numbers, and most have online trading.

Accutrade. 1-800-228-3011. Online trading at www.accutrade.com.

American Express Financial Direct. 1-800-658-4677. Online trading at www.americanexpress.com/direct.

Ameritrade. 1-800-669-3900. Online trading at www.ameritrade.com.

Aufhauser and Company. 1-800-368-3668. Online trading at www.aufhauser.com. They also offer stock information and links to other sites at WealthWEB.

Bull and Bear Securities. 1-800-262-5800, no online trading thus far.

Ceres Securities. 1-800-669-3900. Online trading at www.ceres.com. No-frills trading.

Charles Schwab and Co. 1-800-435-4500. Online trading at www.eschwab.com. High volume and low prices from one of the biggest of the brokerage houses.

Datek Securities. 1-888-GODATEK. Online trading at www.datek.com.

*E*Trade.* 1-800-786-2575. Online trading at www.etrade.com. High volume, very popular site with low prices.

Fleet Brokerage. 1-800-766-3000. No online trading thus far.

Freedom Investments. 1-800-381-1481. Online trading at www.trade-flash.com.

Ichan and Company. 1-800-634-8518. No online trading thus far.

Jack White and Company. 1-800-233-3411. Online trading at www.pawws.com/jwc.

Marquette De Bary Company. 1-800-221-3305. Online trading at www.debary.com.

Max Ule. 1-800-223-6642. Online trading at www.maxule.com.

National Discount Brokers. 1-800-888-3999. Online trading at http://pawws.secapl.com/ncb. Major discount brokerage house with research information available.

Quick and Reilly. 1-800-926-0600. Online trading at www.quick-reilly.com. Offering two online services for trading.

Regal Discount Securities. 1-800-786-9000. Online trading at www.regaldiscount.com.

Savoy Discount Brokerage. 1-800-961-1500. Online trading at www.savoystocks.com.

Tradex Brokerage Service. 1-800-522-3000. No online trading thus far.

USAA Brokerage Services. 1-800-531-8343. No online trading thus far.

Vanguard Discount Brokerage. 1-800-992-8372. Online trading at www.vanguard.com.

Wall Street Access. 1-800-487-2339. Online trading at www.wsacess.com.

The Wall Street Discount Corporation. 1-800-221-7870. Online trading at www.wsdc.com.

Waterhouse Securities. 1-800-934-4410. Online trading at www.waterhouse.com.

Your Discount Broker. 1-800-800-3215. No online trading thus far.

Ziegler Thrift Trading. 1-900-328-4854. Online trading at www.ziegler-thrift.com.

READ ALL ABOUT IT

There are also myriad publications that can be of assistance to investors. These financially oriented newspapers and magazines offer valuable insight about the stock market, including stock tips and articles with a more psychological slant. It's a good place to get ideas about investments, but you still need to do your own investigations. You also need to consider whether or not a given stock that you read about in a magazine fits in with your strategy and your overall approach to investing. Many publications will make stock recommendations and show you how the stocks have fared after a year. To look at a copy before buying a subscription you can check your local library.

Among other resources, you can gain valuable insight about investing from the following:

The *Wall Street Journal*: Published by Dow Jones and Company, The *Wall Street Journal* is a leading global newspaper with a focus on business. Founded in 1889, the newspaper has grown to a daily circulation of about 1.8 million readers. In 1994, Dow Jones introduced The *Wall Street Journal Special Editions*, special sections written in local languages that are featured in about thirty-three leading national newspapers worldwide. The *Wall Street Journal Americas*, published in Spanish and Portuguese, is included in approximately twenty leading Latin American newspapers. The *Wall Street Journal* offers thirteen-week subscriptions for $49, six-month subscriptions for $89, one-year subscriptions for $175, and two-year subscriptions for $299. Eligible students and professors can save nearly half the price on their subscriptions. Online access to The *Wall Street Journal, Barron's,* and *Smart Money* is available for $29 per year for *Journal* subscribers and $59 for nonsubscribers. Call 1-800-568-7625.

Barron's: *Barron's* is also known as the *Dow Jones Business and Financial Weekly*. With its first edition published in 1921, *Barron's* offers its readers news reports and analyses on financial markets worldwide. Investors will also find a wealth of tips regarding investment techniques. The weekly publication can be had for a thirteen-week subscription rate of $39. Six-month subscriptions are $74; one-year subscriptions are $145; and a two-year subscription is $245. Eligible students and professors can receive nearly half off on their subscriptions. Call 1-800-568-7625.

Investor's Business Daily: Founded in 1984, *Investor's Business Daily* is a newspaper focusing on business, financial, economic, and national news. The publication places a strong emphasis on offering its readers timely information on stock market and stock market–related issues. The front page of each issue provides a brief overview of the most important business news of the day. It's published five days a week, Tuesdays through Saturdays, and you can have a six-month subscription for $109.00. For one year it's $197.00; a two-year subscription will run you $327; and a three-year subscription is $439.00. Call 1-800-831-2525.

Forbes: *Forbes* magazine is a biweekly business magazine for "those who run business today—or aspire to." Each issue has more than 50 stories on companies, management strategies, global trends, technology, taxes, law, capital markets and investments. A one-year subscription, or twenty-six issues, is $59.95, a two-year subscription is $99.95, 3-years is $139.95 and a seventeen-issue student rate is $19.99. Call 1-800-888-9896.

Worth: *Worth* is a monthly personal finance magazine for individuals who "insist on being in control and refuse to put their finances on auto-pilot." The monthly magazine features such columnists as Peter Lynch and political economist Walter Russell Mead. Coverage ranges from the current state of the markets (domestically and abroad) to specific portfolio strategies for investing in equities, bonds, and mutual funds. A one-year subscription costs $18 (ten issues). Call 1-800-777-1851.

Equity: *Equity*, put out by the same company as *Worth* magazine, is geared to high-income women. Women and their relationship with money is the overall theme of the publication, which was introduced in December 1998. Among other topics, feature articles revolve around investing money, spending money, and making money. As of this printing, *Equity* is free with a subscription to *Worth*. Call 1-800-777-1851.

Money: *Money* is a monthly personal finance magazine from Time-Warner publications covering such topics as family finances, investment careers, taxes and insurance. Each issue includes tips, advice, and strategies for smart investing. The magazine also features other related matters like finding cheap flights, buying a home, and preparing for tax season. They also offer a substantive annual mutual fund guide. A one-year subscription, or thirteen issues, is $39.89; a half-year subscription, or seven issues, is $21.47. Call 1-800-633-9970.

Fortune: Every month, *Fortune* magazine, a Time-Warner publication, offers analysis of the business marketplace. The publication's annual ranking of the top five hundred American companies is one of its most widely read features. *Fortune* has been covering business and business-related topics since its origins in 1930. A one-year subscription, or twenty-six issues, is $59.95, and for students a one-year subscription is $29.98. Call 1-800-621-8000.

Smart Money: *Smart Money,* a monthly personal finance magazine, offers readers ideas for investing, spending, and saving. The publication also covers automotive, technology, and lifestyle subjects, including upscale travel, footwear, fine wine, and music. One-year subscriptions are $24, with discounts to *Wall Street Journal* subscribers. Call 1-800-444-4204.

Kiplingers Personal Finance: One of the most respected names in financial publications, *Kiplingers* offers investing ideas, updates on companies, insider interviews with top financial experts and fund managers, and very detailed listings of the best-performing mutual funds in a wide range of categories. One-year subscriptions are $23.95, two-year subscriptions are $39.95 and three-year subscriptions are $54.95. A discount rate for a one-year subscription of $14.97 is available to students and eligible teachers. Call 1-800-544-0155.

ValueLine Investment Survey: A weekly publication available at most libraries and through subscription, it offers ratings, reports, opinions, and analysis on about 130 stocks in seven or eight industries on a weekly basis. Approximately 1,700 stocks in about ninety-four industries are covered every thirteen weeks. CD Rom subscribers can also purchase an expanded version containing reviews of five thousand stocks. Call 1-800-634-3583.

Standard & Poor's Equity Investor Services: The services include numerous products, such as the Compustat database, which provides information on nearly nine thousand active U.S. companies—including twenty-right years of market data and a lot more. Other S&P Equity Service products include ComStock, Stock Guide, corporate records, stock reports, and directories of the S&P 500, the S&P Mid-cap 400, the S&P Small-cap Index, securities dealers, pension funds and just about any other type of investment opportunity. A catalog will provide you with a listing of their software and books. Contact them at Standard & Poor's, 25 Broadway, New York, NY 10004-1010, or by phone at 212-208-8786.

Investing comes with certain responsibilities. Keeping up with both national and international events via business publications, the Internet, and/or television is extremely important. Following the latest news—including mergers and acquisitions, new companies entering the marketplace, and dramatic changes in currency exchange rates—often reveals trends that may affect your stocks for better or worse.

INVESTMENT WEB SITES

The Internet has made an unparalleled impact on the state of investing. It has significantly affected the manner in which business is conducted worldwide. It has taken the information once found buried in the business sections of newspapers and made it easily accessible to investors at all levels. In short, the proliferation of home computers coupled with the World Wide Web have brought investing to the masses. Add to that a vast array of software and investment Web sites designed for the investment professional and you have a whole new world of investing, literally at your fingertips.

A majority of the major financial institutions and nearly all of the major brokerage houses offer their own Web sites, most through www. plus the name of the company. The most comprehensive of the many Web sites offered by major investment firms are the following: Aim at www.aimfunds.com; American Century at www.Americancentury.com; Fidelity at www.fidelity.com; Franklin Templeton at www.Franklin-Templeton.com; Prudential at www.prudential.com; and Strong at www.strong.com. Historical information, fund holdings, performance updates, fund profiles, information on

fund managers, libraries of articles and general information, and even glossaries and investor tips can be found on various Web sites. Needless to say, the "investor tips" and "how to" information can lean in favor of the funds offered by a fund family. You usually won't find the virtues of REITs or advantages of muni bond funds discussed by a fund family that doesn't handle them. Nonetheless, you will get a lot of overall information at the Web sites of financial institutions.

While Web surfing, it's to your advantage to hone in on the specific areas that you are looking for, such as tax-free investments, socially responsible investing (try www.coopamerica.org), or information on particular funds. This will narrow down your search and reduce your time spent online, since some Web sites (in all areas) are loaded with promotional material and hype or are simply confusing with numerous "bells and whistles."

There are numerous investing Web sites. Some will give you an overall picture of investing as a whole, and others will focus on a particular area. The following list includes a few of the many investment-related Web sites.

www.armchairmillionaire.com: Armchair Millionaire offers a wealth of information for personal investors.

www.bloomberg.com: Bloomberg's online financial news and information site.

www.bondtrac: If you're looking for bond information and the latest in bond offerings, this site should be of help.

www.brill.com: The Mutual Fund Interactive site is a mecca for mutual fund information.

www.cbsmarketwatch: This CBS financial site has information on stocks, bonds, mutual funds, and more, plus charts and commentary.

www.cnnfn.com: CNN Financial News Network offers a site with an extensive amount of information about U.S. and global markets.

www.cyberinvest.com: Cyber invest has links and information and the latest news on stocks, bonds, banking, global investing, education, etc.

www.dailystock.com: Quotes, news, and a wealth of financial information is available from Daily Stock, which links to numerous other sites.

www.dogsofthedow.com: The Dogs site gives you the "lowdown" on the stocks in the Dow Jones, from historical information to the latest quotes, plus news and updates.

www.dowjones.com: The Dow Jones Business Directory offers you a comprehensive listing of all sorts of financial sites on the Web, even reviewing many of them.

www.fool.com: The Motley Fool provides a wide variety. of information, including a lot of investing basics.

www.global-investor.com: The Global Investor Directory, as the name indicates, provides access to a plethora of international investing information, including performance information on worldwide markets.

www.hoovers.com: Hoovers Company directory can give you the scoop on more than ten thousand companies, from IPOs to industry profiles.

www.investools.com: INVESTools links personal investors with the latest from financial news services and with research information sites such as Standard & Poor's among others.

www.investorama.com: Invest-o-rama's site is a major directory to personal finance and investing sites, linking to more than four thousand such sites.

www.investorguide.com: Investor Guide offers a long list of subjects, with plenty of information and tons of links.

www.invsquare.com: The Investor Square is a major investment source, with information on thousands of mutual funds, numerous companies, as well as stock quotes and more.

www.irs.ustres.gov: The government's Web site for government investments and tax information.

www.mfea.com: The Mutual Fund Investment Center can help you get all the information you need to select the right mutual funds.

www.moneypages.com: Links to stocks, bonds, and mutual funds, plus investment tips for the individual investor.

www.morningstar.net: One of several sites from Morningstar, an institution in the financial community.

www.mutualfundchannel.com: Mutual Fund Channel (with some possible downloading necessary) can help you keep tabs on the mutual funds in your portfolio.

www.pathfinder.com: Time Warner's huge site serves as an umbrella for a number of other information sources, including some of their magazines, such as *Fortune* and *Money*.

www.personalwealth.com: Here you can get words of wisdom from Wall Street experts, S&P stock information, and more.

www.psa.com or *www.investinginbonds.com*: The Bond Market Association sites have legislative and statistical information, research, prices, and more.

www.quote.com: Quote.com, as the name might imply, has the latest and as up-to-the-minute as possible quotes from numerous markets, along with analyses and commentary.

www.reuters.com: Reuters Web site offers all the latest financial news you need.

www.sec.gov: The Securities and Exchange Commission's Web site, with information on companies, brokerage houses and SEC policies and news.

www.smartmoney.com: From *Smart Money*, this is a comprehensive site for all levels of investors.

www.stockinfor.standarpoor.com: Standard & Poor's Web site is extensive, with across-the-board information about companies, sectors, funds, and so on.

www.stocksite.com: Stock picks, quotes, charts, split information, and research are all available.

www.stockmaster.com: Stockmaster has the latest stock quotes plus news and historical information about the companies behind them.

www.thomsoninvest.net: The Thomson Investors Network offers real-time quotes, stock tips, research, charts, a fund center, and more.

www.ustres.gov: The U.S. Treasury Department site has plenty of information on what the government has to offer in the way of investment vehicles. Also see *www.easysaver.gov* for the Treasury Department's new plan for direct deposits from your savings or checking account.

www.winninginvesting.com: This site comes from *Winning Investing*, a comprehensive newsletter geared at the individual investor.

www.wsrn.com: A major umbrella site with investment information and links to numerous other sites.

www.zacks.com: Zacks Investment Research is a research site with market commentary and information.

INVESTMENT LINGO: A GLOSSARY

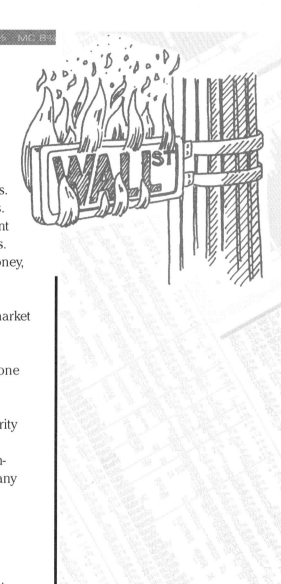

Annualization: Comparing annual rates of various investments.

Appreciation: A positive term, meaning an increase in assets.

Asset Allocation: How you divide up your assets into different types of investments, such as stocks, bonds, or cash instruments.

Bear Market: A bad time in the market, when it's losing money, and prices are dropping.

Bottom Line: After taxes, the true value of the investment.

Bull Market: The opposite of a bear market, it's when the market is on the upswing and prices are rising.

Capital Gains: The appreciation of your investment; taxable income. Long-term are one year or more; short-term are under one year.

Capital Loss: The opposite of capital gains.

Closing Price: The price of your stock, mutual fund, or security at the end of the trading day, once the market has closed.

Dividends: Money distributed to the shareholders of the company, not through the sale of the shares, but because the company is doing well and as an incentive to hold onto your investment and/or buy more shares.

Equity: Another term for stock.

Index: A listing of stocks or mutual funds used to compare prices, among other data.

Investment Return: A percentage indicator of how your investment has done. A 10 percent rate of return means you've gained 10 percent on your original investment.

Laddered Portfolio: This is a portfolio, primarily of bonds, which have maturities due at different times. Setting up such a portfolio will keep a steady stream of interest coming in and allow you the flexibility of liquidating a bond when you need a greater amount of cash.

Liquidity: Basically, how easily your investment can be converted into cash. Full liquidity, a more accurate definition of where you stand financially, means how easily your money can be converted into cash at full face value.

Market Risk: How risky the security is in the market for sales purposes. Market price is affected by the current rate of interest as well as supply and demand, among other factors.

Maturity Date: The date a bond can be redeemed for its face value, or essentially when you "get your money back." Most often if you have a longer maturity you'll get a greater return.

Offering Price: The amount at which a mutual fund is selling, per share.

Par Value: The actual face value of the bond, which is the amount you will receive if you hold onto the bond until maturity or, should you sell the bond, at face value. Selling for "par" is when you sell a 2,000 bond for $2,000.

P/E Ratio: Price/Earnings Ratio compares the price of the stock with the earnings of the company. A high P/E ratio means the stock is overvalued and vice versa.

Portfolio: A compilation of the investments you own or those held by a mutual fund.

Premium: If a bond sells for more than its face value, the profit is considered a premium, or you are said to be selling at a premium.

Prospectus: The document that tells you all you need to know about the investment. You should read the prospectus before buying.

Returns: How much money you are making on an investment.

Risk: How great a chance an investor is willing to take that he or she may lose his or her money. There are a number of subcategories, including market risk, technical risk, interest risk, liquidity risk, tax risk, and inflation risk.

Secondary Market: Where securities are resold.

Technical Risk: How risky your investment is in relation to external factors that affect the market (any investment market), including inflation, unemployment, the interest rate, etc.

Tolerance: How comfortable you are with the concept that your stock may lose money; how well you handle risk.

Volatility: How much an investment will tend to rise and fall.

Yield: The amount paid out on bonds through interest.

Yield-to-maturity: The overall return on a bond, including interest and principal at maturity. This is how bonds are sold, allowing you to gauge how much you will make from both sources of income.

INDEX

EVERYTHING

The Everything HomeBuying Book
by Ruth Rejnis

The Everything HomeBuying Book walks prospective buyers completely through the overwhelming process of buying a home, from open house to closing the deal. If you have a desire to enter the real estate market, you will find something that fits your needs—a great space that is within your budget. And if you never thought you could afford to buy a home, think again. There are literally dozens of options available, and real estate expert Ruth Rejnis has uncovered them all.

Trade paperback, $12.95
1-58062-074-4, 304 pages

The Everything Money Book
by Rich Mintzer with Kathi Mintzer, CPA

The Everything Money Book is written simply to make handling, managing, saving, and possibly earning money easier. It provides suggestions so that anyone can achieve their financial goals: whether it's sending the kids to college, planning a superb vacation, or retiring in another state. The information is shared in easy-to-follow language, so even the first-time budgeter won't be overwhelmed.

Trade paperback, $12.95
1-58062-145-7, 288 pages

Available Wherever Books Are Sold

If you cannot find these titles at your favorite retail outlet, you may order them directly from the publisher. BY PHONE: Call 1-800-872-5627. We accept Visa, MasterCard, and American Express. $4.95 will be added to your total order for shipping and handling. BY MAIL: Write out the full titles of the books you'd like to order and send payment, including $4.95 for shipping and handling, to: Adams Media Corporation, 260 Center Street, Holbrook, MA 02343. 30-day money-back guarantee.

We Have EVERYTHING

More bestselling Everything titles available from your local bookseller:

Everything **After College Book**
Everything **Astrology Book**
Everything **Baby Names Book**
Everything® **Bartender's Book**
Everything **Bedtime Story Book**
Everything **Beer Book**
Everything **Bicycle Book**
Everything **Bird Book**
Everything **Casino Gambling Book**
Everything **Cat Book**
Everything® **Christmas Book**
Everything **College Survival Book**
Everything **Crossword and Puzzle Book**
Everything **Dating Book**
Everything **Dessert Book**
Everything **Dog Book**
Everything **Dreams Book**
Everything **Etiquette Book**
Everything **Family Tree Book**
Everything **Fly-Fishing Book**
Everything **Games Book**
Everything **Get-a-Job Book**
Everything **Get Ready For Baby Book**
Everything **Golf Book**

Everything **Guide to Walt Disney World®, Universal Studios®, and Greater Orlando**
Everything **Home Buying Book**
Everything **Home Improvement Book**
Everything **Internet Book**
Everything **Investing Book**
Everything **Jewish Wedding Book**
Everything **Low-Fat High-Flavor Cookbook**
Everything **Money Book**
Everything **One-Pot Cookbook**
Everything **Pasta Book**
Everything **Pregnancy Book**
Everything **Sailing Book**
Everything **Study Book**
Everything **Tarot Book**
Everything **Toasts Book**
Everything **Trivia Book**
Everything® **Wedding Book**
Everything® **Wedding Checklist**
Everything® **Wedding Etiquette Book**
Everything® **Wedding Organizer**
Everything® **Wedding Shower Book**
Everything® **Wedding Vows Book**
Everything **Wine Book**

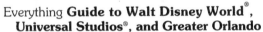